Ellen E Miller

Alone Through Syria

Ellen E Miller
Alone Through Syria
ISBN/EAN: 9783744753418
Printed in Europe, USA, Canada, Australia, Japan
Cover: Foto ©Andreas Hilbeck / pixelio.de

More available books at **www.hansebooks.com**

ALONE THROUGH SYRIA

BY

ELLEN E. MILLER

WITH AN INTRODUCTION

BY

A. H. SAYCE

LATE DEPUTY PROFESSOR OF COMPARATIVE PHILOLOGY, OXFORD
HON. LL.D., DUBLIN

" Memory is the Treasure-house of the mind, wherein the monuments thereof are kept and preserved."—FULLER

WITH EIGHT ILLUSTRATIONS

LONDON
KEGAN PAUL, TRENCH, TRÜBNER & CO., Lᴛᴅ.
1891

INTRODUCTION.

THE proofs of Miss Miller's book have reached me in a place which is, perhaps, the fittest of all others in which to read them. Moored to a bank below the ruined temple of Luxor, I have no need of calling in the aid of imagination to assist me in realizing the scenes she depicts. Here they are actually around me, in the blue sky overhead, the broad river beneath, and the green fields, and yellow sand and purple cliffs, by the side of which it flows eternally. That her words adequately convey the impressions of the moment is more than sufficient justification for the appearance of her work.

No book on the East can be successful unless the author possesses sympathy with the land and its people. It is necessary to divest ourselves to a certain extent of our Western training, to look at the world from the point of view of the Oriental, if we really wish to understand him, and present a lifelike picture of his habits and thoughts. Miss Miller has shown that she possesses this sympathy, and what she has written has accordingly a freshness about it which makes it well worth reading, even by those to whom Eastern life is as familiar as that of the West.

In Syria her experiences were somewhat novel. It is rare for a man to travel there without tents, trusting to the hospitality of the natives or of the monasteries for a night's lodging; for a lady to do so is more than rare. Only those who have themselves undergone the same experience can realize what an amount of discomfort such a mode of travelling often brings with it, or what an insight it gives into the daily life of the people.

I am glad to find that Miss Miller has a good word to say for the Egyptians. The judgments so dogmatically passed upon them by the hurrying tourist, who is ignorant of their language and derives his knowledge of their character from the demoralized population of Luxor, are generally the reverse of the truth. The Egyptians are not, for example, a "dirty people." Any one who has been on the Nile as soon as the cold season is over, will know that men and children alike spend a large part of their time in the water, and that their clothes are washed with a most commendable frequency. There is certainly no European country in which water is so freely used by the labouring classes. Neither are they a lazy people. The fellâh will toil from sunrise to sunset for a miserable pittance, not only without complaint, but with a gaiety of heart which nothing seems able to overcome. The artisans work with the same assiduity and patient industry, and my experience of Egyptian servants is, that they are the most hard-working I have ever known.

The Egyptian, moreover, is intelligent. The poorest fellâh is desirous of sending his children to school, and does not grudge the money spent for the purpose, while the children themselves learn their lessons with a zeal which would excite the envy of an English schoolmaster. The natural cleverness of the pure-blooded Egyptian may be judged of from the fact that the Copts have contrived by sheer intellectual power, during long centuries of Mohammedan domination, to keep the practical administration of the country and its revenues in their own hands. At the present day many of the richest native landowners are Copts. The Egyptian readily assimilates the inventions and civilization of others, but without giving up his old ideas and habits, or in any way denationalizing himself. He is at once receptive and conservative, a fact which was illustrated even by the ancient system of hieroglyphic writing, where the primitive ideographs continued to be used along with the syllabic characters and alphabetic letters which had been subsequently developed out of them.

The Egyptian, again, is honest. Give a donkey-boy or a fellâh a sovereign to change, and he will bring back the exact amount of money required, though he may know that he can carry it away without the possibility of pursuit or detection. Of course there are certain things which servants, for instance, regard as their perquisites, though the European master may take another view, and to these the servants consider that they have a right. Of course, too, there are black sheep in every flock; but, as a general rule, a commercial honesty is more widely spread among the Egyptians than among the inhabitants of any other country known to me, our own countrymen not excepted.

The Egyptian, it is true, is by no means perfect. He has faults, some of which account for the long continuance of foreign rule in the valley of the Nile. He is timid and unwarlike, he has little power of initiative, his actions are seldom disinterested, and his idea of truth is not that which prevails in certain northern latitudes. But he makes a ready and intelligent scholar, and it is possible that the present intimate contact of his country with Europe may bring with it an interchange of habits and ways of thought which will be beneficial both to him and to the European.

Every year this contact becomes closer and more penetrating. The Egypt of Oriental romance which some of us remember is fast passing away, and the traveller has to go forth into the byways and deserts to find it again. So rapid is the change that what was true only three or four years ago has already ceased to be so. It may not be long before Miss Miller's picture of Egypt is as much a picture of the past as is Lane's picture of Cairo fifty years ago.

A. H. SAYCE.

Luxor.

PREFACE.

Women are, I fancy, credited with possessing a faculty, or rather weakness, for exaggeration. I trust I have not fallen into that weakness in the following pages; my endeavour has been to give an exact and ungarnished account of my travels, adventures, and impressions of Eastern life. In that part of the book which has to do with my stay in Egypt I have refrained from any systematic description of the country or of its precious ancient architectural wonders, because such a description would alone fill a volume, and there are already excellent books which supply all such information. During more than six happy months spent in Egypt and Palestine, many of my experiences were unique—in Palestine especially, where I travelled alone and without tents. Some people will say that this last was a mistake, tent-life being "so delightful." I grant it, yet would ask such persons if they must not confess to the remembrance of an occasional *contre-temps*, when, during a storm, perhaps, their tents were uprooted, and themselves and their belongings exposed to the fury of the elements? One such exposure might have proved, in my case, a serious matter, for it was on account of a rheumatic affection in the eyes that I was advised to try the remedial effect of the dry and sunny East; it seemed to me, therefore, only prudent that I should always try to secure a substantial roof over my head. I found the air of Palestine particularly pleasant and salubrious, and during nine weeks' stay all went well spite of a little roughing, which often does one more good than harm.

In Egypt, Messrs. Cook may be said to reign supreme as agents of locomotion; and the solitary traveller, who has not an unfathomable purse, will be as glad as I was to avail himself of their comfortable steamers which, during the season, constantly navigate the Nile. But in Palestine the case is somewhat different. Excellent as their arrangements for the convenience of tourists are in that country also, yet, to not a few persons, it will be uncongenial to visit its hallowed scenes in some haste and in company with strangers; so that, unless a small private party can be arranged, the independent line will probably commend itself to many, and I can testify from experience that it need not prove a more expensive way than the other of seeing the Holy Land.

I have viewed ecclesiastical matters from the standpoint of a Churchwoman, but, I hope, with no lack of charity towards those who differ from me. In many parts of the East, the Anglican Communion is, I regret to say, represented in a manner quite unworthy of her, and certainly not in one likely to promote that reunion with orthodox sister Churches for which so many long and pray; nor yet in a way calculated to attract the votaries of false religions, whose Oriental minds might be impressed by the beautiful yet simple accessories to worship to which we are accustomed at home.

To any who may wish to inform themselves more fully as to the condition of the English Church in Jerusalem and the East, I would recommend the perusal of Bishop Blyth's "Primary Charge" (Wells Gardner, Darton and Co.), which appeared shortly after the completion of my manuscript, and from which I have added, as notes, a few brief extracts.

E. E. M.

CONTENTS.

CHAPTER I.

INTRODUCTORY : A FEW THOUGHTS ON EGYPT PAST AND PRESENT 1

CHAPTER II.

SOMETHING ABOUT CAIRO.

Situation—Street-life—Women—Society—Memphis—Egyptian art—Arabian architecture—Modern barbarians—Mosques—The Korân—Education—Our duty 15

CHAPTER III.

MORE ABOUT CAIRO AND ITS INHABITANTS.

Donkey-boys—Moslem habits, character, prayers—Moral courage—Walks outside the town—An escape—The Copts—Gordon College—A tea-party 32

CHAPTER IV.

A WEEK IN THE DESERT.

Helwân—Tura quarries—Our hotel—Invalids—Climate—Panorama—A meeting—Desert music—Christian persecution—Hermits—The ferry-boat—Across country—Cultivation—Happy families—A nocturnal ramble 49

CHAPTER V.

NILE REMINISCENCES.

Steamer-life—Villages—Pigeons—The inundation—Native traffic—Weather—Scenery—Assouan—Nubian aquatics—Philæ—Beverages—An impromptu bath 68

CHAPTER VI.

INCIDENTS AT LUXOR.

Crowded hotels—Egyptian saddles—A duet—Saucy children—Egyptian sociability—A victory gained—Curiosity-vendors—Deprivations—Epiphany-tide ... 84

CHAPTER VII.

LOOKING FORWARD.

In dock—*Séances* with a Copt—In search of a saddle—Native servants—Small enemies—Means of defence—Heliopolis—Its sacred shrine and famous school—Greek language and learning 98

CHAPTER VIII.

ON THE TRACK OF THE HEBREWS.

Why I went to Suez—Goshen past and present—Cat-worship—Striking contrasts—Ismailîya—Hebrew route—The Red Sea—In the Arabian desert—A clever exchange—A Bedawîn meeting—Return to crowded civilization—A serious loss 114

CHAPTER IX.

ARRIVAL IN THE LAND OF THE HEBREWS.

Embarcation difficulties—Yâfa "the beautiful"—Evening guns—Needful arrangements—Visit to Lydda—Catechizing—The ascent to Jerusalem—A solemn procession 137

CHAPTER X.

AT JERUSALEM.

Reflections—Ancient traces—First ride—Hotel-surroundings—Turkish soldiers—Mount Zion and Mount Moriah—Jebusite steps—The Sacred Rock and its shrine—Old channels—A dearth—Pilgrims—Modern Jews—Converse in a synagogue—Holy Sepulchre—"The place of a skull" 154

CHAPTER XI.

THE GREAT DESCENT.

Walks outside Jerusalem—Christian miscreants—Native alertness—The khan—Need of a Samaritan—In an oasis—Arab wedding—A strange night—A salt bath—Beth-Abâra 181

LIST OF ILLUSTRATIONS.

	PAGE
A STREET IN CAIRO	*Frontispiece*
PRINCE RA-HOTEP AND PRINCESS NEFERT	24
A SHADOOF	77
TEMPLE OF LUXOR	89
AN EGYPTIAN MEAL	136
JERUSALEM, NORTH-EAST CORNER	181
THE FOUNTAIN AT NAZARETH	235
CAPERNAUM	261
A DRUSE WOMAN	*On binding*

ALONE THROUGH SYRIA.

CHAPTER I.

INTRODUCTORY: A FEW THOUGHTS ON EGYPT PAST AND PRESENT.

My first acquaintance with the East was made in Egypt. I travelled with a friend direct from England to Cairo, and, after some stay there, we started in January on the now familiar "Trip up the Nile."

It is a great privilege to have the opportunity of visiting Egypt; so much food for calm enjoyment, for quiet thought, for deep instruction, lies before one in that land of glowing light, of strange mystery, and most venerable antiquity; that Egypt, so long and closely connected with Holy Scripture, and with the history of God's chosen people.

A wonderful fact it is to realize, that this very old land still lives and takes its place in contemporaneous modern history; nay, more wonderful still, a careful perusal of the prophetic utterances of Ezekiel, Jeremiah, and Isaiah concerning Egypt, leads us to believe that God has yet an important future in store for her. What His wisdom intends that future to be, or what part the British nation is destined to play concerning it, is not for us to surmise. We have but to accept His written Words, and wait till His Providence shall make them clear. "And the Lord shall smite Egypt, smiting and healing; and they shall return unto the Lord, and He shall be intreated of them, and shall heal them."*

In Egypt one lives in two worlds—one past, one present. This present is a very fascinating one; we find ourselves basking in a golden and vivifying sunshine, breathed on by gentle balmy airs, and enlivened by all rich and tender hues of colour in earth and sky; —and water too, when towards sunset, and long after it, the mellow afterglow sheds a soft, ever-changing beauty on that strange mysterious river, which is now, as ever, making and remaking the land of Egypt.

Gazing over the yellow stretch of desert which more or less bounds the vision far as eye can reach to east and to west, one perceives, while travelling towards Upper Egypt, that without the Nile there could be *no* Egypt; only the union of two deserts, bounded at intervals by rocky hills. The realization of this fact leads one on to a fuller acknowledgment of, and a growing reverence for, the mighty creative power of Nature. True now, as it was then, is the saying of Herodotus, "Egypt is the gift of the Nile." The Delta is especially so; till about the human

* Isa. xix. 22.

period of the world's history, no vestige existed of this large, fertile, and important region, which consists of nothing but the continuous accumulation of mud deposited by the Nile at its mouth. This originally debouched a little below Old Memphis, into a large gulf of the Mediterranean Sea, since converted into the Delta.

The solemn past, too, attracts us powerfully in Egypt; her wondrous tombs seem to preach to each fleeting generation that visits them : " Ye are strangers and pilgrims on the earth." Dating back, many of them, to a period anterior to any known era, the pyramids still stand in the desert sand, stern, silent, solitary, immovable, as though defiant of the lapse of time. But the busy hands which laboured in their construction—the many, many generations of men, who have in turn gazed on them with wondering eyes,—where are they?

Those vast burying-grounds (one of which—the Necropolis of Ghîzeh—extends for twenty-five miles along the sandy desert near the Nile) indicate to us the past existence of enormous cities once inhabited by a highly civilized and intellectual people ; while their tombs remain, the ancient homes, wherein their earthly lives were passed, have vanished ; mounds of sand and rubbish alone suggest their probable site. It may seem strange that these people could not build houses to endure as their imperishable monuments have done; the fact is, they bestowed little care on their earthly tenements, lavishing their chief attention and resources on what they considered their more enduring habitations after death. Thus they seem dimly to shadow forth to us that Christian aspect of life which, long years after, was to be emphasized by the Apostle Paul.*

These curious sepulchres proclaim, with pathetic voice, the greatness and the littleness of man. How *little* does he seem as we gaze on the contents of the tombs! mere dry bones and shrivelled mummy forms, whose parchment-like and now fast-fading countenances peer forth to us piteously to-day from their glass cases in the Boulâk Museum! Many of them were ruthlessly torn from the resting-places in which they had willed and hoped to sleep their long sleep, secure and hidden from human eye. We can view there the faces of once mighty Pharaohs; men who not only conquered the then known world, but also presumptuously strove to fight against the manifested power of God. Faces also are visible of illustrious and once beautiful queens;—one can still see, in some of the mummies, teeth in the jaw, a lock of hair on the brow; but alas! in their now gradually crumbling condition (since their discovery and uncovering in 1881), they seem likely soon to perish entirely, leaving nothing behind but golden jewels which long ago were laid with them in the grave.

Yet, how *great* in life must have been the men

* 2 Cor. iv. 18; Heb. xiii. 14.

who could originate and rear the massive and enduring structures, which, whether temple, obelisk, or tomb, are still wonders in the world! What a wealth of power, art, science, ingenuity, and perseverance was there in those very far-off ages, which we moderns, in our unknowingness of them, have sometimes presumed to call "dark and mythical"! What searchings, too, after an "unknown God"! What an instinct of worship! We learn much about this, as also about their manner of life, from the wall-paintings and hieroglyphs, the bright colours of which still adorn temple and tomb.

Their religion permeated every part of their life; can as much be said of ours in enlightened England nowadays? The highest acts of their kings were religious functions, and to offer gifts to the gods was their highest privilege. The *earliest* Egyptians believed in the great certainties of judgment after death, and of a future life of rewards and punishments; and they had a high appreciation of the virtues of truth and justice. Amid the bright pleasures and simple occupations of their daily life, the thought of death was never out of sight. As a reminder of it, a mummy was introduced at scenes of festive gathering; and a yet more forcible reminder would be the family tomb, which, day by day, was being reared near by under the eye of the Pater Familias; whilst he was still in the enjoyment of health and vigour, one of the main interests of his life would be the construction of this lasting abode, wherein, one day, his carefully embalmed body, as also those of his family, should calmly repose 'mid the sands of the Western Desert, awaiting the time when the dissevered soul, after its passage through trial, judgment, and long mysterious journeyings, should return to be reunited with its earthly tenement. Kings likewise began, simultaneously with their reign, to found their last resting-place, which was so ingeniously planned that its construction could be extended in perfect symmetry of proportion according to the duration of the reign.

There seems to have been, at a later period, a great falling off in the purity of Egyptian, as well as of other heathen beliefs and practices. Indeed everywhere, a gross moral darkness preceded the dawning of that blessed day when the Sun of Righteousness arose, shining in fulness of mercy on a sinful world.

This brings me to the thought of *another* past which the earnest-minded traveller in Egypt would fain recall. He remembers that he is in the land where sojourned Abraham and Sarah, Jacob, Joseph and his brethren, Moses and Aaron. He tries to picture to his imagination all the great drama once wrought out here by the Most High God, working His wonders by the hand of His servant Moses, and mightily delivering His people from "the house of bondage."

Last and best, he remembers that Egypt has been

sanctified by the Presence of the Incarnate Son of God Himself; that here also His gospel was faithfully preached and enthusiastically received, rapidly growing up into a vigorous Christian Church, in whose ranks were numbered some of the great primitive Fathers, and which was early watered by the blood of martyrs. It must not be forgotten that this Church still exists in a languishing form as the Coptic Church, to which I shall have occasion to refer hereafter.

I confess, it *is* somewhat difficult to realize fully such thoughts in the Egypt of to-day, surrounded as one is on all sides by modern civilization—Cook's steamers plying up and down the great river; trains, telegraph-wires, English soldiers, bustling European travellers, in every direction. One feels disappointed that, near the banks of those turbid brown waters, no trace remains of the bulrushes (probably akin to the papyrus) in which the child Moses was concealed by his Jewish mother. It is curious that no vestige now is left either of this or of the lotus-plant, though the papyrus still grows at Syracuse in Sicily, and in certain streams of Syria. However, the disappearance of the papyrus in Egypt remarkably verifies the words of the Prophet Isaiah: "The reeds and flags shall wither. The paper reeds by the brooks, by the mouth of the brooks, and everything sown by the brooks, shall wither."* The "paper reeds"

---
* Isa. xix. 6, 7.

must signify the papyrus, from which we have derived our word "paper;" and "the mouths of the brooks" denote the system of irrigation in connection with the Nile, the neglect of which, at any period of Egypt's long history, would surely cause all that was "sown" to "wither."

As one ponders over the wall-paintings and hieroglyphs which silently relate the history of past ages, one longs to find among them some definite reference to those "strangers" who sojourned in the land for more than four hundred years—some record of the miracles performed on their behalf, and of their glorious departing. Yet, on reflection, how unlikely would it be that the vain-glorious Pharaohs of that epoch should seek in any way to perpetuate circumstances which terminated in so great a national humiliation! The King, Menepthah, of the nineteenth dynasty, under whom the Exodus took place, and who escaped the drowning in the Red Sea by which his army perished, would, during his after-reign, strive to obliterate all memory of the terrible disaster.

One very interesting wall-painting I saw in a tomb at Thebes: Jewish captives of King Thothmes III., of the eighteenth dynasty, are there plainly depicted as engaged in building part of the great temple of Amen-ra. Hebrews are represented hard at work; some carrying water, others making or drying bricks, while Egyptian overseers with long whips or staves in their hands are overlooking all.

This scene readily recalls the account in Exod. i. 11–14; and specially interesting is the inscription visible near an overseer, who is supposed to be saying to the labourers, "The staff is in my hand ; be not idle." We catch the very echo of Exod. v. 17.

But it was at Karnak, cut in the stones of one of the outer walls of its great temple, that I saw the first pictorial representation affording a *bonâ fide* corroboration of Old Testament history : "And it came to pass in the fifth year of King Rehoboam, that Shishak King of Egypt came up against Jerusalem." * On this wall the figure of Shishak (called in Egyptian "Sheshonk") stands, large and conspicuous, in the midst ; he is leading by long strings the representative prisoners of thirty nations whom he has subdued. Above are cartouches bearing in hieroglyph the names of these nations, that of Judah amongst them. A list also is added of the Levite cities of Palestine. The conqueror is holding by the hair of their heads a group of unmistakably Jewish captives, who all have hands uplifted, and eyes upturned towards the great king, as if pleading for mercy. Below, are seen row upon row of these bearded Jewish profiles, all in the same attitude. The ground having risen considerably above the base of the wall, there are probably many more ranks of these pleaders, hidden by the earth from which the lowest row now visible is emerging.

* 1 Kings xiv. 25.

Recalling the fact stated in a previous chapter of the same Book of Kings, "And Solomon made affinity with Pharaoh King of Egypt, and took Pharaoh's daughter, and brought her into the city of David,"* we may wonder why this Shishak so soon went to war with the Jewish nation, considering the friendly alliance of his predecessor with King Solomon; but Egyptian history and Scripture together make it clear. Shishak, who reigned about 970 B.C., was a foreigner of a new Egyptian dynasty (the twenty-second) and allied himself with Jeroboam, the enemy of Rehoboam, the then King of Judah. Jeroboam had at a previous period taken refuge at the court of Egypt,† and may have suggested to Shishak his attack on Jerusalem. After besieging it, Shishak captured the city, spoiling the temple and carrying away with him the golden shields of Solomon, and many captives, whom I have described as represented on the wall of the Egyptian temple. He afterwards removed his capital from Thebes to Bubastes (called in Scripture Pibeseth, see Ezek. xxx. 17), and initiated a low animal type of worship, elevating the cat to the dignity of a divinity. Shishak is the first Egyptian king mentioned by name in the Bible; I was glad to discover among so many heathen chronicles one forming a distinct link with the history of Revelation.

Other such links have been added through the

* 1 Kings iii. 1. † 1 Kings xi. 40.

medium of the Palestine Exploration Society. It is now well known that under its auspices M. Naville, in 1883, identified near Tel-el-Kebir (close to the fresh-water canal) the site of Pithom, one of the "treasure-cities" mentioned in Exodus. He thus brought to light treasure-chambers built more than 3300 years ago. They are square chambers, very solidly and regularly constructed, the walls being three yards thick and containing no door, so that the entrance must have been from above for greater security. The other city, Ramses, had been previously identified by Lepsius near the ruins of Tel-el-Maskûta. Rameses II., a king, not of the Hyksos race, but of the new dynasty which "knew not Joseph," had commanded the Hebrews to build both cities, when he began mightily to oppress them, making "their lives bitter with hard bondage in mortar and in brick."* It was found, on careful examination of the bricks discovered, that they are composed of sun-dried mud, some mixed with chopped straw and some containing none.† How certainly do these old bricks testify to the truth of God's Word! One of them is now to be seen in the museum at Berlin.

Further exploration within Pithom has unearthed some of its monuments, including two Sphinxes. All are now placed in the public square at Ismailîya. It is easy to imagine that Hebrew slaves must have

* Exod. i. 13, 14. † Exod. v.

assisted in the labour of transporting and erecting these works. But M. Naville has done even yet more valuable service, by identifying the site called in Hebrew "Succoth," to the west of which Pithom stands at a distance of about twelve miles. As Succoth is the first point at which the Israelites halted on their march towards the Red Sea, we have here a distinct clue to the Exodus route through the land of Goshen.

Another indefatigable explorer, Mr. Flinders Petrie, has recently been at work on the old mounds which for centuries were the sole indication of the site of one of the most ancient cities in the world —Zoan, or Tanis, now Sân.* It lies on the Delta about thirty miles to the north of Goshen. We learn from Ps. lxxviii. 12 that the court of Pharaoh was at Zoan at the time of the Exodus. The warlike and conquering dynasty, to which the then reigning King Menepthah belonged, had transferred the capital from Upper Egypt to Zoan as being a more central point. Thence troops could readily sally forth against the various foreign powers, whose retaliating attacks might be anticipated at any weak point of the vast empire.

The threatening attitude, too, which the populous Israelites had lately assumed under the oppressive *régime* of the new dynasty, may have partly induced these Pharaohs to fix the centre of residence in this

* Numb. xiii. 22.

commanding situation, close to the disaffected district. Spite of their present bondage, the Hebrews, during their long residence in Egypt, had succeeded in making their influence strongly felt among the people of the land, many of whom even sympathized with them in their affliction; so that, on the whole, the aspect was one to cause alarm to the ruling power, even before Moses appeared on the scene. *Then*, this Zoan must have witnessed many a stormy conference between Menepthah and the appointed champions of the suffering Hebrews, and thence must have gone forth the Divine fiat for the smiting of the firstborn.

This city, so contiguous to and closely connected with the dwellers in Goshen, possesses an intense interest for the earnest Bible student. It is strange that, during two hundred years of the Israelites' sojourn in Egypt, contemporary sacred and secular history are both alike silent. May there not be voices "in stone," now mute beneath the rubbish-heaps of Zoan, which could, in their own peculiar but most reliable fashion, throw a whole flood of light on the unknown history of that epoch?

Bubastes, another old town in the Goshen region, was in process of being unearthed as I passed it by. Though historically belonging to a much later period than Zoan, this place became the capital of the dynasty whence issued Shishak, the conqueror of Jerusalem, to whom I have already referred. Here, again, we may expect to find much which will illustrate Bible facts.

Indeed, of sites inviting excavation there is no lack. But ample funds are urgently needed for the due accomplishment of the very costly work now being carried on by the *employés* of the Palestine Exploration Society. This society earnestly invites—nay, it claims—the generous support of all who value sacred Revelation and are desirous to uphold its truth, as well as to aid in the development of ancient art, science, archæology, and contemporary history.

CHAPTER II.

SOMETHING ABOUT CAIRO.

Situation—Street-life—Women—Society—Memphis—Egyptian art—Arabian architecture—Modern barbarians—Mosques—The Korân—Education—Our duty.

THE traveller landing at Alexandria will probably not halt there long, but rather hurry on by train (in four hours) to Cairo, where, if new to Oriental life and surroundings, he will find much to interest and fascinate him. This city, the largest in Africa and second in importance of the Sultan's empire, stands on the famous life-giving Nile, well backed by its Citadel and brown Mokattam Hills. Its picturesque gates, its more than three hundred mosques, its handsome fountains and tombs, extensive bazaars and fine palaces; its famous school, "El-azhar" (containing ten thousand students, and free to all Moslems throughout the world), its splendid river and handsome modern bridge, its uniquely interesting Boulâk Museum, its many surrounding excursions (the most popular being that to the Pyramids of Ghîzeh whose soft hazy outline the traveller can discern from afar);

—all these together contribute to render Cairo a grand and valuable city, one which any potentate may be proud to possess.

I arrived on the 23rd of November—rather too early;—for the heat was somewhat oppressive, and fever yet lingered, after an unusually high Nile inundation. I should say that December is the most pleasant month for Europeans to pass in Cairo. The thermometer was then by day about 70° Fahr. in my room,* and there was hardly any rain. The rush of tourists, too, is less before than after Christmas, which I think a point worth considering.

Having time at our disposal, my friend and I were able to investigate in a thorough and leisurely manner this most picturesque, lively, and fascinating Oriental city. Its praises have been so well and frequently sounded, that it will not be needful for me to go into all the details of its charms. You have but to sit quietly in front of your hotel, and behold! a living and varied picture will be constantly presented, as in a kaleidoscope, before your eyes;—one rich in scenic effect, in rapid movement, in all possible blendings of soft and bright artistic tints. In it will be seen mingling every type of the human face divine, varied as are the forms and colours of the costumes which accompany and illustrate each type. A rich field is here for the artist, who shall know how to use

* In Cairo, the mean temperature during the short winter is 58° Fahr., in spring 78°, in summer 83°, and in autumn 66°.

broad and glowing colours, as well as to depict architectural niceties. If he take a stroll, each street-corner will offer a charming subject for his brush; each tiny native shop, with its dignified occupant, will suggest a picture, and there is everywhere plenty of animated life for his foreground. I am thinking especially of those quarters which have been allowed to retain their Oriental character; in some of their narrow streets, the lofty, overhanging houses with bay windows of ancient Mushrebiyeh work, form delightful vistas.

It is sad to have to confess that in Cairo, wherever European style and workmanship have been introduced, the peculiar charm has vanished. Much was done by the father of the present Khedive to bring parts of the city to the level of a modern European town, and with anything but a picturesque result. Neither do sanitary arrangements seem to have been made in a very efficient manner in the European quarter, where modern drainage has been introduced; there is certainly still room for improvement.

Strolling up one of the main thoroughfares, and making his way quietly through the motley, moving crowd, so full of interest to a stranger, the candid observer must own that it is the European costume which here appears ugly, ungraceful, and uncomfortable. Those Englishmen are wise who in a measure adopt the loose flowing garments, so well suited to this climate; it is a pity that the Turk, as

C

also the upper-class Egyptian, is adopting a European style of dress, so inferior in grace to his own.

For the female sex, the case is reversed. We Englishwomen can glory in our freedom—of motion, of dress, of mind and body—indeed, of life generally; and can look with pity on the Eastern woman, whose life is so little free, in any real sense. As far as her outdoor costume goes, the Egyptian woman, whether she be clothed in rich Broussa silk or in coarse blue cotton, cannot but present an ungraceful appearance in her uncomfortable outer garment, which hinders all freedom of movement. Her head must be heated and overweighted with its elaborate coverings; on her thickly veiled face no fresh breeze can blow, and her hands seem seldom at liberty under her voluminous surroundings. All her graces are, I suppose, reserved for the domestic circle indoors, where, it is to be hoped, she finds plenty to interest her, as she can see but little out of her closely latticed windows. Her mind is but very slightly cultivated; the consolations of religion, too, are limited for her, as her soul is considered of far less value than that of a man. In the mosques, where the men constantly flock for worship, but few women are seen, and these, during service, are shut off in a place reserved for them; indeed, the men do not care that they should be there at all, since they look on women, for the most part, as mere human chattels.

European ladies, with their independent habits, have been rather a puzzle to the Oriental, who has till lately looked on them with a kind of suspicion, not altogether flattering to our sex. Now, however, that he has become familiarized with the sight of Western women of all nationalities, he merely sets them down as an eccentric race of beings.

Whilst on the subject of "women," I may observe how unchangeable have been their customs and occupations, like everything else, in the unchangeable East. That very old book, the Bible, vividly exemplifies this fact, by many an incidental allusion. For example, in the grand triumph-song of Deborah written more than three thousand years ago,[*] we read of the mother of Sisera crying "through the lattice," just as an Eastern woman would do now. A little further, the "needlework" is mentioned which Deborah imagines her hero-son to have received for a "prey," as "of divers colours of needlework on both sides." Here is an exact description of the exquisite work done by Eastern women, such as I have lately seen in the bazaars of Cairo and Constantinople. The colours and designs are most varied, and all is so neatly finished off that it is impossible to detect any difference in the two sides.

Though the Moslem religion allows a man four wives, this privilege is too costly to be adopted by the majority, as the husband must provide a dowry

See Judg. v.

for each wife; they are also apt to quarrel a good deal amongst themselves, which creates difficulties unless a separate establishment be found for each; thus monogamy is now, for prudential reasons, the more prevalent state of life among Moslems. The poor wife holds her position on a somewhat delicate footing, as a word from her husband could effect her divorce, though she would be allowed to keep her dowry. It is well that many of the highly privileged women of the West are now charitably co-operating to bring light, interest, and bodily relief into the lives of their less-favoured Eastern sisters.

Society at Cairo presents many aspects. Since the establishment of our Protectorate, it has comprised, in addition to the British troops, a good number of English residents, civilian as well as military. The political, scientific, philanthropic, and pleasure-seeking classes can each find their own sphere of interest. English Cairene society offers its votaries balls, concerts, theatricals, reviews, tennis-tournaments, polo-matches, steeplechases;—in fact, every variety of diversion. Of these the Egyptologist and archæologist usually steer clear, finding more than enough to engage them in their own special line.

The intelligent amateur, who may be anxious to derive pleasure and instruction from all available sources, has but to place himself in one of the victorias, drawn by a pair of horses, which stand before his hotel, and he will be whisked off by his interpreter to view in turn all quarters of the city. For this sort of life a main requisite is a well-lined purse, as nothing is cheap in Cairo. The *pension* in the best hotels is at least fifteen shillings per day in the full season, and a drive of any extent cannot be had under ten shillings. As walking will be found here a somewhat exhausting process, recourse may be had to donkeys, on which tourists are seen scampering through the streets in unorthodox fashion, for to ride donkeys "in town" is considered by the Cairene "bad style." However, these animals will often be found more convenient than carriages, especially in visiting the bazaars which, to many, form a main attraction. Besides their picturesqueness and the variety of their contents, they are generally the coolest places, being protected from the sun's heat by a rough covering of mats, which also produce a pleasant subdued light. A single shop is usually about eight feet high and six feet broad. A row of these, all open in front, form the *sûk*, or bazaar, which is devoted to one special line of business, so that many are congregated together. Many, too, are the guides and interpreters—mostly Coptic boys from the mission schools, who, for a trifling remuneration, offer themselves conveniently to conduct the pedestrian through the motley crowd to the point he is seeking.

The sturdy English soldier forms here rather an incongruous object; yet his homely countenance inspires one with a pleasant sensation. He seems quite at his ease. I have often been amused to watch some of them, when off duty, cantering away, with evident glee, on the little Egyptian donkeys which they would think it quite *infra dig.* to ride at home. They are, moreover, up to making an advantageous bargain ;—an art which every one has to acquire in the East, and often by bitter experience.

Cairo is called by the natives "Masr-el-Kahira," that is, "the victorious." " Masr" is the Semitic name of Egypt, being derived from the biblical Mizraim.* This fact gives force to the probability that the Egyptian race came originally from Asia; their language contains some affinity with Semitic roots. The city may be called, in a sense, "ancient," having been founded by the Arabs A.D. 641, and rebuilt on a larger site A.D. 960. But its chief historic interest is derived from its association in thought with the ancient Memphis, called "Noph" in Scripture,† of which Cairo may be considered the modern offshoot. Much of its old material has been utilized in the building of Cairo, especially in its mosques.

The first known king of that splendid Old Memphis was Menes, the son of Mizraim, who was the son of Ham ; so here we are carried back close to the period of the Flood. This Menes must have been a man of great wisdom, judgment, and engineering resource, since, for commercial convenience, he accomplished

* Gen. x. 6.   † Isa. xix. 13 and Hos. ix. 6.

the feat of turning the course of the Nile at the point where he founded his city. About the same time also rose the mighty pyramid-builders. In the words, "Memphis shall bury them,"* must not the prophet have been referring to the vast Necropolis close by where stood, and still stand, the great pyramids, amid hundreds of other tombs, some of them five thousand years old?

The God-given wisdom, skill, and knowledge with which Adam had been dowered at his creation, descended in considerable measure upon Noah and his immediate successors. In the Boulâk Museum, which contains the earliest known specimens of human art, can be seen portrait-statues, typical of many different races which swayed Egypt at various epochs. It is remarkable that the later stiff conventional style of Egyptian art and portraiture is quite opposed to the grace of outline, delicacy of feature, and realistic truth which *increase* in proportion as we *retrograde* towards the earlier period. Then, there was nothing either hideous or grotesque in Egyptian art; then, too, the woman was the one wife, the true companion and helpmeet of her husband and lord; only at a later period did she descend to a more degraded position, such as had long been common among surrounding heathen nations.

No one can fail to admire the modest, dignified, and speaking figures of Prince Ra-hotep and Princess

* Hos. ix. 13.

Nefert, whose stony yet lifelike countenances gaze strikingly on the beholder from a standpoint of quite five thousand years ago, according to the latest computation. Having belonged to the fourth dynasty, this wedded pair were probably near descendants of Noah.

Not only in delicacy of portraiture, but also in perfection of workmanship, did the first Egyptians far exceed those of a later date. Their earliest artists worked in wood. At Boulâk I saw some panels in beautiful preservation, representing natural life in truest outline and fine execution.

I may mention that the voluminous papyrus rolls, which have been of late years extensively discovered and deciphered, prove to what mental and scientific heights the early Egyptians also attained. Much knowledge in chemistry, medicine, and kindred sciences, which had been thought to have a Greek or Arab origin, are now found to have been derived from the Egyptians. To them we owe the very word "chemistry," from "Kem," or "Ham," that is, "the black," chemistry having been formerly looked upon as a dark science.

The modern traveller on his way to Sakkâra rides over the site of Memphis ; but no vestige now remains of that once enormous city except a colossal statue of Rameses II., fallen prostrate on the ground and washed over during part of the year by the Nile waters. Another larger one, which lies near

PRINCE RA-HOTEP AND PRINCESS NEFERT
(Boulak Museum).

by, has been presented to our nation, but the means do not seem yet forthcoming for its removal; it is walled round, and made a show of for payment.

Memphis, during her long history, went through many vicissitudes, and suffered injury from the various conquerors who, under the later dynasties, overran the land. After viewing its present desolation (in which is fulfilled the prophecy of Ezek. xxx. 13 and following verses), it is difficult to realize the statement made by the traveller Abdullatîf in the thirteenth century A.D. He states that, when he visited the spot, portions of the city were still standing, and many fine buildings intact. It seems, then, that we have to thank *modern* barbarians, from that century down to the present, for having carried away all that remained of interest. Alas! such depredations are still too common.

Many of the mosques in Cairo are handsome, but they are mostly erected on one plan, that of the first, built at Mecca; thus there is a certain monotony about them. It is sad that many of the finest are now being allowed gradually to decay, while new ones of inferior style are continually being begun, though often left incomplete. There is ever a certain untidiness amid the elegance of old Arabian architecture; but the modern Turk knows neither how to build well nor how to restore.

The Mohammedan style in Egypt did not immediately succeed that of the ancient Egyptian, being separated from it by the early Christian epoch—an interval of six or seven centuries. Neither was it then of pure native growth; the victorious Arabs borrowed much from the Byzantines and other Easterns whom they conquered, preserving, however, their own individuality in elegance of architectural form and of surface decoration. The main features of Arabian architecture can perhaps in a measure be traced back to the nomadic life of its founders, the tent having furnished the idea of the dome-life roof; while the long surfaces of plain or decorated walls were first suggested by the tent walls with their carpets, hangings and various textile ornaments.

One distinct feature in Arabian architecture is its appearance of unsubstantiality. The columns do not seem to be in proportion to the weight they have to support. Arab architects found the Egyptian style too solid for them; they preferred the Roman or Greek; and much as they were wont to steal, for their own mosques, the columns of other temples, they never utilized Egyptian ones, unless these had been first remodelled in Greek or Roman temples. They also avoided copying the style of pagan temples, but imitated the Byzantines, especially in mosaic and arabesque work; into the latter, however, introducing a peculiar charm of their own. Their religion forbade them to depict living forms, so they gave their whole attention to beauty of design and ornamental decoration; in this matter far surpassing the Jews, whose art had to be similarly circumscribed. Dean Stanley calls Mohammedans "the Puritans of the East;" they give of their *best* in the construction of their mosques, but the ritual therein observed is of a limited character, and there is not very much to assist worship by an appeal to the senses. Their sacrifices, which are but of rare occurrence, take solely the form of a thank-offering, and are not offered within the mosque, but usually on some tomb or other venerated spot outside.

The Arabs developed great decorative ingenuity in artistic metal-work, enamel, inlaying, etc.; thus the term "arabesque" now stands to express elegant ornamentation. In colour they did not reach the exquisite mellowness produced by their co-religionists in Spain, but trusted a good deal to *contrast* of colour. Their chief resources of beauty, in the interior of the mosque, were lavished on the "Kibla," or holy place; the soft-tinted yellow stone of the exterior walls was often set off by bands of black or some other dark colour, such as is seen in many Italian churches.

While the tent may have first suggested the dome, the Arabs, in developing their elegant minarets, may have had in mind the trees into which the first "muezzins" climbed to call the faithful to prayer. The minarets, square at the base, often rise to a great height, in exquisite symmetry of proportion and lightness of design.

The superstitious idea that outward beauty attracts the "evil eye" has hindered the artistic development of house-architecture, so that the affluence of the inmate is chiefly indicated by the sumptuous interior hangings of his abode, and by the costliness of the jewels worn by the women.

It is interesting to note the zeal with which Mohammedans attend to their religious duties. On holy days the men flock eagerly to the mosques, where, having first drawn off their shoes, and performed the needful ablutions, they engage in a series of solemn genuflexions and prostrations. I have been told that at certain parts of their common worship the whole congregation simultaneously beat the ground with their foreheads, producing a sound somewhat like the rumbling of distant thunder. The public service consists of little else than readings from the Korân, which is held by all in deep reverence. Rows of the holy book are placed on stands on one side of the mosque; and it is a moving sight to behold, on any day, men, young and old, all seated on the ground, with feet well tucked up, each poring reverently over one of the sacred books, and continually swaying the body and muttering in a low tone, during the religious exercise. Others may be seen counting their rosaries while reciting the ninety-nine attributes of "Allah," and constantly repeating solemn invocations to that sacred Name. I refrain from alluding to the wild extravagancies practised by the dervishes during their devotions, since this subject has become very familiar from the frequent description of travellers.

The Korân contains a strange medley of Jewish and Christian traditions, which have led "the faithful" to appropriate a promiscuous selection of saints, whom they highly venerate. To translate the holy book into other languages is considered a profanity. Our Friday is the Moslem Sunday, as being the sixth day, on which Adam was created; then only, is a sermon preached by the "imam," often a layman of very moderate education; he stands in a high pulpit called "mambar," while his hearers are seated on the ground before him. Moslems are adverse to the admission of Christians to their service; a good bakshîsh is the only means of gaining entrance on a Friday, and, when you *have* effected it, they are apt to cast on you unpleasantly scowling glances. Though most of the men attend the mosques on Fridays, business is by no means universally suspended; but, in imitation of Christian practice, the law-courts have lately been closed.

On some points we Christians might well imitate the Moslems. They have an enthusiastic belief in their own creed, and, as a logical sequence, make religion the sole basis of all teaching; every child is instructed in the Korân, and nothing but the Korân, till he is nearly nine years of age. Can *we* be said to be *more* enlightened in *our* policy, who, in Christian England, and in this nineteenth century, seem anxious, many of us, to squeeze the religious teaching of the young within the smallest possible limits, if not to banish it altogether? Is it not because, as a nation, we have not faith enough in our creed, that we seem so slack in laying the foundations thereof in the hearts and minds of our children? That fanaticism or superstition, at which we may be inclined to sneer in some other nations, may perhaps prove less disastrous in its final effects than a miserable indifference and half-heartedness on vital matters. Now, or never, is the time when English Churchfolk should bestir themselves to see that the rising generation be not robbed of its precious heritage—religious education.

Without delay or hesitation, then, shall we not all unite, giving money, time, personal effort, and influence —above all, prayer—to strengthen the hearts and hands of those who, in the forefront of the battle, have in these latter days to "contend earnestly for the Faith once delivered to the saints," and to see that it be handed on in its fulness to their children's children? In this time of danger shall any neglect the public petition, "that religion and piety may be established among us for all generations"?

The prince of darkness, with his myrmidons, is busy in the matter of promoting secular education *only;* he knows that England has received from Heaven a great commission—though one which she cannot eventually fulfil, if the doctrines of her religion be expunged from her own national training. Her emissaries have already gone forth—they are still going forth—throughout the wide world, bearing with them, together with civilization, the Lamp of Truth. Its shining light shall surely continue to spread over and illuminate the globe. Meanwhile, God grant that our own dear little England be not found groping back into a darkness which she herself shall have deliberately chosen! Rather may she ever continue to be as a "light" which "giveth light unto all."

CHAPTER III.

MORE ABOUT CAIRO AND ITS INHABITANTS.

Donkey-boys—Moslem habits and character—Prayers—Moral courage—Walks outside the town—An escape—The Copts —Gordon College—A tea-party.

THE Egyptian lad is usually an amusing and intelligent human specimen; the donkey-boys come most frequently before the notice of strangers; I have found them generally very good-natured and obliging. One calls them Egyptian, though among them there are representatives of very different African races. The three main types seen in Cairo are the Nubian, Egyptian, and Arab, but most of them have a composite pedigree; their Moslem creed unites them more closely than affinity of race.

It is remarkable how much more facility Easterns have for acquiring our language than we Britons, as a rule, have for learning to speak even a *European* one, let alone Arabic. The Egyptian boy, always full of vivacity, is wise enough to seize the passing opportunity, and often makes out of the donkey-ride a profitable lesson for himself; being by no means shy, he freely asks questions of the stranger, and, with his ready ear, soon catches up pronunciation and idiom.

As light of foot as he is quick of sight, the boy flies gaily along after your galloping beast, under the burning sun. *You* find that the change to rapid motion raises a refreshing breeze before your face; but for *him* the experience cannot be so pleasant. When, relaxing speed, you try to communicate something to him, his keen eye seems at a glance to read your thought, while the bright smile of intelligence lights up his countenance. What a charm do his beautiful white teeth impart to that smile! They must be made of very different stuff from *ours;* for, though taken no care of, nothing seems to hurt them.

When you enter a village you will see almost every idler gnawing a sugar-cane, which is both a very tough and a sickly-sweet substance, as I found by experience. The donkey attendants usually have their pockets full of the small cucumbers and various gourd-like vegetables which abound; these they nibble raw as they go along and wholly demolish, tough outside and all!

As regards personal cleanliness, I should say that they are far superior to those of the same class in England; their simple linen garments are easily washed, and frequent bodily ablutions are enforced by their creed. What can be said in favour of the old fustian suits worn by our people at home, the dark colours of which conceal so much that is undesirable? I may further ask, Has the old Roman passion for the public bath, of which so many evidences remain in England, descended in any measure to the lower classes of our modern population? Nay, till very recently, were cheap baths at all within their reach?

The people of Cairo and of the Delta are frugal; their bread is generally made of maize, or *durra*—wheaten bread being only the portion of the rich; it looked to me very tough and uninviting, and is eaten with a little salad or fruit. I have often seen workmen engaged at their midday meal, seated on the ground, near their work; their drink is usually either water or coffee. The chief meal of the day is the supper, when the family sit round the one bowl, which contains a hot mixture, often of onions and butter, for which linseed is sometimes substituted; each member takes his portion on a long-shaped piece of bread, which he dips into the bowl —knives and forks being never used;—so it has been the fashion to eat in ages past, and *will* be, in this land of continuity and in other adjacent countries.

Frugal as the Egyptians are, they have that keen greed for money which has become, I fear, a universal failing. When the time arrives for the donkey-boy or man to receive his bakshish, his bright expression will soon be changed to a gloomy one;

for he is sure *not* to be satisfied, whether you at first offer him less or more than his due;—so it answers best to begin with a modest sum, increasing it gradually up to a certain point, after the manner of Eastern bartering.

The vivacious lad becomes at middle age a grave and somewhat indolent character. I fear that at *no* period of life can *truthfulness* be called his strong point. The older men often get a stern, hard expression, which becomes sometimes defiant towards Christians. It is curious that all Moslems have a certain look in their face, by which those well acquainted with them can distinguish them from Christians. Humility and purity are virtues to which they have not yet attained—nor yet charity, at least in *our* sense of the word, though they often exercise much kindliness and liberality among themselves. "An eye for an eye," and "a tooth for a tooth," still holds good in some quarters, and vengeance is sweet and imperative.

A young Englishman whom I met, verified this to me from his own experience in Morocco. Happening to be in a great crowd one day, he had the misfortune to knock out with his elbow the loose front tooth of an old woman who was pressing against him; she and all her sympathizers were furious, and in spite of his humble apologies and regrets, demanded of him, in compensation, one of his own front teeth! The situation was very unpleasant, and he thought it prudent to retire for awhile as fast as possible from the scene. However, the old woman's avengers pursued him to his retreat. He found he must either leave the country, or let them extract one of his good front teeth; he would not tell me which alternative he chose.

We must not be too hard on the follower of Islam, for his creed does not help him in the cultivation of those great virtues in which he is deficient. While diligently worshipping the one God Who is the Father of us all, and acknowledging Him constantly as great, good, and merciful, the Mohammedan does *not* know Him under His aspect of Infinite Love, which the full acceptance of the doctrine of the Incarnation can alone reveal to man. The Korân, however, by its restrictions, *does* conduce to a quiet, decent condition of outer society. Thus, wine and gambling are forbidden, or at any rate a public indulgence in them. The meeting together in coffee-houses, where they chatter, or, as they smoke and sip their coffee, listen to the recitation of some wild tale,—this, or something akin to it, forms the mild amusement of the people of the lower class. They are exceedingly credulous, easily entertained, kind and hospitable in their habits.

Islamism means "resignation to God's will," and it certainly promotes, in its votaries, a brave, devout, and resigned character. The Moslem is easily moved to religious excitement; he is also bold to confess and uphold his faith before all men. I venture to think that, in this matter as also in that of reverent posture in worship, we may again learn something from our Moslem brothers.

Of the five hours for individual prayer, as instituted in the Korân, the three most generally observed are—that of sunset, of sunrise, and of noon or about three hours later. Most Eastern travellers have been impressed by the solemn earnestness with which these religious duties are attended to; they are considered a regular part of the day's business, which must not be crowded out nor slurred over, whatever may be the surroundings of the worshipper; he, of course, *prefers* a *quiet* spot, if he can get it. Having turned himself in the direction of Mecca, and spread out his prayer-carpet, he begins his prescribed form of recitations and bodily movements, which repeatedly bring him prostrate on his carpet, a certain spot of which he touches now and again with his forehead. The banks of the Nile are a favourite place for these devotions, water being there at hand for the necessary previous washings; at sunrise or sunset, its margin, dotted with male worshippers, offers an interesting spectacle to the stranger.

One morning, as I was entering a bank at Cairo, I remember seeing a man spreading his carpet on the top step before the door of the bank, evidently with the intention of seizing there a short time and a place for prayer, while his master was transacting business within. On board our Nile steamer, too, we frequently, at noon or soon after, had the opportunity of watching the men of our crew; each in turn fulfilled his religious routine on the fore-deck as he could be spared from his work. No matter how public the position, nothing deters Moslems from this duty.

I had not been long in Cairo before feeling the desire to get somewhere beyond the city precincts, and where in my walks I might breathe a purer air than its streets afforded. It is not very easy to do this. Cairo total covers a large surface of ground; for within it are included its straggling ancient quarters, old rubbish-mounds, sandy cemeteries (where lie buried the Khalîfs and Memlûks)—and also Boulâk, its chief commercial centre. The nearest walking point I could discover in the direction of open country was a very rough, sandy, and untidy-looking road along the side of a canal, where bustling country-folk now and then passed along, either riding upon or walking behind their well-laden asses; their light garments flowed wide in the wind, which was blowing violently the day I was there. I noticed that each man held in his hand the universal stout walking-stick or staff. All seemed to stare at me, *en passant*, as if it were unusual to see an Englishwoman walking that way.

The fellâh is patient, good-natured, and well-conducted, and superior in character to his town brother. He is a careful farmer, industrious and ingenious at his work; also a kind father, and anxious for the better education of his children; not remarkable for self-reliance or truthfulness, but the Turkish misrule and extortion under which he has long groaned would not be calculated to develop these virtues. In his own village, the sheikh and his subordinates exercise a kind of patriarchal sway; but, beyond that limit, all have been the helpless slaves of their rulers; the fellâh is kind and civil to strangers, and is worthy of the better state of things now, let us hope, dawning for him. I was told that for each date-palm which he possesses (and *one* is often his sole wealth) he has been accustomed to pay a tax of £4 per annum. This amiable peasant must not be classed with the noisy rabble who mob every traveller, shouting for bakshîsh.

I had here, outside the town, an opportunity of observing the habits of the women. Those dwelling in the country make no attempt to conceal their faces, wearing only a slight veil fastened on their dishevelled hair and flowing behind. Their whole costume seemed to consist of a long, loose, straight garment, without sleeves, made of red or yellow print; it clung ungracefully close to the figure in the strong wind, somewhat after the fashion of a bathing-gown. The children are often quite nude.

During my walk I noticed many of these women flitting to and fro from their little mud hovels; they were constantly going to the banks of the canal, and laying down or taking up something; I soon found that the banks were covered with good-sized round cakes, placed there to bake in the sun; they are composed of a mixture of mud and dung, and it seems to be the chief occupation of the women to make these cakes, and bake them in this fashion, for use as fuel. Wood is now very scarce in Egypt, so substitutes have to be found.

As may be supposed, there is no great demand for fuel among the poor for house-warming purposes, yet it is constantly needed for feeding the ovens, which form a prominent feature amid every collection of huts; indeed, the round-shaped oven-building is often nearly as big as the hut itself. The bread has to be slowly baked in hot ashes, and, as each household makes its own bread, the ovens must be kept constantly heated.

Another day I tried a walk in the direction of the so-called "Windmill Hill," but it was weary work, wading through deep layers of dust at its base, and the view on the brown, bare summit did not repay me; for, turning toward the side away from the city, nothing could be seen but successive lines and hillocks of dust and sand, which appeared to fill the air. On that occasion I was accompanied by a gentleman; he soon after took the same walk alone, and returned with a story most amusing to his auditors, but not so much so to himself. Reclining on the top of the hill, he had taken off his hat, and, holding his umbrella over him against the hot sun, remained some time in a state of quiescence. As he lay there, he casually observed two or three large birds hovering aloft; but did not heed them, till he was suddenly aware of a good-sized round stone descending rapidly from a great height straight in the direction of his head, which was bald. He had but just time to avert the stone with his umbrella from so dangerous a contact with his skull; then, thoroughly aroused from his reverie, he trudged home in a state of some little perturbation. It was a buzzard which had attempted this experiment on the pale, pink skin of his head, which it had marked from afar as a delicate-looking morsel. These birds have a remarkable instinct, which teaches them to select smooth stones, which they carry in their beaks as they soar upwards; then, their keen glance having discovered in the world below some object which promises an appetizing dinner, they drop their missile with wonderful aim in order to secure their victim.

Long before going to Egypt, I had felt interested in the Copts, and anxious to know more about them; a desire which I have been able in some measure to gratify. These interesting people now form about one-fifth of the population of Egypt, and have extensive colonies in Upper Egypt. They are lineal descendants of the old Egyptians, and their present type of physiognomy still bears striking resemblance to that of the earliest inhabitants as handed down to us by primitive Egyptian art. Their aspect and character vary in many points from other dwellers in this land. They are smaller in stature, more delicately formed, fairer in complexion, have more brain development, and a tenacity of character which, under their long oppression, has produced a certain gloominess of disposition. They are somewhat avaricious and reticent, and without the generous spontaneity and dignified bearing which distinguish the Arab; the Copts' deportment is more cringing, a natural result of past suffering and terror. Though free from the vice of polygamy, they are addicted to intemperance, which is not uncommon even among the priesthood. The Copts have quick mental faculties, and an aptitude for mathematics, which causes them to be sought for as clerks, accountants, etc.; they are also employed in the more refined trades, and now often attain to high mercantile positions. The freedom and respect which they have gained will doubtless help them to develop more breadth of character than heretofore.

The history of this people presents no less interest to the ecclesiastical historian than to the ethnologist, since the Copts are Christians who still represent the great primitive Church of Alexandria founded by S. Mark, though they have not, alas! kept the whole of the Apostolic doctrine, acknowledging only the Divinity of our Lord, in which they believe His Humanity to have become absorbed. Sad though this be, we Anglicans cannot but feel respect for a Church which through long and bitter trials has steadfastly clung to Christianity. During the first three General Councils she was at one with the whole Catholic and Apostolic Church, but refused to acknowledge the decree of the Council of Chalcedon, A.D. 531, by which the Eutychian heresy was condemned, into which she had fallen.

The Copts, after a bitter inter-Christian strife which raged fiercely during the sixth and seventh centuries, broke off all allegiance to the Byzantine Church, and gladly submitted themselves to the victorious Saracens. Yet they staunchly refused to embrace the Islam creed, choosing rather to stand alone as a schismatic Church in the midst of aliens. They were at first leniently treated by their new rulers, but later had to suffer bitter persecution at their hands. From this depressing state of things they have but lately emerged to a footing of equality with other Ottoman subjects. They were formerly compelled to wear dark clothing, to distinguish them from the more privileged classes; this they in some measure retain, and by their sombre-coloured turbans may be easily known.

Coptic churches are somewhat similar to those of the Greeks, having a nave terminating at the east in an apse, and having aisles which contain galleries. The nave is divided by wooden screens into three sections; the first forms the vestibule, and has in the floor a trough for water; the second is for the women, and the third for the men; next comes, slightly raised, the choir, where, besides the singers, stand the officials, who read the lessons, etc. Shut off by a close screen, which has a small central door, is the Sanctuary, or Tribune, with the Altar in its midst. The screen is often richly adorned with mosaics, gems, and ancient pictures. The priest within celebrates the Holy Mysteries weekly. The laity communicate seldom, and only after confession; but small loaves are distributed among the people by the priest, who lays his hand of blessing on each individual; the kiss of peace also passes through the congregation. The service begins early, and, as it is very lengthy, and there are no seats, crutches are provided on which weary ones may lean. The whole partakes of a social as well as a religious aspect; conversation is often indulged in, and children are allowed to act as deacons.

Spite of much laxity, Coptic worship breathes a primitive atmosphere, and, according to Dean Stanley, this may be considered the most interesting of all Eastern Churches; its ritual is more ceremonial than that of the Greek Church. The Patriarch is elected from one of the five chief monasteries; he is consecrated by the act of breathing, and can never be translated from one See to another. The Fasts of the Copts are long and severe, even eggs and butter being forbidden, and the fare chiefly confined to bread, with onions, and beans, or salad.

For the sake of mutual protection, these long-oppressed people have been in the habit of building their houses and churches in close proximity, and in somewhat isolated situations, surrounding their quarters with lofty walls. In one of these enclosures the oldest Coptic churches of Cairo are to be found; the exterior walls convey the idea of a fortified position. I am glad to say the Copts have lately been able to erect for themselves a handsome church in the best part of Cairo, and are now free to follow their own worship unmolested. They have a serious difficulty to contend with in the ignorance and indolence of their priests, who are fast losing the little knowledge they had of their venerable Coptic tongue, in which the service is still rendered, though unhappily now little understood either by clergy or people; indeed, it is likely to become a dead language.

Let us hope that increased light may soon be granted to these Christians, whereby they may be guided to a reformation of their Church, and to a reception of all the fulness of revealed Truth. Then shall their light, kindled so long ago, but since partially obscured, again be set on a "candlestick," to lighten the "land of Ham."

Our own peculiar position at present in Egypt gives us, nationally, a great opportunity of assisting the Copts, if we will seize it at once, and use it in a right direction. To proselytize them from their old historic, though clouded faith, into communion with a modern Protestant sect, does not seem quite the best line to pursue; yet this is nearly all that has been hitherto attempted of spiritual work by English-speaking people in Egypt. Those who have laboured there have done so with true zeal and Christian love, and they have succeeded in making many converts; but does not God's Providence seem now to be emphatically calling on our great nation, and its pure branch of the Church Catholic, to come forward in the gap and lend a helping hand to this weak, erring sister—*not* by urging her to forsake her old foundations, but rather to clear round about those foundations, and by sympathetic and judicious efforts to endeavour to assist all, priests and laity alike, within the Coptic pale, to press forward into the paths of enlightenment and truth? The "Society for Promoting Christian Education in the East" has already made an effort in this direction, by the foundation at Cairo of the "Gordon Memorial College." I fear it was not begun on quite the best lines, as its success did not come up to the expectations formed, and it has been closed since my return to England. I am glad, however, to hear that there is a probability of its being re-opened;—I trust with the full consent and co-operation of the Coptic Patriarch, without which permanent success would be dubious.

I must not omit to mention Miss Whately's excellent and well-known school for natives, which I visited. She was, I believe, the first to open an Anglican school in Cairo, and long and faithful has been her work.

Having obtained an introduction to an Englishman belonging to the staff of Gordon College, he kindly invited myself and another lady to an "afternoon" there, which we found very interesting. We were introduced to, and conversed with, about a dozen of the senior Coptic students, who had been asked to tea to meet us. They were nearly all grown up, and mostly engaged in commercial pursuits, some being in positions of affluence. All spoke English, some remarkably well and with a good accent; the questions they asked us concerning our country and ways at home showed them to be intelligent and thoughtful. I should say that the classes which were formerly carried on here, in Church history, English language, literature, and other excellent things, had had very good results; however, none of the young men under instruction have been led to offer themselves as candidates for the priesthood, which was one of the ends hoped for by the establishment of the Gordon College.

I have added, as an Appendix,* the "Prayer for the Land of Egypt," which was in use at the college.

* See Appendix A.

CHAPTER IV.

A WEEK IN THE DESERT.

Helwân—Tura quarries—Our hotel—Invalids—Climate—Panorama—A meeting—Desert music—Christian persecution—Hermits—The ferry-boat—Across country—Cultivation—Happy families—A nocturnal ramble.

I WAS anxious to start for Upper Egypt in the vigorous health which forms so large a factor in real enjoyment; to this, as I have already hinted, a prolonged stay in Cairo would not seem likely to conduce. I also wished to make a more intimate acquaintance with desert life than I could do from Cairo, and therefore decided to spend a week at Helwân—a small place in the desert, on the eastern side of the Nile, fourteen miles distant from Cairo, with which it is now connected by a short railway. Its pure air recommends it as a health resort for those invalids who fear to remain at so remote a place as Luxor. It also possesses sulphur springs, the properties of which are similar to those at Aix-les-bains.

I persuaded Miss —— to accompany me, though

it was for a day or two only, as she, with a prudent regard for comfort, was not willing to renounce her pleasant room at Shepheard's; I, more reckless, gave mine up. In order to secure good donkeys, with side-saddles, it was necessary to send them on from Cairo, which we did; I engaged mine for the week, with a reliable donkey-man, whom I knew well.

Our train conducted us along the foot of the Mokattam Hills, which are of limestone formation, full of curious fossils. We passed the quarries of Tura, where remain the subterranean chambers from which the old Egyptians hewed the stones for the great Pyramids; these we could see just looming opposite in the distance. The modern Arab workmen still excavate stone from this quarry, but in a very inferior fashion to those great primitive workers; for now they cut the stone above ground just as it comes, regardless of selecting the best in quality; their superstitious feelings make them afraid to work underground.

The one hotel at Helwân is not remarkable for its excess of comfort. It met *our* needs; but one could have wished to obtain a few extra luxuries for the many sadly consumptive patients whom we found there, this climate being much recommended for chest complaints. The bedrooms, as is common in the East, are accessible only from an open-air gallery, leading by an open staircase into the *salle-à-manger*, etc. The temperature of the air becomes much colder at night, and to this trying change after the hot day the invalid must often be exposed. Meals in his room would be but a doubtful experiment, as there are no bells in Egyptian hotels; so he may often have to stand for some time clapping his hands in the open air before obtaining any attention to his wants. One could see that some of these poor people had come here too late. The sight of their sufferings was the one thing which marred my pleasure at Helwân.

I looked out from my windows in each direction on a boundless expanse of earth and sky; the sun by day, and the moon by night, reigned in a cloudless vault. The air was particularly pure, fresh, and invigorating, and Nature seemed to present her calmest aspect. Helwân is not a natural oasis; what it possesses in the way of vegetation has been obtained by man's artificial labour. There was a nice green garden belonging to our hotel, into which the water which percolated everywhere, had to be conveyed from afar. I was glad this garden was not round the house, but quite disconnected from it, so that nothing impeded our open view. The poor invalids sat out all day in the garden, being too weak to walk or ride. The little town contains, besides the baths, several straggling European houses, including one belonging to the Khedive; but the street had an ugly, dreary appearance.

I shall not easily forget my sensations on taking

a walk that first evening, towards sunset, straight away in the direction of what looked like boundless desert. The sand was mostly firm and crisp to walk upon, and frequently sprinkled with salt which crackled under my feet. The pure health-giving air inspired me with a delightful sense of buoyancy. Casting my eyes westward, a unique panorama was before me; for there, in the distance across the Nile, were mapped out the whole successive groups of Pyramids—those of Ghîzeh, of Abusîr, of Sakkâra, and of Dashûr, covering an extent of thirty miles, and all thrown darkly into prominence by the sinking sun, soon to disappear behind them. What a glorious sunset it was! and the afterglow even more beautiful, as the whole desert and sky gradually seemed to blend together and glow in richest colours, fading by-and-by into the palest of ethereal tints, then soon to merge into the cold blue shades of night. I had to hurry back, as darkness here comes on apace.

Next day we took our first donkey-ride; it was my friend's first and last, as she returned next day to Cairo. How delightful it was, cantering along that firm crisp sand! The hot morning sun was tempered by such a deliciously fresh air, that we did not find it too overpowering. Returning, we met some ladies of the Khedive's harêm walking out with their male attendant. I rejoiced to see these poor ladies able here to enjoy comparative freedom, for in Cairo they only drive out in broughams with closed windows. The Khedive is very wise to keep a residence where he, as well as his family, can occasionally enjoy this good country air. He seems a popular and amiable prince. I had the pleasure of a bow from him one day in Cairo; I was riding a donkey in the Shubra Avenue—not quite the correct thing—when suddenly my attendant drew the animal up short at the side of the road, and there we waited while his Highness passed by. We happened to be that day cutting a poorish figure; for the pommel of my saddle had been hurting me, and my donkey-boy—it was a great proof of his good-nature—had unwound from his head the long turban which all wear twisted round the tight-fitting felt cap, and had utilized it as a bandage for my pommel, thus relieving my discomfort, but not adding to the neatness of the *tout ensemble*.

To return to Helwân;—my donkey seemed to profit as much as I did from the change of air. When we got quite into the open desert, he was wont to assume a most jaunty and gay demeanour; sometimes, as we were cantering along, he would suddenly, with his enormous ears well erect, give forth such an animated and resonant bray as almost to stun me; this he would continue, and resume at intervals for some minutes. I must say his music is not so discordant, nor certainly so melancholy, as that of his English relative, to whom he is, in many points, quite superior, being of a more sensitive and high-mettled nature. My attendant informed me that these sagacious animals are accustomed, in the desert, to give forth this note—of warning, is it?—whenever they catch sight of a Bedâwy, or any such wanderer, approaching in the far distance. To my near-sighted eyes, on this occasion, nothing at all was visible till some time after, when we were met by a handsome mounted Arab, with whom we exchanged salutes. This kind of thing constantly occurred, and became so comical, that I found my laughter often forming an accompaniment to the donkey's bray.

But though the desert conduces to health and good spirits, it is also suggestive of many solemn thoughts. When one has become accustomed to the new surroundings, and spent some quiet hours alone, under the canopy of heaven, a sense of peace, of repose, of nature's harmony, and of the Infinite above and around, steals over one, so that it seems good to be there. I was led back in thought to those holy men who, before the end of the third century, had established monasteries in this very Arabian desert, on the margin of which I now found myself. They were Copts, for the Egyptian Church furnished the first instances of Christian anchorites, as also, soon after, of Cœnobite communities.

It was in the third century that the persecution of Christians became severe throughout all the Roman Empire, and specially in Egypt, where the fire of

Christian zeal then burnt so ardently. When one realizes what life in Eastern cities has always been, and was then especially ; a dense population crowded into very close quarters ; individual life lived almost entirely in public ; but few places to which the pious soul could retire for communion with its God ;—then again, when one thinks of the gibes and insults which the pagans were ever heaping on those early Christians, even during their intervals of respite from public persecution,—it becomes easy to understand what an attraction this desert life must have had for them. Here was the Lord's "holy Temple," in which the whole earth kept "silence before Him ; " here, alone and undisturbed, they could pour out their hearts to the Lord of heaven and earth. Among them were lowly ones, "heirs of faith," who had learned to mortify the flesh ;—"of whom the world was not worthy . . . they wandered about in sheep-skins and goat-skins, being destitute . . . they wandered in deserts, in dens and caves of the earth."

Such a one was S. Anthony ;—he lived in Upper Egypt about sixteen hundred years ago, and was a young man of wealth and influence. One day, while reading his Gospel portion, it spoke to him with a living voice: "Go and sell all that thou hast, and give to the poor." He obeyed to the letter, and, after settling his worldly affairs, retired to this Arabian desert, a few miles inland from the Nile, opposite the modern Benisoef, and some few miles south of Helwân.

There he spent twenty years in an old tomb, living on bread and water, and, being a man of mental power as well as ardent piety, his fame soon spread, and crowds flocked from the populous Nile banks to receive from him teaching and healing. He became the friend of Athanasius, who had sent for him to Alexandria, and who commissioned him to preach against the Arians.

Later in life, S. Anthony was led to found a religious community, not far from the scene of his own seclusion. He became a man of authority, whose advice was sought by all, including even the Emperor Constantine. Then came the snares of vanity and spiritual pride. He began, like Elijah of old, to reckon himself as the most lonely and self-devoted of men. From this state of mind he was mercifully delivered by a voice, which revealed to him the existence of the holy Paul of Thebes, who, in a region of the desert further east, had lived for ninety years a hermit life, almost unknown to any but God ; in him Anthony would see truly exemplified the beauty of childlike faith, humility, and devotion.

Obedient to the vision, Anthony started in search of the aged saint, and after three days found him dwelling in a cavern of the great Thebaid solitude, with a fountain and a single palm tree close by. Eagerly and thankfully did Paul welcome his visitor, as one sent by God to bury him, for he knew that his end was near. They held sweet and holy converse for some days in the cavern; the fountain furnishing them with water, and bread being conveyed to them by a raven, which had for some time past brought the hermit his daily food. Full of years and full of peace, Paul of Thebes passed away, leaving to his aged and lonely friend the task of providing him with burial. This was no easy matter, for S. Anthony was feeble with age, and had no tools at hand to aid him. He reverently wrapped the corpse in a cloak, which he had fetched from the distant monastery for the purpose, and was wondering how next to proceed, when he saw two lions near at hand, pawing a hole in the desert sand; this done, the beasts, with gentle aspect, approached S. Anthony and his sad burden, helped him to push it towards the hole, and to cover it with sand: truly "by faith they stopped the mouths of lions." S. Anthony lived fourteen years after this, dying at the ripe age of a hundred and five years. The oldest monastery remaining in Egypt is called "Deir Antonios."

My donkey, its attendant, and myself had got quite to understand each other; the youth was most civil and well-conducted, and he knew enough English to be able to carry out my wishes. The poor fellow was one day very doleful, for a co-occupant of the shed where he slept (I fancy in company with his donkey) had, during the night, stolen his pair of new shoes—bright red leather ones, with upturned toes, such as all wear ;—but of which they take great care, walking barefoot on smooth rocks and sandy paths, and reserving the shoes for the protection of their feet on stony or rough surfaces.

As the time for my departure for Helwân drew near, I formed the idea of returning to Cairo in a more unconventional and independent fashion than that by which I had come. I would cross the Nile, then ride straight ahead through the Egyptian plain towards the Pyramids of Ghîzeh, spending the night at the comfortable new hotel there; thus I could renew by moonlight my acquaintance with those dear old friends, and ride into Cairo on Saturday on my faithful beast. There seemed no difficulty in the way, at least my attendant made none ; so I engaged another strong lad to carry my large bag, which he did by fastening it round his neck with a cord, and letting it fall behind across his shoulders.

Then off we started early one lovely morning, making straight for the Nile, one hour's ride. We had to cross the river (here very wide) in a native ferry-boat—for me a novel experience. There are no landing-places on the Nile banks, and often, close to it, patches of shallow water remain from the overflow ; so, unless you wish to reach the boat with wet feet, you must submit to be hoisted on the back of a native. My bearer seemed to stagger under the weight of my long limbs, but deposited me safely in the barge ; the same process had to be gone through again on the other side. It became a familiar one later on in the "Nile trip," especially at Luxor, where, in order to reach the grand Theban ruins, one has to be carried over many marshy overflows. It was often comical to see fat ladies and gentlemen of my acquaintance hoisted up in this unceremonious manner.

For the poor donkeys the process of embarkation and disembarkation is no joking matter; indeed, it must be most disagreeable, and looks dangerous. Having been divested of all burdens and trappings, they are whipped and urged through the water; then, by vigorous pushes behind, made somehow to get their fore feet up within the edge of the boat, the hind quarters having to follow in such a scrambling, heterogeneous manner that you think some bone or muscle *must* get hurt. When the time for exit comes, they are pushed head foremost down into the water, and must be thankful enough when they again find themselves safe on *terra firma*.

Like every other Eastern arrangement, this ferry is a very slow mode of travelling, and it was quite an hour before I could land on the opposite side. The process of depositing passengers and goods at the various tiny villages was a prosy one; we seemed sometimes to be going backwards instead of forwards However, the whole scene was very pleasant and picturesque, for, as we kept making many curious turns and bends, the river and its banks assumed continually new aspects, and the shadows were reflected sweetly on the water. I fancy that our ferry-boat, with its many long-oared rowers, and its motley cargo, was not the least picturesque feature in the landscape. The boat was crowded with Egyptian men and boys; several donkeys, too, were compressed into as close quarters as possible, at one end of the craft, though rather too near to us to be agreeable. I, being the only European and a woman, was, of course, an object of general curiosity, but it was respectful and quiet curiosity; my donkey-man (conversing in Arabic in an undertone with the boatmen) was, I suppose, giving a little history of what he knew about me.

Shortly before midday, most of them produced their dinner from their pockets; it was only bread, and a salad of some kind. They seemed anxious that I should share it, so I pulled a piece off one of their large flat loaves; it was baked to a dark brown, and very tough to bite, and as there seemed nothing *but* this epidermis kind of thing, I found it very difficult to get through any of it; I did my best, but it was anything but pleasant food. In baskets at the bottom of the boat were large, curious-looking fish, some of them yet alive, which had evidently been just caught in the Nile, and were no doubt to be conveyed for sale to one of the neighbouring villages.

One exciting occurrence broke the prevailing calmness of our atmosphere. Among the passengers was a man quite different in appearance from the rest; his uncovered head was crowned by a bushy crop of dark, matted hair; his complexion was very swarthy, and his dark eyes flashed fiercely when the dispute began —apparently about his fare. He was a Copt, intending to land near his monastery; but certainly did not seem a specimen of a *peaceful* Christian. I learnt afterwards that he had some cause for exasperation, as his Mohammedan ferryman was venting a little religious spite, by making him pay more than the others;—so money was, as usual, at the bottom of the dispute! In two or three minutes, all the crew, except myself and the donkeys, were joining hotly in the discussion which ensued, amid such fierce looks and gestures that I felt quite frightened, not knowing then anything of the cause. All was noise and confusion till the offending Copt having been got rid of, we fell once more into quietude.

When, after landing, I had started again on my donkey, a little *contre-temps* occurred. The animal stumbled, and, the saddle turning right round, rolled me on to the ground; fortunately it was a soft place, so I only suffered a little delay, while the girths, which had given way, were being patched up. This kind of thing is of frequent occurrence in Egyptian donkey-rides, but my poor beast had never stumbled the least with me before; I fancy his legs must have been still suffering from the effects of his ungainly struggles to get clear of the boat. All went well afterwards. I felt that the bearer of my heavy bag had the worst of it ; as he ran along in the hot sun, his neck must have been terribly chafed by the cord, to which it was attached ; however, he did not complain, nor did my attendant offer to relieve him of the burden.

This little expedition gave me an unusual opportunity of seeing the byways of Egyptian scenery and country life, as we were making a cut, through the middle of the land, which is rarely made by travellers. The day was cloudless, and all looked smiling and full of life—vegetable, animal, and human. This last fact was most literally true ; for when, tired and hungry, I alighted and sought a sequestered spot in which to eat my luncheon, I could find none. The country being flat and open, and the tufted foliage of the palms high above their slender trunks, everything here is *en évidence.* As my last resource, I seated myself in a dry ditch ; but even there children and fellâh women found me out, and came curiously round, no doubt anxious to share my repast. I, however, could spare them nothing, as there were yet many hours of travel in prospect, and my attendants, seated at a respectful distance, were looking out for some of my viands to supplement their more slender meal.

This verdant Egyptian plain was one vast garden, full of edibles of various kinds, but no flowers, either wild or cultivated, in our sense of the word, were to be seen. Our poor English farmers, who so often have to get in their hay crops under stress of weather and other difficulties,—what would they think of the green crops here, which spring up as though by magic, and are cleared off the ground with scarcely any harvest labours?

There *is* labour, though, only it is all at the beginning. First, in preparation of the ground; then, by careful and patient irrigation. In the soft, loamy soil, tiny channels are traced in little squares with the foot; after water has been admitted into these furrows, the seed is cast in; next the fellâh, with his foot, again lightly covers the seed, by passing over it the little ridge of earth which had been left. I have often seen them doing this, and thought how it exemplified the Scripture passage, "a land, ... not as Egypt, whence ye came out, where thou sowedst thy seed, and wateredst it with thy foot, as a garden of herbs." * The work of irrigation must be continued daily, if good results are desired. Have we not here also a beautiful illustration of the sacramental system of our Church? From our Lord's Humanity, that one infinite reservoir of grace, flows forth the water of life, which is the Holy Spirit, into prepared channels, which are the means of grace appointed by God in His Church. He comes in fulness of power and mercy to fructify and refresh human souls, first uniting them to, and then strengthening them in,

* Deut. xi. 10; see also Exod. xi. 1.

their union with the great Fountain-head. God's own commissioned labourers are the ones solemnly charged to guard these sacred channels, so full of blessing to all hearts made fit for their reception. But here the parallel ends ;—whilst the parched earth ever gratefully imbibes the refreshing streams offered to it, man, through his prerogative of free-will, can, if he please, so harden the soil of his heart that the stream of grace cannot find an entrance. God's condition is, " Open thy mouth wide ;" then comes the gracious promise, " and I shall fill it."

The hay crops were not often of ordinary grass, but mostly of beautiful clover, which, in January, I noticed, was bright with deep-crimson blossoms ; this dainty fodder is the essentially "green meat" of the beasts in the very early spring they have here. Some is cut and taken while fresh into the town, but the greater part of these crops is not cut at all ; a variety of animals are tethered at intervals round about one spot, under the watchful eyes of women and boys. When all is eaten clean, they are moved on a little further, and so on. I have often seen quite a menagerie of domestic animals thus grouped together —a cow, an ass, a camel, a donkey, a goat—all feeding within a small area, and apparently forming one happy family. It can be imagined what a curious and populous aspect these flat fields assume when occupied by such incongruous groups and their attendant watchers. I did not see horses in the open country, nor are they employed often for labour, but rather for the use of Europeans and the upper ten thousand in town. Neither are the buffaloes turned into the clover-fields; *they*, poor things, have to do the main drudgery of heavy work and are not treated to such dainty fare. They are patient, laborious beasts, but hideously ugly; much of the milk sold in Cairo is that of the buffalo.

When we seemed drawing at last near the venerable Ghizeh Pyramids, I began to realize how much I should enjoy a good dinner and a good rest after my long day's outing. But we came unexpectedly on a considerable sheet of water left by the inundation; it was too deep to be forded, and not till we had made a long *détour* did I thankfully reach my destination. I had rather expected to meet some acquaintances, but, having just missed them by a day, found myself alone in the comfortable little hotel. I did not object to this, for I was dwelling literally under the shadow of the mighty pyramids, and that was company enough! The Italian *chef* provided me with an excellent dinner, and after two hours' rest, I was ready, at 9 p.m., to fulfil the remainder of the day's programme. Under the care of an Arab guide recommended by the *padrone* of the hotel, I sallied forth to admire by moonlight these wondrous creations of man;—so very old, yet ever presenting a new charm to the appreciative beholder.

For an hour and a half we two wandered about

in and out of the dark pyramid shadows. It was enchanting. All around breathed of awe and mystery, and the famous Sphinx, whose intelligent countenance is now, alas, by daylight, so disfigured through loss of the nose, seemed to gaze at us in renewed beauty under the moon's tender rays. I and my guide were the only living creatures moving in the desert sand that night, save the jackals, one or two of which I caught sight of, prowling stealthily along under the shade of the tombs. By day this spot is full of eager tourists, who doubtless leave behind enough trace of their banquets to afford a feast to these nocturnal visitors. The deep sand was very uneven, and full of large, loose stones; and, amid the many smaller ruins below the pyramids, there was plenty to stumble over. It was hard work, climbing up and down the sand-hills in the dim light, and I should have fallen head foremost more than once, but for the strong arm of my gentle protector, which I clutched vigorously.

At last my comfortable bed was acceptable, and sleep soon followed; but before daybreak I was awoke by the sound of a howling and shrieking wind, such as I imagine is rarely heard in this country, where fine weather is usually taken for granted day after day. However, it seemed that now I was to prepare myself for an awful storm—probably a thunderstorm, which I had never yet experienced in Egypt. When I looked out, to my astonishment all appeared clear, cloudless, and tranquil as usual; for no branches were here to bend to the hurricane. The grand pyramid, which stood just in front of my window, gazed as calmly as ever at me from its moonlight shadows, all regardless of the tumult raging around. As I still listened to that mysterious shrieking wind, it seemed as if the spirits of the air must be engaging in a nocturnal contest with the spirits of the departed ones, whose bodies had been long ago consigned to that huge resting-place. Whatever had been the cause of this disturbance of nature, all was calm and hushed, as well as bright and cloudless, when I arose later in the day.

After a quiet morning among the pyramids, I rode back to Shepheard's Hotel in the afternoon, cantering at a good speed along the pleasant shady carriage-road which has been made by the Khedive between Ghizeh and Cairo. My donkey behaved well to the end, and I had every cause to be satisfied with the week's outing. I felt also well fortified for the enjoyment of Nile life, which was to be my next Egyptian experience.

CHAPTER V.

NILE REMINISCENCES.

Steamer - life—Villages — Pigeons — The inundation — Native traffic—Weather—Scenery—Assouan—Nubian aquatics—Philæ—Beverages—An impromptu bath.

THE run up the Nile is now made easy ; in one of Cook's first-class steamers you are taken to the First Cataract (about six hundred miles from Cairo) for the sum of £50, including the return journey—nineteen days being allowed for the whole trip. If you choose to prolong your voyage to the Second Cataract (more than two hundred miles further), you can do so at an extra charge of £20, and by spending an additional six days in a smaller steamer, which starts above the First Cataract. The period I have mentioned allows time for visiting all the interesting points on the route; they lie often at some distance from the river-banks, and are reached on the backs of donkeys of various degrees of speed and sure-footedness. Our passengers, all told, made up a pleasant party of sixty persons, and often many a droll and noisy scene was enacted before we could be fairly started on the ride.

These exciting donkey excursions, which usually include a pleasant *al fresco* repast in the immediate vicinity of some venerable ruin, form an agreeable diversion from the placid monotony of the Nile steamer life; however, on one bank or the other, if not on both, there is generally some object worthy of attention. If not—well, one falls into a rather dreamy condition, to be suddenly roused, perhaps, by a jolting and scraping of the boat on a sandbank. But the *contre-temps* are few. As the steamer casts anchor at sundown, the prudent traveller, by retiring early, can secure his fair share of undisturbed repose before the early morning start, which, by-the-by, is effected by this Oriental crew in a far less noisy and fussy way than it would be by an English one. The hours, too, of sunrise and sunset vary but little here throughout the year, in comparison to what they do at home; so in Egypt one is not awakened in the small morning hours by the sun intrusively peering into one's chamber and eyes, when one would wish to be oblivious of him and everything else.

To return to the Nile. The little villages which, as we steam along, constantly come into view in turn with more important-looking places, present to the English eye a curious aspect. "Mud" is not altogether a pleasing substance, neither does its presence presumably conduce to the charm of a landscape; yet *here* this lowly substance must be spoken of most respectfully, since "mud" forms the real riches of Egypt in every possible way. Hovels, composed of dried Nile mud and with flat roofs covered in only with mud-plastered reeds and interlaced branches, with neither door nor chimney, but just a few small holes to let in light,—erections such as these are generally to be seen crowded together on eminences high enough to protect them from the Nile inundation. In colour these villages are all one with the ground on which they stand, and the uniformity of tint would become monotonous unless glorified and transformed by the subtle and variously beautiful effects of light, which the generous sun so freely sheds over the face of Eastern nature; the mud huts, too, are generally relieved by the graceful foliage of the feathery date-palm clustering around them, and, as we go further south, also by the picturesque-looking Dôm, or ivory-yielding palm, the fantastic spreading branches of which form such a contrast to its more slender neighbour.

In these villages the picturesque-looking pigeon-towers add much to the interest of the scene; they are lofty erections, terminating at the top in a rough dome, in which are inserted oval earthenware pots forming a battlement around it. The whole of the tower bristles with long stalks of dried Indian corn emerging from loopholes in the walls and serving as perches for the pigeons, which are seen in hundreds hovering round; and each pair finds its own separate home and shelter in its own pot. Pigeons are much valued in the East generally. In Scripture the name is often synonymous with "dove." A heathen poet writes—

"Let the white dove, revered in Palestine,
  Uninjured through the crowded cities fly."

In Egypt the bird is chiefly prized on account of the manure it yields.

The constant sight of these quaint, conspicuous towers reminded me of that curious passage, "Though ye have lien among the pots, yet shall ye be as the wings of a dove covered with silver, and her feathers with gold." * The Revised Version, by substituting "sheep-folds" for "pots," does not seem to help in the elucidation of this difficult passage. Could the word "pots" have been retained, the following might appear a simple explanation: As the birds emerge from their close quarters in the "pots," to take wing in the pure brightness of their gold and silver plumage, *so* the Israelites, who at the Exodus were delivered from the "burden of making the pots," were to be at liberty henceforth to enjoy, if they would, a life of freedom and happiness.

I have often wished that, during the inundation, I could be there to see the transformed Nile valley; but at that season the great heat would make this a doubtful pleasure for a European. *Then* these raised villages, which I have been describing, become

* Ps. lxviii. 13.

veritable Noah's arks—cattle, poultry, human beings, all huddled together in most intimate proximity. Woe then to those slothful or incredulous peasants who have neglected to collect their live stock together, while due warning was given! The fellâh may perhaps be deceived in his judgment on the matter, as the rate of rapidity of the Nile-rising is somewhat uncertain; but the Egyptian Government officials, who possess a most correct means of measurement in the Nilometer at Cairo, are only too eager to proclaim, and even exaggerate, the daily ascertained elevation, since no land-tax can be levied till a certain water-level has been reached.

Then, proclaiming messengers are sent hurrying throughout the land, shouting forth their news in the loudest of voices. I have been told that the dogs, which form an inevitable element in village society here, are accustomed to bark away with unerring instinct as the Nile approaches a height likely to imperil the low-lying lands. This rapid rise takes place about the middle of July, coinciding in time with our "dog-days;" the Egyptians also commenced their civil year on July 21, the day when the dog-star Sirius (which they formerly venerated as the goddess Sothis) appears here, simultaneously with the sun, on the morning horizon; thus it announced to them the rise of the river, as well as the periodical return of their civil year.

I may mention that, as the uniform fall of the

Nile, in its course through Egypt, is seven inches per mile, the mean average between the high and low water-level varies according to locality; being about twenty-five feet at Cairo, and forty-nine feet at Assouan, in Upper Egypt. The Nile makes a pause for about fifteen days, towards the end of September; then continues to rise again, attaining its highest level in October; the lowest is reached between April and early June. I think these statistics in connection with the wonderful river will not be found uninteresting. It is not surprising that the ancient Egyptians worshipped the Nile as a deity, since, though not the largest of known rivers, it is certainly, through its course of more than four thousand miles, the most wonderful and beneficent in its working.

The land is at present so carefully irrigated, that the Nile overflow is mostly guided into prepared channels and reservoirs, whence it can be poured forth on the cultivated ground as required; thus the general aspect is not quite that of a small deluge, as might be imagined, excepting in the lowest-lying land. There, the natives, being penned up in their protected villages, can find exit only by boat, or along the few artificial causeways which have been thrown up permanently in the direction of the main lines of traffic near the Nile.

The lively, inhabited appearance which the plain of Egypt usually presents (and markedly so in contrast with its desert boundaries) is, I think, a good deal attributable to these high embankments, which will not admit of much more than marching in single file; so, when you cast your eyes over the flat plain, every man and beast is seen moving along the raised road, in clear-cut distinctness against the bright background of sky;—there goes the well-to-do and gracefully costumed Egyptian gentleman, trotting along on his gaily caparisoned white ass, with saddle poised almost on the tail, and feet stretching well forward towards the neck of the animal;—there goes, too, the humble fellâh, with his heavily laden donkey; the trader, with his long procession of wellfreighted camels, etc.;—this is the real luggage-train of Upper Egypt, the only other means of transit being by dhows which navigate the river. All this passing life gives the impression of a well-inhabited land which, in its wider portions, is also a well-cultivated one.

The camels are made to bear very varied burdens. They object, strongly and noisily, while kneeling to receive their load; but, once erect on their legs, and the luggage well poised on their backs, all discordant murmurs cease, and they do their duty nobly, accepting the inevitable in a truly philosophic manner. I remember once seeing a curious spectacle; in the distance a file of camels was marching along, each camel bearing a heavy load of fresh-cut branches, which were so piled upon the animals that their bodies and heads were quite concealed from view, the legs only being visible; their appearance thus was suggestive of the Birnam Woods in "Macbeth."

As our steamer advances at a good rate of speed, we often pass by, with a feeling of superiority, some helpless dahabîyeh moored to the river-bank, the occupants of which are impatiently awaiting the breeze which shall waft them on their way. It is not to be denied that these little crafts add far more to the picturesqueness of the scenery than do the very unromantic-looking Cook's steamers, which are little in harmony with graceful Oriental surroundings; however, they meet the demands of the eager rapid traveller of to-day, and have therefore tended to diminish the traffic in dahabîyehs, which can now be had at far less exorbitant charges than formerly.

In connection with the mention of "desired breezes," I may say that on board our steamer we sometimes had *more* breeze than was desirable; in fact, a decidedly cold wind, from which little shelter could be found, as it usually cuts directly in front of the boat's track. Fortunate, then, were those persons who had provided themselves with a sufficiency of wraps; many travellers deem it unnecessary to cumber themselves therewith in such a latitude—though, too late, they learn their mistake by experience. I must further confess that there *are* occasional dull days, when one sighs for the charm of the landscape which has vanished. This is a meet opportunity for the sturdy Briton to betake himself to his old insular habit of grumbling, which may have seemed for a time to have been baked out of him by the warm genial sunshine; he has indeed become, in his way, a sun-worshipper, somewhat after the manner of the ancient Egyptians. So, in the temporary absence of that heavenly orb, he feels himself entitled to grumble away *ad libitum*, till the sun's returning embrace restores him to serenity. 'Mid his full, sunshiny enjoyments, is he, I wonder, oblivious of the poor Londoner at home who, in this same month of January, is patiently existing in more or less of foggy darkness, and gratefully appreciating an occasional register of "twenty-five minutes' sunshine at Westminster"—more often of none at all? Thankfulness for small mercies is truly a good habit to cultivate everywhere, and one which brings its own reward in peace of mind and sweet content.

> "Some murmur when their sky is clear
> And wholly bright to view,
> If one small speck of dark appear
> In their great heaven of blue;
> And some with thankful love are filled,
> If but one streak of light,
> One ray of God's good mercy, gild
> The darkness of their night."

It was almost too much to expect never to experience rain in Upper Egypt; yet I had been told that the natives are puzzled at sight of an umbrella, not

A SHADOOF

knowing its use. This must be an exaggeration, for we had a few drops of rain even close to the First Cataract, and, nearer Cairo, occasionally a heavy shower.

The Nile scenery of Upper Egypt must be called, on the whole, curious and interesting rather than beautiful. The prevailing drab tint of the mud banks and of the villages, together with the bare bounding hills, conduces to form sometimes, one might say, a tame scenic effect. Palms, acacias, and tamarisks are almost the only kind of trees to be seen.

The shadoof forms quite a peculiar feature in the landscape; this primitive method of irrigation is worked on the bank by two men in nature's bronze livery who, with a pulley, draw the full water-buckets up, to be poured over the thirsty land, the weight of ascending water being balanced by a lump of Nile mud. Above Thebes, where the breadth of Egypt becomes very limited indeed, the shadoof is more and more frequent, and the poor labourers work away with their buckets all through the burning heat of day, and at night also, producing a creaking monotonous sound. The typical English farmer is wont to consider himself aggrieved, and often with some reason. But what a serious item would he have to add to his usual catalogue of hardships were he obliged to employ so laborious and continuous a method as the shadoof in order to obtain sufficient water for his crops!

Quaint-looking, long-legged birds haunt the riverbanks; especially among them may be noted the famous ibis, to whose sacred corpses the old Egyptians dedicated a special cemetery, from which tiny mummied forms have been unearthed in modern times. Monarchs of the air, such as the eagle, hawk, and vulture, hover high overhead, watching for their prey; and in parts, wild ducks and other game abound to delight the heart and eye of the sportsman. The crocodile, alas! is now mostly conspicuous by his absence till after the First Cataract has been passed; the ply of the steam-engine, does not seem to suit his constitution, so he will probably continue to retire further and further from European civilization! I express the regret of a tourist desirous to see all strange sights; the people who live near the Nile have doubtless no objection to the withdrawal of the horrible monsters.

What I have said about Nile scenery refers only to the character of it as a whole; exceptions must, of course, be made. There is the beautifully situated Theban plain, rich in splendid ruins and embraced by its amphitheatre of mountains, which are of some height, and are varied in outline. Then, again, at Assouan, the last town in Egypt, we enter a most picturesque district; opposite to it is the island of Elephantine, where we find ourselves in a new region —Nubia—and see there, in its swarthy natives, a new type. Nubian women wear large nose-rings, enormous pendant ear-rings; also arm and ankle rings, which are fixed on them when children, and thus become part of themselves; of ordinary clothing they are somewhat scant.

In busy Assouan one sees a great variety of African physiognomy, and its bazaars are full of strange and rough-looking articles made in the Soudan, and professing mostly to come from Khartoum. Rough knives, *kurbages* or native whips, glass and shell ornaments, baskets and shields of dyed grass, red pottery made from Nile mud; also the curious article nicknamed "Madame Nubia"—it is a girdle with narrow strips of leather hanging from it, adorned with shells and well steeped in castor-oil, and forms the only garment of young Nubian girls, except in cold weather.

On leaving Assouan, the ride of two or three hours through the desert formed a pleasing variety from our steamer-life. We passed first the quarry from which the ancient Egyptians obtained material for all their most important works. One can still trace on the rock the marks of their tools, and it is interesting to note that the same are used for a like purpose by the modern Egyptians. Fine old granite and syenite abound here, and chaotic-looking rocks surrounded us throughout the ride, some of them inscribed with the records of travellers of long-past ages. As I was expressing my appreciation of the stern and wild desert surroundings, a clerical acquaintance remarked, "So *you* like the desert? *I* prefer the oases of life." "Do you?" said another of the party; "but the oasis can only be *in* the desert." How much is conveyed in these simple words!

At last we found ourselves above the First Cataract, and just opposite the island of Philæ, to which we crossed over. I need not dwell on the beauties of that sweet island, which are well-known. I think I expected to see a rather more luxurious vegetation than it now possesses. This sacred spot —for it was called "Holy Island" in days of yore— contested with Abydos the honour of being the burial-place of the great and favourite god Osiris; many were the pilgrimages once made here by the pious, and many the corpses brought for interment near his tomb. Now the island is quite deserted; only picturesque ruins remain of the old pagan temples, where heathen rites were carried on as late as A.D. 453; that is, forty-six years after the edict of Theodosius had caused them to cease in other parts of the empire. At last Christianity was introduced, and a Coptic Church sprang up in the midst of the chief heathen temple. It gave one pain to see there still, the deserted credence-table, and part of the overthrown Christian altar. The ruined pillars are covered with representations of heathen gods, among which the Coptic Cross has been roughly inscribed, and is still in places visible. The Coptic Church has now died out in Nubia.

Our programme for this day's excursion was a varied one; from the calm solemnity of Philæ, we were transported in a little boat to a spot on the mainland, whence, on mounting to a cliff, we looked down on the cataract beneath. Here a somewhat exciting scene awaited us; swarthy Nubian men, whose naked bodies were lustrous with castor-oil (the graceful bush grows close round about), were preparing, for bakshîsh, to take headers from the cliff into the surging waters below, and then to swim down the cataract. It was dreadful to watch them struggling with the angry rapids. Some paddled with pieces of rough wood, others used only their hands and feet; but they seemed none the worse for the exertion, and, once out of the water, came skipping up the steep cliffs again with the agility of wild goats, to stand before us—dripping, shining, panting, their dark eyes rolling, their white teeth gleaming,—while they clamoured loudly for their reward. That obtained, they were ready and eager to start off and repeat the feat.

The return ride, by another way, brought us back to our comfortable steamer at Assouan, where a nice tea awaited us on the deck. The Nile water makes excellent tea; in fact, I found it, under all circumstances, a most wholesome and refreshing drink. How often afterwards, in Syria, did I long for some of that sweet, health-giving water! but in this case, as in so many, appearances are deceptive, for it never

G

looks perfectly clear. It should be left to stand for some time in one of the porous earthenware vessels, called *kullehs*, which are manufactured for the purpose; it then becomes inviting to the eye, as well as cool and refreshing to the taste. I used to chuckle inwardly at my own economy in the matter of beverage, when I saw many around me spending quite a little fortune on wines and mineral waters, because they would not trust themselves to Nature's precious fount, from which the Egyptians drink freely. It is certain that, in such climates, the less stimulant one takes the better, and Englishmen are often unwise in not considering this fact.

I ought to have mentioned that, before being allowed to enjoy our tea, we had, each of the sixty, to submit to a thorough dusting process. As soon as we set foot on the steamer, swarthy stewards were at hand, who, after violently shaking our nether garments, belaboured us from head to foot with a long-handled brush. After all, this desert dust is a very innocuous appendage to the toilette, if one is wise enough to abstain from wearing dark colours. English dust may too often be truly called "*dirt* in high spirits," while mud would be "ditto in low spirits;" the same need not be said of these fine sandy particles, which partake of that purity which the desert imparts to all its surroundings. Of course, this does not hold good in the immediate neighbourhood of towns and villages; but I can well understand that the desert traveller, in the absence of water, finds sand a good substitute for cleansing purposes. It is also used by the Mohammedans, under the same circumstances, for their religious ablutions. I have often seen the naked children outside the villages basking and rolling contentedly in the hot sand, which provides them with an *ad libitum* hot bath, of which the sun is the mighty heater.

CHAPTER VI.

INCIDENTS AT LUXOR.

Crowded hotels—Egyptian saddles—A duet—Saucy children—Egyptian sociability—A victory gained—Curiosity-vendors—Deprivations—Epiphany-tide.

MY friend—more ambitious than myself—proceeded from Philæ, with a pleasant party, to the Second Cataract, whilst I decided to return to Luxor hotel and vegetate there alone for a time. One of the chief drawbacks to Egyptian travel is, I think, the insufficiency of hotel accommodation in proportion to the large number of tourists, who, for a short season of the year, flock to the Nile. My own experience was an illustration of this. The common saying, "blessings are never realized till they are lost," came true in my case; for all the calm comfort of the late aquatic life returned vividly to my memory as soon as I had set foot on shore, where I at once found a heap of difficulties awaiting me.

Standing alone on the river's bank, I had, with equanimity, watched the steamer which I had just left, as it ˊglided fast away toward Cairo—for I knew that a good room had been bespoken some time ago at the hotel, and promised to me for this 18th of January, the date of my arrival; moreover, I had already obtained and paid for coupons, at the rate of fifteen shillings per diem, which was to be my charge *en pension*. But, on walking to the hotel, I was sadly *désillusionée!* The room shown me as my domicile was a miserable little damp-looking hole, built right away from the house, on a level with the garden, in connection with the laundry, and well overlooked by every passer-by! It was only just large enough to contain a bed, chair, and washstand, so that my luggage would have to remain outside in the garden;—and *this* was to be mine for *fifteen shillings a day!* I went off indignant to the Bureau, and was there told that it was the only room then available, that the hotel was crammed, that many persons were sleeping in tents in the garden, and many others in dahabiyehs kept on the Nile for that purpose.

Thanks to the kind intervention of an influential friend, who opportunely came to my aid, and a little, I think, to the persuasive power of my conversation, in his vernacular, with the Italian *direttore* (who was most anxious to please every one), I at last obtained a faint hope of better things. Our joint cross-questioning had elicited the fact that the room—which had been promised as mine—was still tenanted by a gentleman who had given due notice of his departure that day. But unfortunately, owing to a fall from a camel, he had damaged his nose, which had to be plastered up, and in this disfigured condition he refused to vacate, or, indeed, to show himself at all to public view. I mildly suggested that the mutilated member might possibly attain to convalescence in a less commodious chamber than the one which was now mine by right; after which expostulation I seated myself forlorn in the garden, and, surrounded by my luggage, patiently awaited my fate.

In the space of about an hour and a half matters were somehow arranged, and I had the satisfaction of being conducted to my much-desired room, and a tolerably fair one it was. Having made it as habitable-looking as the limited contents of my portmanteau would permit, I found it pleasant to settle down peacefully, and to review in anticipation the varied attractions which lay before me in this beautiful, salubrious, and classically historic region.

However, fresh anxieties soon arise; first, on the part of the hotel authorities, who seem as eager to get you *out*, as *you* were to get *in* to the room which, for the nonce, is your only "castle." After three or four days you are politely interrogated as to the "probable duration of your stay;" and this question is reiterated daily, so that you have to cultivate the art of dissimulation to an unpleasant degree; moreover, your *amour propre* is getting touched, and you begin to feel a ruffled sensation, being, in your own estimation at any rate, quite an inoffensive and well-conducted individual.

But there is another side to the question. The hotel-keepers have a vision before them, which will soon prove a reality, of another steamer arriving, with its cargo of tourists, who have all been promised accommodation, but for whom none will be forthcoming unless some of the present inmates turn out. There *is* another hotel, in a beautiful situation; but when I was at Luxor, its arrangements were not, I believe, quite as good as in the one in which I was staying. I found plenty of kind, pleasant people to beguile my solitude; at *table d'hôte* there was often an enjoyable "polyglot" kind of conversation. In the pretty, well-irrigated garden, the murmur of tongues was seldom absent, and there often mingled with it the notes of rare and curious birds, which form an interesting feature in Egypt.

Being fresh to Eastern life, I had a new experience in listening to the animated duet kept up at night by the dogs and jackals, whose blended voices cannot be said to produce the most melodious music, nor to conduce particularly to sleep. The dogs consider themselves at night fully masters of the situation in every sense, and tumultuously oppose the invasion of the jackals, who sneak in from their neighbouring country lurking-places to see what they can get in the town or village. One easily learns to distinguish the short sharp bark of the jackals from the more violent demonstrations of the dogs.

The habits of these dogs recalled to me the wonderful veracity with which the Bible portrays the smallest incidents of Eastern life ; thus we read in Ps. lix. 14, 15, " Let them make a noise like a dog, and go round about the city. Let them wander up and down for meat, and grudge if they be not satisfied." It is proverbial that the dogs are rapacious, nocturnal devourers of all that comes in their way, and that they do " grudge " any other creature a taste of what they consider theirs by right.

Around the site of famous old Thebes excursions can be made in great variety ; donkeys and vociferous donkey-boys are there in abundance ; but, for ladies, there is often a difficulty, through the great scarcity of side-saddles, which become the prize only of the few who have exercised superior forethought and diplomacy ; thus many are doomed to be disappointed for that day, at any rate. Such saddles are only in demand by Europeans, as Egyptian ladies ride in a gentlemanly kind of fashion ; but they seem timid, their animals being usually led. Seated all of a bunch on their queer little saddles, I must say they present a more unprepossessing appearance even than when on foot. Alas ! one cannot know what redeeming beauty of feature may be hidden under the ugly black " burko " which only allows the eyes to be visible.

TEMPLE OF LUXOR.

A few pleasant strolls may be made by pedestrians in the immediate vicinity of Luxor. One can explore the ruins of its beautiful temple, whose lotus-bud columns stand, solemn and imposing, looking down on the Nile below; or one may saunter along the banks of the river, whence can be enjoyed a splendid sunset view; the declining orb, casting his long shadows across the wide Theban plain, flashes back a glory of blended colours on the venerable ruins eastward of the Nile, whose waters reflect, as in a mirror, all the beauty of sky and ruin; then comes the tender afterglow, when even the far-away Arabian hills catch rich tints of crimson, amethyst, and gold.

You must not mind plenty of dust in your walk; it is thick under your feet, and a gentle breeze will blow it into your mouth and eyes; but happily, in the month of January, one does not often experience that hot wind from the desert, which compels the traveller to sit down and envelop the head till the sand-cloud has rolled past.

If you *wish* to be alone in your stroll you *cannot* be so, pleasant as it would be for a little while amid such scenes; the children hereabouts are remarkable for their precocious audacity and extreme sociability; they *will* not leave you alone, but run round you, behind you, before you, kicking up the dust in your face, and clamouring loudly as usual for bakshish. Tiny little girls, who have but lately learnt to run, will come up staring and laughing saucily, and toddle in front of you, raising the dust with their little head-veils, which trail behind them on the ground;—even if they have no further toilette, it is *de rigueur* that the smallest girls should have their heads covered. These little Arab children usually wear, as their only garment, what looks like a loose night-dress, often of red, pink, or yellow cotton, probably of Manchester manufacture, as a large number of cotton fabrics, of Oriental design and colour, are exported thence to the East.

Being of an active temperament, I preferred— when not engaged in an excursion to some distant temple or tomb—to extend my walks a little beyond the immediate precincts of Luxor. The first time I did so, I induced a lady in the hotel to accompany me; but this proved a failure, as she found some good pretext for an early retreat to our starting-point, so I afterwards went alone—at least, I intended to do so, but generally had a volunteer escort of noisy, clamorous children for about half a mile out of the village. They are most pertinacious in their attentions. I found the best plan was to pay no heed to them, but to walk on at a firm even pace, which at last tired them out, so that they fell back.

It is very enjoyable to explore on foot, for the first time, such a new land as Egypt was to me. Walking between the well-cultivated crops, which here succeed each other rapidly, I could fully realize the luxurious fertility of this country. Already, in the month of January, were to be seen splendid barley in full ear, odoriferous broad beans, and clover-blossoms of richest crimson and twice the size *we* are accustomed to; while the tall sugar-cane would soon be ready for cutting.

It was pleasant to be at last alone in these green pastures; I began to look about for a spot where I could sit down and ruminate, as one cannot keep up, in this climate, one's native walking powers. But a nice seat is a difficult thing to find; there is neither fence, nor stile, nor division of any kind, to mark out the land, except an occasional tumble-down wall. Against one of these I was leaning, when I suddenly found I had become an object of interest to some labourers in a far-distant field; first one and then another coolly left his work, and came sauntering towards me, hoe in hand,—and there they stood staring at me, just as cows, in an English field, stare at any stranger seated on a stile near them. As their immediate presence did not conduce to a feeling of repose, I trudged on again, till I saw I was approaching a village. Wishing to be unobserved, I halted outside it, and sat down on a heap of stones near the river's edge, where I had before me a fine view of plain and hill, lit up by the now fast-declining sun.

The little villages are usually surrounded by a rough high outer wall. I thought no one could see me, as there were no windows looking my way; I was, however, mistaken. In five minutes about a dozen men and boys appeared on the scene; they came strolling up one by one, and sat down, forming a half-circle in front of me; very well-behaved they were, as they smoked away, casting occasional glances at me, and chattering a little together in a subdued tone. I always carried a book, which I now opened and read vigorously, just looking up now and then to smile at them. This quiet little drama had lasted about a quarter of an hour, when I thought it was time to be turning homewards; my friends hitherto had asked me for nothing, as they sat round in grave conclave, but I knew my departure would be the signal for their voluble importunity,— and I was right. Rising from my lowly seat in a very sudden and energetic fashion, I gave them my blessing, in one of my few Arabic sentences, "*Naharîk saîd*," which is something equivalent to our "Good evening," and then marched off at a sharp pace.

Of course, they all followed like a flock of sheep, bleating for bakshîsh. I turned round once or twice with a negative nod, saying, "*Mafîsh*," which means that I had nothing with me; then, as I took no further notice, they began by degrees to fall back. But when I thought I had got clear of all, a fresh intruder presented himself from some unknown corner; he had a different aspect from the village men, and looked rough and disagreeable, whereas *they* had all seemed good-tempered. When I found he was going to follow me some way, bellowing loudly in my ear for bakshîsh, I thought I would try on him a curious kind of attack, which I had often found successful in frightening away children. Facing suddenly round upon him, and with a threatening gesture, I opened my sun-umbrella full in ·his face; this had an excellent effect, and the cowardly bully disappeared as suddenly as he had appeared on the scene. After this I was able to reach the hotel in peace, though, of course, a fresh concourse of children, donkey-boys, and curiosity-vendors accompanied me through Luxor.

These latter seem as remarkable for their keenness of vision as for their patient pertinacity. They never fail to spy you out, and to pester you with their wares. The chief object of many travellers in Egypt seems to be to pick up so-called "ancient" curios, which are but too often only modern fabrications. I fear our American cousins have done much to encourage this class of vendors, and to embolden them to ask a preposterous price for their rubbish, among which, however, one may now and then find a treasure.

I cannot conclude my Nile reminiscences without reference to the state of Church affairs, which, I regret to say, is not satisfactory. At Cairo there is a nice little English Church, with reverent services; but, on starting thence in the direction of Upper Egypt, a spiritual wilderness is entered so far as concerns outward means of grace. Messrs. Cook have to exercise the wisdom of the "children of this world" in providing supplies in proportion to the demands of their tourists, and I fear the facts prove that these demands are far more urgent for bodily than for spiritual provision. It is well advertised that every steamer plying on the Nile has on board a fully qualified doctor and a pharmacy; the same are to be found in the few hotels in which tourists can sojourn in Upper Egypt. Indeed, without such an arrangement, the thousands of travellers who flock up the Nile would not risk themselves six hundred miles or more beyond the civilized world. When it is remembered that amongst these thousands the largest proportion are English-speaking people, professing to belong either to the Anglican or to the American Episcopal Church, and for the most part possessed of ample worldly means for ministering to their own comfort and needs, one sorrowfully wonders why they have not already made some effort to obtain an organized system of Church ministration;—for such one must trust to the kindness of any clergyman who may happen to be of the party. Even at the Luxor hotels, where many travellers linger for weeks, and sad invalids sometimes for months, there is no permanent chaplain.* No room is set apart for religious

* Since writing the above I am glad to learn that a season chaplaincy has been established at Luxor.

services, nor are any holy vessels provided wherewith to celebrate the Sacred Mysteries of our religion.

The Epiphany Festival arrived as we were voyaging up the Nile. I was sorry that it was allowed to pass without public notice, either on the day itself, or during our little service on the following Sunday. Where could a scene have been found more fitted to inspire all with true Epiphany gladness? To right and left of us were visible deserts such as the Magi must have traversed long ago. We could descry dignified-looking Arabs riding on gaily-decked camels; they, with their long retinue of baggage-animals, might well personify those faithful men of old bearing their costly gifts for presentation to the Infant King Whom they sought. In their journey they must have been lighted and warmed by that same majestic sun, which ever "cometh forth as a bridegroom out of his chamber, and rejoiceth as a giant to run his course," and which seemed to speak to us travellers, as he may have done to them, of the blessed "Sun of Righteousness," to the brightness of Whose rising they were coming.

At night, too, we could realize that the same glorious vault, the sight of which touched us with awe, had also overarched those faithful pilgrims of nearly two thousand years ago. In the absence of the moon's silver light, the heavens were yet radiant with the tender glory of millions of stars, some of them of wondrous size and brilliancy; and as one kept a fascinated gaze directed upwards, the larger stars seemed gradually, in turn, to dilate before the vision, as if beckoning one towards some distant goal! Must not this same nocturnal aspect have been presented to the Magi, but with this difference—that, when *they* gazed, they could thankfully recognize now and again, amid that starry host, the *one* guiding star which was leading them joyfully onwards to the true Light of the world? The psalmist wrote in holy jubilation, "The heavens declare the glory of God, and the firmament showeth His handiwork." We Christians, as we look up to them, can add our yet higher note of triumph when we sing, "Blessed be our God . . . through Whose tender mercy . . . the Day-spring from on high *hath visited us* . . . to be a light to lighten the Gentiles."

From among these Gentiles, of whom the three Eastern sages were the firstfruits, have we all been called unto the hope of "the glory of His people Israel." When kneeling in lowly adoration before the Infant Messiah and presenting to Him their prophetic gifts, little did the Magi, perhaps, deem that they were fulfilling the sure word of prophecy,[*] and striking a mighty chord, the music of whose refrain should echo on for ever:—

"Kings shall bow down before Him,
And gold and incense bring;

---

[*] Isa. lx. 3.

All nations shall adore Him,
  His praise all people sing ;
To Him shall prayer unceasing
  And daily vows ascend ;
His kingdom still increasing,
  A kingdom without end."

CHAPTER VII.

LOOKING FORWARD.

In dock—*Séances* with a Copt—In search of a saddle—Native servants—Small enemies—Means of defence—Heliopolis—Its sacred shrine—Famous school—Greek language and learning.

I CANNOT say that I returned to Cairo in a jubilant mood. The well-praised salubrity of Luxor had beguiled me into a rashness upon which I should not have ventured in our English climate ; though it was but the mild dissipation of strolling out after sunset, to enjoy by moonlight the majestic beauty of the temple ruins. The time of sunset is always dangerous in hot countries, and in the verdant and well-cultivated portions of Egypt dew falls heavily ; it benignantly refreshes the thirsty earth, but is not always equally beneficial in its effect on any weak member of the human body. So, at least, it proved in my case, for next morning I awoke to find one of my eyes attacked by an old enemy. The usual remedies, which I always carry, had become, alas! dried up, and the pharmacy of the hotel did not prove equal to my demands upon it; so I had to spend a week in a sorry plight with a bandaged eye, longing for the arrival of a steamer to carry me back to Cairo.

Miss —— having just returned from the Second Cataract, I had been looking forward to revisiting, with her, all my favourite haunts; but such dreams were for the present dispelled. On the seventh day I thankfully hailed a return steamer, which, in five long days more, landed me in Cairo. Off I went at once to Dr. Brugsch, the oculist, and, thanks to his careful treatment, my eyes in about a month regained what is for them a fairly satisfactory condition.

It was on the 5th of February that I again arrived in Cairo. I must own that I found the weather there, for a time, rather damp and chilly. January and February are usually the two coldest and most rainy months in Egypt, and in Cairo especially. The natives say that European intervention has altered the climate of late; the great number of trees which have been planted in the city, and the proximity of the Suez Canal, have probably tended to attract damp, for there is certainly more rain and fog in Cairo than formerly. Walking there after rain is exceedingly disagreeable, as the soil then assumes a slimy character; also, one is dripped upon everywhere by the thick *lebbekh* trees—a handsome kind of acacia, bearing large yellow pods. These disagreeables are usually over in March, when one has to expect another for a few days, in the oppressive breath of the hot Khamseen wind, during which it is wisest to stay indoors.

This spring season in Cairo was to me one of anxious suspense; for, after considerable treatment, I had to await the verdict of my oculist before daring to entertain the fulfilment of my long-cherished desire to visit Palestine. I passed this interval in the private pension of M. Amici Bey, which is situated in the best locality, and which I gladly recommend to any who may prefer a much quieter house than "The Grand" or "Shepheard's" Hotel. I was glad that I had already become acquainted with the many attractions of Cairo, since now I could, without any compunction, devote myself to nursing my weak member,—doing and seeing nothing particular.

I engaged as my newspaper-reader a young Copt, who was a teacher in the American Missionary School of Messrs. Lancing and Watson. He had himself been educated there, and had gained an excellent knowledge of English; this may be inferred from the fact that, with only slight bungling, he was able to read the *Times* aloud, intelligibly to me and to himself. When he came to an account of some philanthropic work or institution at home, he would shake his head, exclaiming, "That is good!" I was amused to see how well he could take in the political aspect of things. One day, after reading one of those audacious dicta which too often now disfigure the oratory of our Imperial Parliament, he remarked that for saying such a thing in Egypt a man would quickly "lose his head." He was a good little fellow, and we got quite to understand one another. I even ventured on Sunday to make him read me one of Canon Scott Holland's sermons, which he seemed fully to appreciate.

I looked with respect on this descendant of the old Egyptians; he had a very intellectual forehead, and quite the type of countenance which one learns to recognize as having belonged to them. I observed that, during our *séances*, he always kept his thick red fez cap firmly planted over his dark hair, contrary to our English custom, although it was then hot weather. I was curious to see how he looked without the fez, so pressed him to take it off while in my room. This he seemed very loath to do; but at last, to oblige me, he complied. It was a great stretch of amiability on his part, for I found afterwards that it is considered quite against etiquette for Copts to uncover their heads.

I have always known this rule to hold good among Mohammedans; one obvious reason for it may be, that they would look such frights with their bald heads, on which they are allowed to retain but the one tuft of hair by means of which the angel is to lift them into Paradise! Out-of-doors it is, of course, imperative that all, in order to avoid sunstroke, should keep the back of the neck well covered; for the head, a thick felt cap is the best protection. The only opportunity I had of seeing the "tufts" was in the country, on the heads of little nude boys, who strutted about, looking much like wild Indians, and seemingly impervious to sunstroke or anything else.

Being now quite alone, I had plenty of time to cogitate, and make what preparation I could for the somewhat rash enterprise I was contemplating, for all who knew my intentions urged me *not* to go alone to Palestine. In the Preface, I have already alluded to some reasons why I wished to do so. This desire was now strengthened; for my friend was returning home *viâ* Athens, and, were I to join a party, I might perhaps, unwillingly, be the cause of delaying its progress, on account of bad weather, which I was unable to face. At the risk, therefore, of appearing obstinate and strong-minded, I came to the decision that, if I went at all, it should be alone.

I was influenced in some measure by a fact which I had already ascertained from a well-informed traveller on the Nile, viz. that it would be possible for me to visit the greater part of Palestine without tents, though this would entail some extra fatigue. My recent experiences at Luxor had taught me that I could not risk the exposure to chill or dew, which is almost unavoidable in tent-life, especially in the early morning, when one has to turn out for the general packing-up before the fresh start. At night,

I fancy, the tents are rather *too* air-tight, when not blown down!

I gained many valuable hints from the gentleman I have alluded to. One was the desirability of taking my own lady's-saddle to Syria, if I wished to spare myself unnecessary discomfort. So here was an interesting object of search in my present enforced retirement. But *how* to set about it? I consulted the heads of the chief hotels, who sent me in turn, from Egyptian shops, a variety of most excruciating-*looking* side-saddles! To look at them, however, was not enough; so I directed their swarthy bearers to deposit them, one at a time, in my room. A saddle is an unusual and not a pleasant addition to a lady's bedroom; but I knew not where else to keep them safely and close at hand, in order to try them. This I did as well as I could, by propping them up, one by one, on chairs. Such a set of narrow, hard, *mountainous* saddles, I should say, had never before been brought together. I felt in despair!

The man who waited on me had ushered in the first bearer of these commodities, with a curious, puzzled look on his face; for though it is quite the thing for ladies to ride in Cairo, they do so in proper "Rotten Row" style, whereas *my* equestrian preparations seemed rather peculiar.

I may say, *en passant*, how desirable it would be if English maids could take a hint from the white-robed, white-turbaned house and parlour *men* in this country—so quiet and gentle in gait and movement, so light of tread, so obliging and respectful in their service. Unless looked after, they may not always be as cleanly in their work as we should desire, but this is not a fault quite confined to the East.

To return to the saddle. When on the Nile, I had been introduced to an English officer from a station thereabouts, who had visited our steamer in search of friends; from him I had obtained an address which eventually procured me the desired object. From a very small hotel, which I had great difficulty in finding, emerged the bearer of what *had* been once a first-rate French saddle — large, strong, well padded, though the white chamois with which it was covered was now in a most disreputable-looking condition. The first time it was brought to me I declined it, as the price asked was too high; but when, after long waiting, nothing better nor so good turned up, I was glad to become the possessor of the saddle for the sum of £3. I had afterwards continual cause to be thankful for this new possession, though more than once its safe custody cost me some trepidation.

I had reason also to be thankful for a few other acquisitions, made rather vaguely, while I was still uncertain how far my Eastern travels would extend. Most people know that several small, but very irritating personal inconveniences, have to be put up with in Egypt. I may classify the three most persistent ones as—flies, fleas, and mosquitoes. Of the first I would say, as I have before said of the donkeys here, that they are of a more developed type than the English ones, certainly more audacious and larger, and that they possess extraordinary vitality.

It is hardly necessary for me to allude to the well-known fact, that Egyptian mothers willingly allow flies to remain settled on the eyes of their little children, and to crawl all over their faces; to drive them away would be considered unlucky; thus many, while quite young, get their eyes inoculated with disease, and bad eyes often mar the otherwise fine Egyptian physique. If you pass through a bazaar in the middle of the day, you will observe that all edibles are black with flies, while the grave shop-keeper sits amidst his wares, calm and thoughtful, as though engaged in some deep intellectual problem, and apparently quite regardless of the bold insects, which, besides covering his goods, walk in a most ticklish fashion over his nose, eyes, hands, or any other part of him, where the skin is visible.

It is very well to say that these little creatures are harmless; in their *moral* effect on the individual they are not always so! Whenever I wished to read or write with any sense of enjoyment, I had recourse to a large square of thin muslin, which, after throwing over my head, I let fall over my hands as far as was possible while using them. My appearance thus must have been somewhat mysterious, but it did not seem to frighten my sociable little friends! The reader will say that this was a hot, stuffy arrangement, in such a climate; true, but sometimes one is driven to a choice of evils.

With regard to the second of the small nuisances, I fear I can give no decided receipt to guarantee freedom from attack. Travellers in Italy find that "Keating's Powder" is scarcely strong enough to check the liveliness of Italian fleas, so the most experienced resort to "*Persian* Powder;" and I should certainly recommend plenty of this in the East, where the little vermin is so very strong and active. The "Levinge Bag" is a good means of defence, though not a comfortable one in a hot climate. It is an ample-sized calico bag, to which is added on one side a double flap, open at the end; through this aperture you creep into the bag, which you have first deposited within your sheets, then fold the flap over you, and sleep as well as you can in such a constrained situation; the bag does *not* throttle your neck, being affixed round the top to a small circular mosquito-net, which you have first fastened to the head of your bed. In some parts of Palestine I was very thankful for this means of protection. Of course, in good hotels, such as Shepheard's, there is not much cause for complaint on this score.

Of the third nuisance—mosquitoes—I need say

but little, since most European travellers are well acquainted with their habits; indeed, from causes which I will explain, they may often suffer *more* from their attacks than do Egyptian tourists. In some parts of Europe—the Riviera, for instance—mosquito-nets are often but a snare and a delusion: they are either made gracefully flowing, and so allow these clever insects to walk easily up their ample folds; or, they are very short; or are hung up by rings from the bed-top, festoon-fashion, thus enabling the mosquitoes to enter the citadel from above under cover of the ornamental frilling.

In Cairo the mosquito-curtain is arranged in a practical manner, and is usually satisfactory. It is made quite plain and very long, and *so* scanty that the traveller has some difficulty in penetrating through it to his desired haven; this should be done as expeditiously as possible, and the curtain then well tucked in all round, which is a difficult matter to do for one's self. Prudent persons will have their bed-curtains kept down all through the day; even during the short interval of bed-making one or two of these astute little creatures may intrude, and succeed in hiding themselves till the small hours, when the sharp attack usually begins, continuing till sunrise. If all the precautions I have mentioned be observed, I think a good night may be secured, unless the light sleeper be disturbed by the angry trumpeting of the disappointed mosquitoes outside the curtains.

I hold, with the poet, that "sleep is the chief nourisher in life's feast," and concur also with the adage that "discretion is the better part of valour;" so, when travelling, I provide myself with a small, portable mosquito-net, which may be easily packed with one's wrappers. This net, and also the "Levinge Bag," can be obtained from Messrs. Thresher and Glenny, 152, Strand. I think that, after what I have said, my reader will understand, as I did after a brief time spent in Egypt, that it is possible to realize what *some*, at least, of the ten plagues enumerated in the Book of Exodus must have been, since they were but the enormous aggravation of a constant annoyance.

One of the most interesting drives near Cairo is that to Heliopolis, the Greek name for "On," in Egyptian, "An;" called also in Holy Scripture "Beth-shemesh," that is, "the house of the sun."* I visited it many times, but have reserved the mention of it till the last period of my stay in Cairo, because, when standing on that site, I was already within the confines of the land of Goshen, which I soon contemplated traversing *en route* towards Suez. Heliopolis is only five miles from Cairo, and forms the southern apex of a triangle, which extends in a north-easterly direction through the Delta, and embraces the ancient land of Goshen, now known in part as Wady Tumilât. This city contained, with the exception of Memphis, the

* See Jer. xliii. 13.

oldest of all Egyptian shrines, and here was worshipped the sun-god "Ra" (in Greek, "Helios"), to whom the light-coloured bull, Mnevis, was sacred. Similarly at Memphis, the black bull, Apis, was revered in the early sanctuary of Ptah, but he was afterwards transferred to a special sanctuary, and buried in his own cemetery outside that city.

There can be no doubt that Aaron and the Israelites had in memory this bull-worship of Egypt, with which they had become so familiar at Heliopolis (On), when they set up the golden calf in the wilderness as a new object of worship. To the same source we may refer Jeroboam's idolatry. Recalled by the disaffected tribes from his refuge in Egypt to be made king over Israel, he immediately afterwards set up for worship two golden calves—the one at Dan, the other at Bethel.*

The temple at Heliopolis was very rich, and its service was connected with magnificent rites. The obelisk, emblem of the sun's ray, originated among the Egyptians, and it is probable that a great many of these unique monuments once stood in this city so devoted to the worship of the sun. Always in pairs, a number of obelisks must have once composed a lofty avenue before the great Temple of Ra. Of the one pair which survived as late as the twelfth century A.D., only a solitary obelisk now remains; it is sixty-six feet high, but the greater part

* See 1 Kings xii.

of its height is lost under the increasing accumulation of earth. Its clear-cut old-empire hieroglyphs inform us that it was erected by Usertasen I., a king of Upper and Lower Egypt, belonging to the twelfth dynasty.*

When Cambyses overran the country he wrought much havoc; portions of buildings, however, remained till the Mohammedan period; but its desolation now literally fulfils the words of Jer. xliii. 13. Excepting the one obelisk, nought remains, in that wide expanse of plain, to denote the site of a great city, save in one direction, where a small ridge of earth is supposed to indicate a portion of the old outer wall.

Gazing on this scene as tranquilly as the worrying children, who assault one on all sides, will permit, one's thoughts naturally revert here to the great Hebrew, Joseph, who probably passed many happy days in On, since he married the daughter of the priest of its sun-god; he may even have had a country residence in the neighbourhood (like the present

* It is worth mentioning, as illustrative of the accuracy of Holy Scripture, that the *reed* was the appointed emblem of the kings of Upper Egypt. Contemporary with Hezekiah, King of Judah, was Shabako, King of Egypt, who had reconquered Upper Egypt, and once more constituted Thebes his capital, thus reuniting for a time the upper and lower kingdom. His successor, Shabataka, was an ally of the Jewish king. These facts give force to the words of Rabshakeh, who, when sent as envoy from the King of Assyria to Hezekiah, ironically said, "Lo, thou trustest in the staff of this broken (cracked) *reed*, on Egypt; whereon if a man lean, it will go into his hand, and pierce it" (Isa. xxxvi. 6).

Khedive), Heliopolis being not far distant from the then capital, Memphis. This interesting obelisk must have met the eyes of Joseph, just as it did mine, only then nearly the whole of it was visible. Nay, more; being the oldest but one of all Egyptian obelisks, it must have been standing long before the time of Abraham, who, during his sojourn in Egypt, probably visited this famous city.

Passing over an interval of about two hundred and fifty years, we are reminded of another great and holy Jew, Moses, God's own appointed lawgiver, who, at the renowned school of On, must have obtained that thorough education which made him "learned in all the wisdom of the Egyptians." Hither, too, Pharaoh's daughter, his foster-mother, may have often resorted from Zoan, in order to worship at this most sacred shrine.

Later, all great Greek scholars came to study at Heliopolis, including Plato, the father of philosophy; Herodotus, the father of history, etc. Strabo tells us that when he visited the place (*circ.* 60 B.C.) this university had ceased to exist, having been transferred to Alexandria. But Heliopolis was still a great city at the time of our Lord's birth, and the oldest tradition has it, that to its neighbourhood S. Joseph conveyed "the young Child and His Mother" when warned by God to "flee into Egypt."

Thus on this spot, I think, can best of all be embraced in one vast mental vision, the past glories of Egyptian worship, learning, and culture,—as well as our own biblical records connected with the place —from the time of Joseph the governor, on to that of Moses the prophet; and thence, forward again, to that greater Prophet (of Whom Moses was so eminent a type), the light of Whose Presence for a time shone upon this favoured land.

Further, it may be said that the whole later intellectual training of mankind can be traced mainly to Heliopolis. From its great school, which was coeval with the history of Memphis, were transplanted, in after-years, to the new university at Alexandria, the precious traditions and learning of the old school. There they grew into a mighty tree of knowledge, capable of sheltering under its capacious branches, for many centuries, the most ardent searchers after philosophy and truth.

Through the wise providence of God, the beautiful, rich, and pliable Greek tongue became in Egypt, before the Christian era, and afterwards, in Asia and Europe, the prepared channel through which we moderns were to receive the Divine revelations. When Greek learning, under the auspices of the Christian Emperor Constantine, was transferred from Alexandria to Constantinople, the subtle Greek language, which could so well interpret the thoughts of the acute Greek mind, became, and continued to be, the vehicle of the thoughts of all theologians, philosophers, and *literati* throughout the known world.

The Christian Church, the while, was called to be the specially appointed keeper and interpreter of the oracles of God now enshrined in that tongue, as well as in the Hebrew Scrrptures.

It is known to all students that when at last, in 1453, Constantinople fell into the hands of the infidel, its rich intellectual treasures became the precious prize of European scholars in general. Greek refugees carried their learning with them to all parts of the civilized world, so that it became, in England as well as in other countries, the seed-plot of modern literature.

Thus, in many ways, do past and present blend before the mind of the traveller as he stands musing near the solitary Obelisk of Heliopolis.

CHAPTER VIII.

ON THE TRACK OF THE HEBREWS.

Why I went to Suez—Goshen past and present—Cat-worship—Striking contrasts—Ismailîya—Hebrew route—The Red Sea—In the Arabian desert—A clever exchange—A Bedawîn meeting—Return to crowded civilization—A serious loss.

WHEN my hotel acquaintances heard that I contemplated going on to Suez, they seemed to consider me rather crazy; that point appears to be beyond the ordinary routine of tourists, unless it be intended to proceed further towards the Indian route. To some persons, I suppose, the charm of past association lends less than it does to me towards the enjoyment of localities which may present in themselves but slight attraction. "Why go," I was asked, "all the way to Suez, a horridly barren, dusty place, where there is nothing to be seen?"

It was enough for me that I should traverse the old land of Goshen. I would try, mentally, to see that land as it had been long ago, beginning with the time when the patriarch Jacob with his followers entered it, leaning upon his staff;—then onward to the period during which his descendants prospered greatly there while pursuing their simple shepherd-life; until, in accordance with God's appointed discipline for His chosen ones, arrived that bitter time when they were called to exchange freedom and prosperity for slavery and misery. Next, and last, would follow the bright picture of the triumphant and hasty departure of the long-oppressed people, bearing away with them costly gifts from the Egyptians, and also the precious mummied relics of Joseph, their great forefather.

The journey from Cairo to Suez, a distance of forty-nine miles, is now accomplished by train in seven hours. Many will feel, as I did, that the iron thraldom of a railway is not the means of travelling the most conducive to aid one in meditating over scenes of a vanished and buried past; however, as the latter portion of the route lies through solitary desert sands, and as I was quite alone, without interpreter or aid of any kind, I felt thankful to be in so safe and comfortable a place as a first-class railway carriage.

Even on the station platform where first we halted, I was able to recall the Bible account of Joseph's meeting with his father and his brethren. For there I saw a stately old man of Arab type, with fine aquiline features and flowing beard, literally falling upon the neck of a young man—I presume his son—

and kissing him; then the young man "fell on his neck." May not any one of the ancient Jewish patriarchs have presented much such an appearance as did this old man in his rough striped *abba*, thrown gracefully across his shoulders and partially covering his ample linen nether-garments; while his head and neck were shrouded by the graceful *kefîyeh*, which shaded and half concealed his countenance?

A run of two hours and a half brings the traveller to Zakâzîk, forty-eight miles from Cairo, where he finds himself in the midst of the Bible "Goshen" (called in Egyptian "Gosen"). Near here are the sources of the springs which formerly rendered Goshen so productive; they fell into the Bitter Lakes, and were conducted thence by canal to the Red Sea. At Bêlbes we first approached this very interesting old Fresh-water Canal, about twelve miles before reaching Zakâzîk. The canal was in existence long before the Israelites entered Egypt, having been the work of one of those early Pharaohs, who showed here, as in so many other instances, their great sagacity and engineering skill. The canal must have been in connection with the Nile, since Herodotus graphically describes how, on its becoming connected with the Bitter Lakes, those acrid waters were rendered sweet, and became the home of fish, wild fowl, etc., and it must have communicated with Lake Timsâh (Crocodile Lake), the name of which indicates its Nile source. Herodotus further states that this canal was carried as far as to the Red Sea, which was known by the ancients as "Yâm Sûph," probably from the weeds which grew near the outflow of the fresh water into the salt; I may mention that similar green weeds now grow round the point where the waters of the modern Sweet-water Canal debouch into the Red Sea.

I was much interested in watching the course of the old water-channel which continually intersected our route; it had been allowed to fall into decay for centuries, till rediscovered by the French explorers of 1798. M. de Lesseps was more than once guided by the direction of its ancient course while in the construction of his great work. The old canal must have been intended for purposes of navigation and commerce, and is still utilized for conveying the sweet waters of the Nile to Ismailîya and Suez.

The country round Zakâzîk, once so fertile and productive, had, under long Turkish misrule and neglect of irrigation, fallen into barrenness, till of late years redeemed from this state by European enterprise and energy;—though to Mahomet Ali, in 1826, must be attributed the credit of first resuming its careful cultivation. It is now regaining the smiling aspect which Goshen must have worn when Pharaoh offered it to Joseph's father and brethren, as "the best of the land of Egypt."* Zakâzîk, the present capital of this district, is a thriving semi-

* Gen. xlvii. 5, 6.

European town, the centre of an extensive trade in Egyptian cotton and grain, and likely, from its favoured position, to become still more flourishing.

Its station presented, as we halted, a strange and animated medley of civilized and uncivilized life; but my eyes were attracted beyond it, to the barren mounds on the left, which I knew formed the tomb of a buried city. The Arabs designate all such accumulations under the term " Kom." The mounds are three quarters of a mile distant from the station, but in this clear atmosphere looked to me much nearer, and I could discern the forms of workmen, who, under the direction of M. Naville, were busy disentombing the old Bubastes (the Hebrew Pi-beseth).

I have already, in the first chapter, referred to this scene of excavation. Its beautiful temple filled Herodotus with admiration; and he speaks of his astonishment at the vast crowd of pilgrims (seven hundred thousand when he was there) who resorted to the shrine of the goddess Sekhet or Bast (corresponding to the Artemis of the Greeks, and the Ashtaroth of the Phœnicians). It was customary for pilgrims of both sexes to make an annual pilgrimage to the sanctuary of Sekhet, who was represented as a lioness having a cat's head. Statues of this hideous divinity are seen in many parts of Egypt; the cat was sacred to her, and a whole cemetery of mummied cats has recently been laid bare at Bubastes.

At the later period of Egyptian history, and

coeval with this city—that is, from about 780 B.C.—
its religious worship had already begun to show signs
of corruption and depravity, which were evidently
conspicuous in the time of Herodotus; and a striking
warning was pronounced by the Prophet Ezekiel
against the wicked young men of Bubastes and other
adjacent towns.*

Dearly should I have liked to visit those mysterious
mounds and pore into the excavations already opened
in them; but "time and (train)-tide wait for no
man," and, there not being any hostelry there fit to
receive me for the night, I had to content myself
with purchasing a few small unearthed treasures
which vendors were offering for sale on the station
platform. I was pleased thus to become the owner
of a very sanctimonious and ancient-looking little
cat-statuette, which had doubtless aided the devotions
of some pious soul in life, and, further, had been
imagined to be able, by its presence, to hallow the
tomb of the departed; it is quite perfect, and very
curious.

Leaving Zakâzîk, one passes through what was
once the centre of the land of Goshen; it is still
very fertile,—especially in the western portion,—producing excellent fruits, and particularly good dates.
Farmers and peasants, by means of the Fresh-water
Canal, are now able to carry their agriculture to considerable perfection.

* Ezek. xxx. 17.

As I gazed, everywhere, on green gardens bathed in sunshine, my thoughts reverted to those terrible three days of darkness in which the adjacent land was once plunged, whilst the children of Israel could in Goshen still rejoice in the blessed light, which is " God's own glorious shadow." Yet another contrast presented itself,—I thought of that mysterious midnight when the "great cry" arose in Egypt—the cry of desolate mothers weeping over the death of their firstborn ; while in this Goshen, God's chosen ones were all the time gladly and hopefully watching for the dawn—the happy dawn which was to herald their freedom. With them, too, there was death; but only that of innocent lambs, which the believing Israelites were hastily preparing, in order to partake of that first great Passover meal ; pledge to them of coming deliverance, and precious type to all future generations of a far greater and more enduring one.

As my eye fell here and there on village huts scattered about, I liked to fancy that, similar to them, may have been those of the faithful Jews of yore, who, through the obedient blood-sprinkling of their doorposts, were delivered from the destroying angel. In towns one is still somewhat reminded of this circumstance by the curious pictorial adornments which are permitted to be painted round the doorways of those Mussulmans, only, who have made the pilgrimage to Mecca.

About twelve miles from Zakâzîk begins a desert

region. Those barren sands are a mysterious power which would be ever encroaching on the cultivated lands, but for man's constant effort and watchfulness. Familiarity with Egyptian scenery enabled me to appreciate more fully even than before the truth of the beautiful words of the late Canon Mozley: "Nature in the very act of *labouring* as a machine, also *sleeps* as a picture!" In Egypt, whether one gazes on the fertile water-fed plain, or on the bare stretch of desert sand, Nature ever presents herself under an aspect of calm repose; though she is all the while actively at work through two mighty agencies—the one producing increase and blessing, the other loss and destruction.

We soon reached a tiny station, the name of which, "Tel-el-Kebîr," is so familiar to the ear of a Briton. With sad interest he gazes on the little plot, surrounded by desert and neatly fenced in, where repose peacefully the bones of his gallant countrymen, who fell in the victorious struggle with Arabi in 1882. Close by is the site of ancient Pithom, already referred to as having been identified by M. Naville. So the next fourteen miles of desolate country which I passed through must have been, thirty-three centuries ago, the very scene of the laborious drudgery of the down-trodden Israelites during their long bondage.

On arriving soon after at another very small station, the ear is suddenly arrested by another familiar name, "Ramses." Familiar it is; but whence and how? From our Bible * we have learnt the name, as being that of the other treasure-city which the world-wide conqueror caused to be built, and named after himself. What memories—very old and also very new—come rushing together into the mind, as one hears consecutively called out the names of these two tiny stations: "Ramses!" "Tel-el-Kebîr!" They lie only fourteen miles apart.

By-and-by the bright waters of a large lake appear on the left, their lovely blue tint forming a striking contrast with the golden yellow of the surrounding sand. My map tells me that this is Lake Timsâh, on which stands Ismailîya. A few minutes more, and, as if by magic, we are transported from our lonely desert tract into the smiling vicinity of this little town, which—'mid sparkling waters, neat rows of modern houses, green gardens, trees, and squares—looks like a miniature Paris transplanted to this barren neighbourhood, and is a veritable oasis in the desert. On arrival, all seemed life and vivacity, and inviting to a short sojourn; however, I thought it best at once to go on direct to Suez, hoping perhaps to return there later.

What a chasm of thought and feeling lies between ancient Goshen and the great highway of all nations which I now saw before me!—for Lake Timsâh forms part of the great Suez Canal, through which, from

* Exod. i. 11.

the ends of the earth, pass and repass ships of all descriptions and of all nationalities. Yet, by a strange coincidence, that modern embodiment of science and perseverance trenches closely on scenes of former mighty achievement in the Eastern Delta, where, buried under reedy marshes or rubbish-heaps, are to be found the sites of some of the greatest glories of ancient times.

Between Ismailiya and Suez extends a district almost entirely desert; it is one which must, even in the time of the Israelites, have been more or less barren, producing only a scant pasturage, and that at limited seasons of the year. Now, all the green that meets the eye anywhere is a very narrow rim of verdure on the immediate border of the Fresh-water Canal, which frequently intersects the line.

But engrossing thoughts continue to occupy the mind during this somewhat dreary journey. Many modern critics are of opinion that the site of " Etham, in the edge of the wilderness,"* which was the next camping-place of the Israelites after Succoth, is to be placed somewhere near the table-land now known as " El-Gisr," at a short distance from Ismailiya. If this supposition be correct, Moses, when conducting his people out of Egypt, must have intended to follow the northern route, which is that usually taken by travellers between Egypt and Palestine, namely, by the wilderness of Shur, towards Gaza.

* Exod. xiii. 20.

So the vast tract of sand through which I was now passing had once been the marching-ground of that mighty concourse of human beings, more in number, perhaps, than any army which had ever invaded the land—"about six hundred thousand on foot, besides children," and "the mixed multitude which went up also with them." How eagerly and hopefully must all that vigorous and able-bodied Jewish host have pressed forward! for, when once they should have got clear of the fortified posts protecting the strategic points of the Delta, all might be well, as they would soon after find themselves in freedom and safety.

But lo! suddenly, all is reversed. Scarcely have they encamped in Etham, when the Divine word goes forth, " Turn ! " * Mysterious at the time must have seemed the order, thus completely to reverse their course from north to south. Yet God condescended later to make known to His people the *reason* for this change. " God led them not through the land of the Philistines, although that was near ; for God said, Lest peradventure the people repent when they see war, and they return to Egypt."† We learn elsewhere that the Philistines were at that time in alliance with the Egyptians, so that they would certainly have come forth to fight against the Jewish hosts, had they passed through their territory. " Truly in His mercy He led them."

* Exod. xiv. 2. † Exod. xiii. 17.

At this crisis did the Lord also vouchsafe them special protection, through the "pillar of cloud by day, and of fire by night." Strange phenomenon indeed would such a pillar be in this country of clearest atmosphere, and how awe-inspiring to the pursuing Egyptians!

It is believed that the Red Sea formerly extended further north than is now the case, and that the so-called "Bitter Lakes" formed then an arm of the sea; the mixture of salt and fresh water which they contain renders them brackish, whence their name.

Pi-hahiroth (the "place of reeds"), where the Israelites were next ordered to encamp, after leaving Etham, is supposed to have been near the confluence of the fresh waters with those of the Red Sea, at some point nearly midway between Ismailîya and Suez. The scriptural account says that Pi-hahiroth was "near the sea, and over against Baal-Zephon," probably a distant mountain on the Asiatic side.

It was, then, possible, nay probable, that while pursuing my journey towards Suez I was, at some one point of it, near to and parallel with this very spot—Pi-hahiroth—where the memorable crossing once took place. Right away to my left it must have all happened—the thought was a thrilling one! Had the crossing been *below* Suez (or *opposite* to it, as some hold), there would not have been enough desert space left for the three days' march, which the travelling host had to make before water could be obtained ; this would not be found until they reached the oasis of Ayûn Mûsa, probably the " Marah " of the Bible.

When one looks back to contemporary history in connection with that mighty exodus which was to be so pregnant with results for the whole future world, one can see how marvellously God's providence had been preparing the way for His people by gradually weakening the internal resources of the Egyptian empire. Thus, while the immediate predecessor of Menepthah, Rameses II., had been much engaged in Asiatic wars (especially with the powerful Hittites), and gaining laurels for himself abroad, his garrisons at home had probably become more or less demoralized in the absence of his autocratic eye. During the succeeding reign of his son Menepthah, the country had to repel an invasion of Ethiopians from the south, at a time when it must have been already considerably weakened by the strain of foreign war. Humanly speaking, these considerations might account for the facility with which the Israelites were able to elude the fortified positions of the Delta.

While I had been musing on so many things of the past, the shades of evening had been creeping on apace ; and the grand rocks of the Atâka Mountains, which bound the head of the Red Sea to the west, stood out black and solemn against the pale sunset-sky as I entered the station of Suez. Shortly after, I gladly found myself in the Suez Hotel, which is kept up in comfortable English style, and stands in quite the best part of this ugly town.

What my friends had said about Suez was true; —it *is* a very dreary-looking place; yet, from its position, must always possess a certain amount of commercial importance, and continue to be a centre of telegraphic and other business communication. In 1864, when M. de Lesseps had begun his great work, Suez rose from a state of utter dulness to become a considerable town; it has, however, lately been superseded by the rapidly developed Port Said, and has lessened in prosperity since the P. and O. steamers have ceased to make it one of their halting-points.

Uninteresting as the town may be, from the windows of the hotel one can enjoy an enchanting view down the Red Sea, which almost washes the walls of the house. Its lovely greenish-blue waters are bounded closely on the right by the bold mass of the Atâka, the rugged rocks of which vary constantly in colour and shadow, according to the direction in which the sun's rays fall upon them. To the left, on the Asiatic side, the eye ranges over a yellow stretch of desert; beyond it, again, to a hazy line of distant mountains. Over these, especially at eventide, is often cast a beautiful veil of tender colour, such as an Eastern atmosphere only can produce. There is a fascination in gazing in that direction, and one which comes more from what one sees *not*, than from what one sees; for, right away towards the south-east that mysterious-looking chain gradually merges into the lofty and gorgeously tinted rocks of the Sinaitic group, culminating at last in Sinai, the "Mount of God."

It being part of my travelling plan to visit places leisurely, I did not, as many do, rush away from Suez immediately after reaching it. It was pleasant to ride along the shore of the Red Sea, picking up there many objects new to the European, for the fauna of this sea is quite different from that of the Mediterranean. I found pieces of sponge, lovely little bits of coral, and a variety of beautiful shells, some very tiny, others quite peculiar. This sea is very deep in the middle, but bordered by extensive coral reefs, which render navigation dangerous, and compel large vessels to keep well in mid-stream. The primitive, picturesque Arab crafts can steer dexterously among the reefs, and prefer generally to hug the shore, that they may be able to run into creeks in case of storms of wind, to which this sea is liable.

The mother-of-pearl shells, found in these waters, are an extensive source of profit to the Bedawîn, who employ slaves in summer to dive for them, and find a ready market at Jedda, the sea-port of Mecca; tortoise-shell is also found here. It is remarkable how sparsely inhabited its coasts are; chiefly, I suppose, on account of its dangerous shores and rocky or desert surroundings.

I was not content to gaze only on the famous Red Sea and ride along its shores; I wished also to sail on its waters and land on its Asiatic side. All this could be embraced in the excursion to Ayûn Mûsa, or the "Springs of Moses," where it is thought probable that the triumph-song of Moses and Miriam was sung. It is certainly the first point they could have found fit for an encampment, after the three days' march along the Asiatic desert-border. Ayûn Mûsa is eight or nine miles south-east of Suez, and about an hour's walk from the Red Sea. Travellers usually sail some distance down and then land, riding to the oasis on donkeys, which have been ordered to meet them.

There seemed to be no one in the hotel whom I could ask to join me in this excursion—indeed, on arriving, I was almost the only lady there; so I had made arrangements for proceeding alone, when, on the day previous to that fixed on, I had the pleasure of meeting at *table d'hôte* an English naval friend, who accompanied me on my long outing. Unfortunately, the violent wind, which so often blows on this sea, was dead in the teeth of our rowers, so the boat portion of the route had to be shortened, and the donkey ride extended; however, we gained thereby a better opportunity of seeing the entrance to the Suez Canal, which is at some distance from the northern point of the Red Sea, and is indicated by buoys and stakes.

K

It was not a favourable day in any sense, for the wind, which had impeded our boating, maliciously and pertinaciously annoyed us as we proceeded on the donkeys; I began to realize how disagreeable desert travel *can* be. The sky was cloudless, and the sun beat with intense power upon my head; the heated air seemed to shimmer before me, and the burning wind blew the fine sand straight into my mouth and eyes. Our donkeys, too, were not of the best, mine being disposed to stumble at every step. Turning round to accost my friend, who (suitably equipped from head to foot in a suit of white flannel) was at the moment a little in the rear,—an amusing sight met my eye; for I beheld him in the very act of being thrown over his animal's head, whilst a ginger-beer bottle was flying in mid-air, to waste its sweetness in the desert sand! It was a shame to laugh at his misfortune, but the scene was too funny; it looked quite a John Gilpin incident. While he had been quietly trying to quench his thirst, the naughty donkey had played him this bad turn! I was not sorry when the oasis appeared in sight, as I did not wish to repeat any part of the comedy with my stumbling beast.

With a sudden revulsion of feeling from the comic to the tragic, I remembered that near here, in 1882, poor Professor Palmer had started on that sad expedition which proved fatal to him at no great distance from this spot.

Ayûn Mûsa was the first literal oasis I visited, and it was passing strange to me to see, emerging from the burning sand, date-palms, tamarisks, stunted acacias—and a green garden. I was surprised to hear that the place is private property; it is in a measure inhabited, as a few Arabs dwell in wooden hovels outside the fence of opuntia paling which encloses the garden; they cultivate the various vegetables which it contains. In its midst, well forth wonderful little springs from tiny holes in funnel-shaped basins, at a temperature varying from 70° to 84° Fahr.; some are drinkable, but others nauseous.

As we were seeking a cool spot wherein to refresh ourselves with the viands brought from Suez, an inharmonious buzz of loud voices, and clatter of plates, knives, and forks, greeted our ears; soon we saw, seated in a kind of open-air restaurant, about twenty young Germans, all well engaged, and evidently making the repast the *summum bonum* of their day. They had preceded us by less than half an hour, and were off again immediately after the meal.

Wishing to enjoy quiet in the oasis, we determined to keep our fast a little longer, and make an inspection of the whole place on foot. We proceeded to a raised hillock, about ten minutes distant, crowned by a few solitary palms. This proved the best point for observing the action of the springs. From a pool about four feet in diameter and one and a half in depth, gurgled up the water, here very salt and bitter, and filled with myriads of water-fleas. A foreign geologist states that he discovered this hill to be formed entirely of the deposited skins of these tiny insects;—thus strangely and wonderfully has minute organic life walled in channels, without which these remarkable waters, as soon as they had issued from the devouring sand, would have been surely absorbed in it again.

When we at length returned for our meal, the noisy Germans had vanished, so we were able to enjoy the grateful restfulness of the place. My donkey-boy had effected, in my absence, a clever exchange, which conduced much to my comfort in the return ride. The donkey which I had ridden the day before, and had intended to ride this day, had been appropriated by one of the German party. My boy espied it amid the many animals which were unsaddled and turned out to refresh themselves in the oasis; so he adroitly exchanged saddles on the two donkeys, and the German rode off on my stumbling animal, quite unobservant of the trick, though he would probably find it out later, to his cost. As *I* had not concocted this fell device, I felt no compunction in profiting by it.

The wind had somewhat abated when it was time to return towards Suez, and we were able to enjoy the lovely tints of the descending sun and the picturesque rocks of the Atâka, now full in front of us. But very loath did I feel to turn my back on the mountains of Gebel-el-Tih, to which I had, during the ride to the oasis, been drawing somewhat nearer; they belong to the great Sinaitic chain, and I knew that from Ayûn Mûsa I could, on a dromedary, have reached Mount Sinai in a few days. However—

"The distant landscape draws not nigh, for all our gazing;"

I had made no preparation for going further, and the journey would have been, for me, a rash one.

On our homeward way we met an interesting group of mounted Bedawîn, who suddenly appeared from an intersecting path on our right. The sheikh of the party was a grand-looking fellow, mounted on his gaily-decked camel; he held in his hand the head and beautiful antlers of a very recently captured ibex, for the poor creature's glassy eyes were hardly yet closed in death. The fine pair of horns was offered to us for the sum of something less than three shillings. As I had no means of conveying them, my friend bought them to send to his ship till he should return to England. He had made no bargaining in the purchase, which seemed so to astonish the Bedâwy that he, in most simple manner, offered something else as compensating bakshîsh; to soothe his conscience, I suppose, for he knew that at first he had, according to wont, asked more than he expected to get.

These children of the desert are in character a strange mixture; profuse, yet covetous; full of generous hospitality, yet often treacherous as though half-savage. The religion of the Bedâwy partakes largely of superstition ;—he knows well how to overreach, yet has his own code of honour; for when once he has given his word, it becomes his bond. My heart went out to these Ishmaelite brothers, descendants of the great Abraham, who is, through faith, the spiritual father of us all. Courteous and dignified was the bearing of this picturesque group ; they had been hunting in the Sinaitic mountains, which are invested with so sacred a halo for Bible-readers. Our excursion had been on the whole fatiguing, but most interesting.

I spent a quiet Sunday at the Suez Hotel, where it had been advertised that divine service would be held. This was of a hearty and reverent character, conducted by a layman, who was supported by an excellent little choir. The few English persons (about sixty, and mostly young men) who have to reside at Suez, have set apart a room, which they have rendered quite fit for its holy purpose, and maintained at their own expense for some years. I felt very sorry to find that they can but rarely obtain the ministrations of a priest, which they would thoroughly appreciate. I saw lately in the *Worker* an article written by Bishop Blyth, of Jerusalem, on " English Church Work in Egypt." I have added * a short extract from it concerning Suez needs, in the hope

* See Appendix B.

that some persons may be induced, on reading it, to assist in providing a chaplain there.

It was my intention, if possible, to pass through the Canal in a large ocean-steamer; thence, well raised above the banks, one is better able to view the surrounding Delta, which, marshy, flat, and unattractive as it is, contains so many interesting ancient associations. However, as none was expected to arrive at a time convenient to me, I returned by train, on the 15th of March, to Ismailîya, and spent two nights at the neat little hotel, which is surrounded by a shady garden. At first I had it all to myself, and the repose and freshness of everything was very enjoyable; I even, for the first time, extricated my precious saddle from its sack, that I might ride on a donkey round the place. Not till afterwards did I discover that some naughty boy had stolen the crupper before I repacked it.

My peaceful enjoyment was transient; the next afternoon the hotel was flooded by upwards of fifty "Cook's tourists," all *en route* for Palestine. I was fortunately secure in a comfortable bedroom; but there seemed neither beds nor food enough forthcoming for this invading host. So I was not sorry that I had to start on the 17th for Port Said, having long ago engaged my berth in a steamer, which was to start thence for Jaffa on that day. After all, I had to content myself with travelling through the canal in a common little steamer, which started very early.

Most people know that this wonderful canal is a hundred miles long and twenty-six feet deep; that it was cut with enormous labour and skill through an isthmus which, at its narrowest part, measures seventy miles; that it was begun in 1858, opened in 1869, and has proved a huge commercial success.

I cannot say that I enjoyed the canal-transit; the wind was too cruelly violent, for it blew, right off my head, the beautiful white felt helmet which I had purchased at Thresher's, in the Strand. I had put it on because I knew not where else to stow it, having left my big trunk at Cairo; now it was gone for ever! I saw it gracefully floating away—puggaree, veil, and all—in the direction of the Red Sea. Meanwhile every one was considerately calling out to me, "Take care of your head!" for the sun was broiling. I did the best I could, and immediately on reaching Port Saîd had the pleasure, or rather anxiety, of searching for another. This was the last place on my proposed route where there would be much chance of success, so I was thankful to get one there, though it was a heavy, clumsy, and unbecoming one, somewhat like those worn by our soldiers in Egypt.

AN EGYPTIAN MEAL.

CHAPTER IX.

ARRIVAL IN THE LAND OF THE HEBREWS.

Embarcation difficulties—Yâfa "the beautiful"—Evening guns—Needful arrangements—Visit to Lydda—Catechizing—The ascent to Jerusalem—A solemn procession.

I SAT down to luncheon at Port Saïd with a considerable number of English-speaking tourists, who, under Messrs. Cook's auspices, were, like myself, that day bound for Jaffa by the Austrian Lloyd Steamer, which was to start at five o'clock in the afternoon. I felt no anxiety as to obtaining a berth, since one had been booked and paid for, weeks before at Messrs. Cook's office in Cairo. However, hearing at *table d'hôte* rumours about the steamer being very overcrowded, I soon hurried off to the Bureau to secure the number of my berth,—but was there dismayed, by the intelligence that not one remained vacant.

Of course, they were full of apologies for the mistake which had been made; a crowd of German pilgrims from Trieste, in addition to a large party of tourists, had proved too much for the accommodation of the boat, and the officials were at their wits' end how to stow away the passengers. The offer was made to return me my fare; but the alternative of waiting alone at Port Said for a fortnight would have been far from pleasant, and the delay would have disturbed all my plans. So I had to put a bold face upon it and embark, not knowing where I was to be put for the night. The weather was fortunately very bright, and the sea calm; some others who, like myself, had been "done out" of their berths, were intending to sleep on deck, but I was afraid to risk such a night-exposure, and was contemplating the unpleasant time I should have, seated in a sofa-corner of the dreary saloon (the other corners were to be occupied by three gentlemen), when the dear old Italian stewardess, who had seemed much distressed at my dilemma, came in the evening with great glee to tell me she had discovered a vacant berth in a cabin for four ladies, to which she conducted me with all despatch and secrecy. The three ladies, who had disposed of all their extras on the spare bed, did not seem pleased at my entrance; but I was indeed thankful to be able to spend in quiet this eventful night, which was to usher me into Palestine.

On that glorious Sunday morning of the 18th of March, I left my stuffy cabin early, but only to find the deck crowded with people;—no quiet, no privacy anywhere. When passing to the upper deck, I had espied a venerable-looking Greek priest, who, planted in a corner among the ropes, seemed to be trying hard to concentrate his mind on his Holy Book; but the individuals so occupied were few. Telescopes were busily in use, guide-books open, and the clatter of tongues was incessant.

I made my way to the fore-deck, where was a more interesting spectacle. Huddled together there, were many Eastern pilgrims—Copts, Abyssinians, Armenians, etc., apparently "on holy thoughts intent," and looking with straining eyes towards the land of their desire, to visit which had cost them much weary labour. There it lay before us, distinct in the clear morning light, though we were still four hours distant. The coast presented a flat monotonous line, but we were able soon to discern, towards the south, the bright yellow band marking the desert towards the land of the Philistines; this sand, by its gradual encroachment, seems likely, unless checked, to swallow up the margin of alluvial land near the coast.

When the railway between Jaffa and Jerusalem shall have been accomplished, it is intended that the line shall probably be extended southward, in the direction of Gaza and El-Arîsh, to Port Saîd, thus opening out to Palestine easy communication with the world and its commerce—no doubt a desirable object financially. I am most glad, however, that I have been permitted to traverse those hard and rocky roads on which time has been able hitherto to effect so little change, before they have been marred by the introduction of railway lines.

Specially appropriate on *that* Sunday morning seemed the beautiful Psalms for the day. Did I really see before me the very land which God had chosen for His people, and where He had been their supreme " Refuge from one generation to another "? —the land into which His children had been brought by the Everlasting One, in Whose sight " a thousand years are but as yesterday "? His promise standeth sure : "The Lord will not fail His people, neither will He forsake His inheritance." *

The view of Jaffa as seen from the sea has been made familiar by sketches and photographs; it is called in Arabic, " Yâfa," or " beauty." The town rises bright and compact on rocks above the sea ; its whitewashed houses, which are approached by the most tortuous and painfully rocky paths and steps, are piled irregularly one behind another on the steep ascent. The little domes, which form the roofs of the houses, give the place a thoroughly Oriental appearance; they probably came into vogue on account of the scarcity of wood now in this country, and for the same reason are extensively adopted at Jerusalem. The dome is surrounded by a flat surface for walking on, which is enclosed by a parapet made of earthenware pipes cemented together and arranged in patterns. To have a " battlement " to the roof is

* Ps. xciv. 14.

strictly in accordance with the Divine direction,* and the Arabs may in this respect, as well as in many others, have carried on the Jewish custom.

Though the somewhat limited area of Jaffa (in Scripture, Joppa) can never have been much more extended than at present, it must always have been a place of some importance, since from time immemorial it was the only port existing on this coast until the point near Mount Carmel is reached, about fifty miles distant. This is one of the towns which can trace a continuous history from a very remote time down to the present day. From the early Israelitish records,—on through the period of inroads by various Eastern conquerors, till that of the Roman occupation; then later still, on to its capture by Crusaders, Saracens, and, last of all, by Napoleon I.,—Jaffa has survived all vicissitudes, to be still a bustling, prosperous port, and the *only* port of Jerusalem.

Bad as the landing is, how many, many generations of men—kings, prophets, apostles, crusaders, merchants, soldiers, pilgrims,—must this Jaffa through long ages have witnessed, struggling anxiously to land through its dangerous reefs; and what precious freights, from the time of Solomon onward, must have been carried up that hazardous ascent where to-day—tourists, luggage-bearers, laden camels, mules, donkeys, all jostle together in an alarming manner!

* Deut. xxii. 8.

Jaffa still retains, in many quarters, its picturesque Oriental aspect, but has of late acquired several European buildings: among them a C.M.S. mission station of some years' standing; an excellent school for more than eighty native boarders (besides day-scholars), conducted by an indefatigable lady, Miss Arnott, who, though a Presbyterian, works in harmony with the C.M.S. chaplain; a hospital under the care of English nurses; and other good things which I trust have made their mark felt in this place. Perhaps to some practical minds it may appear an equally good thing that steam saw-mills have of late been established, and the old walls of the town pulled down; further, that even a railway station will soon be planted in ancient Joppa. Thus "the old order changeth," even in the East;—but all this is pain and grief to the lover of the antique and its associations.

By an unfortunate arrangement, steamers in these parts frequently arrive or depart on a Sunday. To have reached the Holy Land on that day would not have seemed incongruous, could we have landed early; but we did not get to Jaffa till one o'clock, when a very unsabbatical scene of confusion and turmoil ensued. First, there was the troublesome landing; to be followed, after struggling through the intricate streets and alleys in the midday sun, by a rush for rooms in the two crowded hotels.

It proved fortunate that the larger one, the Méditerrané, was too full to receive me, as I thus became an inmate of Howard's Hotel, the proprietor of which proved my kind friend and helper. He installed me at once in a charming terraced room at the back of the house, looking over an extensive orange-grove, the sweetness of which was almost overpowering. How delightful it was to settle myself in this haven of rest, after the excitement and noise of the last few hours, and to realize quietly *where* I was! I could not do this till considerably past three o'clock; I had already ascertained that the only service still available would be Holy Communion, at 4 p.m., certainly not a fitting hour; so I remained musing quietly in my room.

The refreshing green of the orange-groves, as also the fragrance of a flower-garden just below my window, was most enjoyable to eye and sense after the barren regions in which I had just lately been staying. What heavenly brightness glowed over the landscape! What glorious weather was this wherein to make acquaintance with the Holy Land, type of our promised Canaan!

Evening drew on quickly, to be succeeded by an equally exquisite night. I was ere long attracted by the popping, at intervals, of small guns, apparently from all directions and corners of the vast plantation of orange trees and vineyards which lay mapped out before me. I was told that the firing was necessary, in order to keep off foxes and jackals, which at this season are prone to do much harm among the tender blossoms and fruits. How truly did this help me to realize that I was in a Bible land! "Take us the foxes, the little foxes, that spoil the vines."* Oranges are now cultivated here even more than grapes, and their fine quality is universally acknowledged. These intermittent sounds of warfare continued till between eleven and twelve o'clock, when, perhaps, sleep may have overpowered the would-be thieves, as it did me, for I heard no more.

Next morning, whilst I was enjoying my breakfast and the lovely view, Mr. Howard entered, and, after a graceful Oriental salutation, asked me to accompany him to a room facing the street. Thence I beheld a curious and interesting scene. A party of fifty tourists of both sexes, mounted on a promiscuous-looking selection of horses and ponies, were just jogging off down the street. The heads of many of the equestrians were protected against the sun by head-gears more ingenious than ornamental, but which lent variety to the cavalcade. The ride to Jerusalem being too long to accomplish in one day, they were all to sleep at Ramleh, arriving at the Holy City on the following evening.

How thankful I felt that *I* was not one of that heterogeneous party, but should be free as air while in Palestine, to come and go as I would! No waiting companions, no puffing steam-engine, no inexorable "conductor" to hurry me unduly forward! These

* Song of Solomon ii. 15.

poor travellers could scarcely have had time to feel that they had really arrived in Jaffa, before receiving orders for the early morning start, with the prospect before them of two long days' riding on horses which they had had no opportunity of trying previously.

My landlord at once saw that I should require some help in making a start. As he spoke English fluently, I had no difficulty in getting him to understand that my first requirement would be a trustworthy man of well-known probity and good behaviour, whom, though I should need him as my guide, I should prefer to look upon as a servant receiving his weekly wage, rather than precisely as a dragoman. Fortunately he had a young man close at hand, who seemed likely to possess the needful qualities, and who owned the promising name of Solomon. I engaged him on Mr. Howard's recommendation, and always found him respectful, well conducted, and strictly honest, though as a guide he was not always quite efficient, because at that time he knew but little about the north country.

My next important requirement, a good horse, was not easy to obtain just at this season, when so many are drafted off to meet the constant requirements of Messrs. Cook. The charge for horses is usually five shillings a day—at least, that is what I paid. Followed by my new groom, I made trial of horses in several interesting rides. The one most worthy of mention was that to Ludd, the "Lydda" of the New, the "Lod" of the Old Testament. It lies buried in palm-groves, nearly ten miles distant from Jaffa. Though a most interesting expedition, it proved to be a very tiring one, as my horse possessed the heaviest of heavy trots. The way, moreover, lying mainly along the hard high-road, I suffered a small purgatory in shakings and joltings, so was thankful to be deposited for rest in the house of the C.M.S. native catechist of the place.

He most kindly, after introducing me to his nice wife and children, gave up his sitting-room, in order that I might there quietly eat the luncheon which I had brought with me. This I did in grand style, having the rare luxury of a good-sized table. The catechist, who had a beautiful and intelligent countenance, and spoke English fairly, was anxious to conduct me himself to view what remains of the fine church, built and dedicated to S. George, 315 A.D., and rebuilt by our Richard Cœur de Lion, on the same and supposed site of the healing of Eneas by S. Peter. After an hour's repose, I gladly availed myself of my new friend's escort, though the sun was still very powerful.

This Lydda was the home of very early Christian saints; its grand ruin, standing on the very spot where S. Peter, in the power of his ascended Lord, healed the palsied man, possesses much interest for all, especially for an Englishman, since the church, besides being reared by our own pious and valiant king, was, according to tradition, both the birthplace and burial-place of S. George, the patron saint of England. In the crypt I was shown a modern tomb, in which his remains are said to lie. Moreover here, before a council of bishops, in 445 A.D., the British heretic Pelagius was tried.

This church was brought to ruin, like so many more, by the mighty hand of Saladin; but it still preserves its magnificent Gothic tower. The interior has been better preserved than many others of the same date, probably from the fact that part of it has been turned into a mosque, while part still belongs to the Greek Church, and into its walls many massive stones of the old masonry have been built. A splendid and lofty central arch has been preserved, and there are traces of many others which must have formed part of a noble cathedral nave.

Before my return for Jaffa, the missionary asked me to catechize the native children, boys and girls, comprising the C.M.S. school under his care. This I was pleased to do, as far as I was able, he acting as Arabic interpreter. The children presented a happy and comely aspect, and answered intelligently, and so vivaciously that I had to suggest to them the propriety of cultivating a somewhat more reverent manner while replying on sacred subjects. Let us hope that "saints" are still being reared at Lydda.

I shall long have a happy reminiscence of that my first introduction to a native house and family.

The bearing of its inmates towards me was one of courtesy, dignity, and kindly sympathy, though all around them was of a most simple and homely style. As far as I could judge, civilization and Christianity are in Lydda—as I trust in many other places—working hand-in-hand together.

During my ride home towards the evening of this delicious day, it was strange to reflect that I was probably traversing the very same road which S. Peter had taken, when, in obedience to the message of the two men sent from Joppa, "he arose and went" in haste to exercise his newly bestowed apostolic gift at the bedside of Dorcas, the deceased and much-mourned saint, whose name has since become identified with feminine good works. I passed the traditionary scene of the miracle, which lies near the high-road, more than a mile outside Jaffa.

On another occasion I visited this interesting spot, which is situated in the grounds of a Russian gentleman. I was conducted through a large garden, where the notes of singing-birds and the perfume of orange-blossoms sweetly mingled, to the ruins of an ancient little building, nearly buried underground. We descended by some rough steep steps, and then, bending low through a very small doorway, found ourselves in a tiny square chamber, which I was told had formed part of a Jewish sepulchre containing several divisions. Probably early Christians eagerly desired that their bones should repose near this spot of resurrection memories. In the same direction an old cemetery has lately been discovered, containing rock-cut tombs.

The neighbourhood of Jaffa is assuming everywhere a prosperous aspect. A body of German enthusiasts, called "The Temple Society," and founded by Dr. Hoffman, have recently established colonies near here, as also at Haifa and other places. They are a well-conducted and persevering community, who, by their agricultural efforts, have tended to develop the material resources of the neighbourhood, and also have, I am told, exercised a good influence by their moral example. It is due to their efforts that a rough cart-road now exists between Jaffa and Haifa, and one also in connection with Shechem.

The numerous gardens of Jaffa contain, under their sandy surface, a layer of rich soil; they are provided with good wells, and have increased fourfold in productiveness. In the town a fair amount of business is carried on; I am glad to add that the tanning trade still exists there. The traditionary house of "Simon the tanner" is the first point of interest to the traveller, and often the only one he has a chance of seeing at Jaffa.

Passing above the small mosque which occupies the ground-floor, I ascended, by a few rough outer stairs, to a small flat roof, which must be almost identical with the place where the Apostle Peter received, in vision, his great commission to open to all believing Gentiles the gates of the kingdom of heaven. Close below ripples the Mediterranean Sea; and far ahead the eye of S. Peter must have ranged, as mine did, over the bright blue waters, whereon should soon fly "happy, happy sails—happy with the mission of the Cross!"

The most satisfactory link of identification is found in the courtyard, where stands a very ancient and deep well still full of water, which would always be a necessary adjunct to a tan-yard. In the margin of the well is a deep furrow, telling of the constant working of ropes long ago.

I would fain have lingered yet awhile in beautiful "Yâfa;" round about it are found many pleasant nooks, their charm enhanced by the distant sparkling of the clear blue sea. The air, too, felt delightfully fresh and invigorating, and, in spite of the hot sun which shone in a cloudless sky, there was usually a pleasant breeze. Moreover, it seemed fitting to make a preparatory halt before entering the city of the Great King.

But as I wished to be installed in Jerusalem before Holy Week, a move had to be made; so, on the 23rd of March, I started in a rough kind of vehicle drawn by three horses. The distance of forty miles is accomplished in eleven hours; owing to the extreme roughness of the road in places, one has to submit to some violent shakings. The latter part of the journey is a continuous and rugged ascent, as

ARRIVAL IN THE LAND OF THE HEBREWS.

Jerusalem stands two thousand six hundred feet above the sea.

It was tantalizing to observe, often parallel with our old road, a nice new one, which I believe has been some years in making; it seemed, when I was passing, to be finished, yet no vehicles were allowed to go on it. Rough indeed, and hasty of construction, must have been the roads which contemporary history, and the Bible also,* tell us used anciently to be thrown up before the arrival of a royal potentate—a custom still observed in the East, in quarters where European science has not developed practicable roads. How lonely and dangerous the road between Jaffa and Jerusalem was some few years ago, may be guessed from the fact that huge sentry boxes (now empty) stare grimly at one at frequent intervals.

I halted at Ramleh to view the desecrated ruin of its handsome Crusaders' Church; the lofty tower is preserved, and from its summit one enjoys a grand view extending far over the Plain of Sharon.

After passing, first the hill-boundary, and later, a portion of the fertile valley of Ajalon—scene of the rout of the Amorites by Joshua on the great occasion when sun and moon stood still—I drove for some time through a very bleak and hilly country. At last, picturesquely planted at the foot of a green hill, appeared in sight—Kirjath-jearim ("place of

* Isa. lxii. 10, 11.

forests"). Ajalon means "place of deer;" and we can easily gather, from these two names, what a contrast this whole region must have once offered to its present barren aspect. It has been remarked by a recent explorer that the only traces of any forest remaining in the district are found near Kirjath-jearim. This village possesses considerable biblical interest, as having been for twenty years the resting-place of the Ark of God in the house of Abinadab.

During the remainder of the drive, I was haunted by the thought of those wondrous events in connection with the Ark, which probably took place on this very road; for, as in parts it is but a passage cut in sheer rock, it may have then formed the only approach, from this side, toward Jerusalem. From Kirjath-jearim that glad procession issued, headed by great King David himself "playing before the Lord." But, too soon, the triumphant journey had to be shortened; for we read in 2 Sam. vi. 10, that King David, "displeased," "carried the Ark aside" into the house of Obed-Edom the Gittite. On one of the green knolls to my right, I could fancy that I saw that happy dwelling, whose household God so blessed, on account of the Holy Thing which, for three months, rested within it.

At last, came the time for the Ark's triumphant instalment "in the city of David." On the same steep road by which I was ascending, "oxen and fatlings" had, on that occasion, been freely offered in joyful sacrifice; here, too, the devout young king had then been seen dancing "with might before the Lord;" the solemn refrain had been rising continually to heaven: "Arise, O Lord, into Thy rest; Thou, and the Ark of Thy strength,"* while the bright air everywhere re-echoed with "shoutings and the sound of the trumpet." Thus the Holy Ark arrived safely within "the gates of the daughter of Zion."

* Ps. cxxxii. 8.

CHAPTER X.

AT JERUSALEM.

Reflections—Ancient traces—First ride—Hotel-surroundings—Turkish soldiers—Mount Zion and Mount Moriah—Jebusite steps—The Sacred Rock and its shrine—Old channels—A dearth—Pilgrims—Modern Jews—Converse in a synagogue—Holy Sepulchre—"The place of a skull."

WE pass, for the first time, within the precincts of the Holy City with very mingled feelings. There is, first, thankfulness at having been permitted to reach this place, for eighteen centuries the much-desired but unattained goal of many, many pious souls; then, soon, a sense of shame and sorrow must steal over one, as come rushing to the mind the dread catalogue of sins—rebellion, idolatry, stubbornness, selfishness, pride, unbelief, malice, murder, yea, even the murder of the Son of God, which have been cherished or perpetrated within this city.

Yet pity lingers also in the breast; pity for that spiritually blinded and long persecuted race, who, up to this very day, are reaping the fruits of their own past words and acts, who yet cling with such warm affection to the memory of their ancient shrine, and who, still remaining throughout all the world a separate and peculiar people, present to mankind a long and never-ceasing miracle, as also a firm testimony to the fact, that "verily there is a God that judgeth the earth." Next, one feels indignation towards the Turkish unbelievers who now rule in this most hallowed place, as in so many others dear to Christian hearts. With indignation at sight of the waving crescent mingles, too, vain regret that the flag of the Crusaders should have so long ceased to float over the fortresses of Palestine.

Last and best, comes—

> . . . " Hope, that thrills so keen
> Along each bounding vein,
> Still whispering glorious things unseen."

Hope, first, for this people, on whom the Lord, spite of anger, still looks in "pity," and to whom, by the mouth of His prophets, He has revealed great and precious promises, which, however rich in typical meaning for ourselves, must nevertheless be intended in some measure to have a literal fulfilment for His people Israel. Among numberless passages, that in Ezek. xxxvi. 8–11 may be cited as holding forth to the Jews promises temporal as well as spiritual, and applying to their land as well as to their nation. But hope also "thrills keener here" for us Gentiles, "graffed" late into the olive tree. As we muse sadly over the "Jerusalem which now is, and is in bondage with her children," the glad word of the great S. Paul comes ringing in our ears, bidding us "Rejoice!"* Yes, in the fulness of Christian *hope*, shall the faithful heart be lifted in joyful thought towards that free "Jerusalem which is above, which is the mother of us *all*." Truly, "the Past bears in her arms the Present and the Future!"

Many people whom I have met in England have said, "I should not wish to go to Palestine, because I know all would be so disappointing." Much depends on what this "all" is intended to comprise, and on the expectations with which the traveller visits this land. If it be to trace out in Jerusalem, one by one, the sites connected with Old Testament history, and, while riding through the country, to gaze on picturesque and smiling landscapes, such an expectation will be disappointed, and it is a most unreasonable one. To any person who believes his Bible, can it be a "disappointment" to realize at every turn that God's Word "standeth sure," and that the land *once* "flowing with milk and honey" has become for many centuries "desolate," though beginning now to bear traces of the renewal which seems part of God's promise for His people in the "latter days"?

A sober consideration of the past history of Jerusalem, of the terrible vicissitudes to which she has, at all periods, been more or less subjected, especially

* Gal. iv. 26, 27.

since the Christian era, will lead any thoughtful mind to expect, what really is the fact, that scant trace of any building of the Jerusalem either of the Old or New Testament, can be found in the present city. The *débris* of centuries of warfare and destruction has accumulated over the old foundations, which are in places buried as much as seventy feet underground.

Such a foundation can still be traced under the traditional site of the house of Pontius Pilate, on which now stands a convent belonging to some Roman Sisters. There seems but little doubt as to the correctness of this site. The house stood towards the north-east, and near the Tower of Antonia, where was stationed the military garrison. The Sisters are most kind in allowing strangers to descend, by many stairs, to a crypt; here remains of an old building foundation are visible, partly constructed in the solid rock; while the ground is the old Roman road, in which the marks of chariot-wheels are still engrained, as in so many places near Jerusalem. One looks with deep interest on this rocky surface, over which may have passed the Feet of our Lord, when going before Pilate the governor.

The only *bonâ fide* remains of old Jerusalem, now easily seen, are contained in the outer walls, which, often rebuilt, still encompass the city. Especially towards the *lower* portion of these, are found massive stones of splendid Jewish workmanship, many of them probably dating from the time of King Solomon, and which have never been equalled either in Christian or Mohammedan times. The south-west and south-east corners contain the finest specimens, but the main part is buried beneath the heaps of rubbish which have risen round the walls to a height of from sixty to ninety feet. Sir Charles Warren, when excavating in 1867, discovered in the south-east corner, deep underground, some huge stones inscribed with mysterious masonic marks in red characters; these have since been proved to be of Phœnician origin, and to correspond with marks discovered on similar stones found near Tyre. How forcibly does this discovery illustrate the Bible account of the building of Solomon's Temple! We read in 1 Kings v. 17, 18, "And the king commanded, and they brought great stones, . . . hewed stones. . . . And Solomon's builders and Hiram's builders did hew them, and the stone-squarers." We know that Hiram was King of Tyre, and that Tyre was the capital of Phœnicia at that time.

But though so few visible vestiges of man's handiwork can be found in the city, nature's boundaries and defences, within and around, remain almost intact. As we "walk about Zion, and mark well her bulwarks," we observe that we are on a foundation of massive and impregnable rock, such as no power of man would be able to remove. This "rock of defence" did God choose for "the place of His habitation;" for it is pretty certain that Solomon's Temple was placed somewhere on the large rocky eastern platform whereon now stands the Great Mosque. From this point, or some other high position commanding the outer surroundings of the city, we can see how "the hills stand about Jerusalem," just as they did when the psalmist wrote of them as so sweetly figurative of God's mighty and sure protection of His people. "The strength of the hills is His."

One can see, moreover, that "Jerusalem is built as a city that is compact together;"* for its deep surrounding valleys, as well as its hills, add to the strength and isolation of Jerusalem; those of Hinnom and Kedron circumvent it on all sides except one, acting like a vast separating moat. The only point from which the city could in olden times be dominated was the north, so *there* strong fortifications were always placed. Titus was encamped on the northern hill of Scopus (Nob) during the remarkable siege in which he was at length victorious.

To sum up what has been so far said,—I think, then, that there *is* a satisfaction in standing on the site of old Jerusalem ; that *there*, as also when making excursions near it, one *does* find faith in Gospel narrative growing stronger, and hope purer and brighter.

"Nor by the wayside *ruins* let us *mourn*,
Who have the eternal towers for our appointed bourne."

The best way to obtain a general geographical idea of the locality is to make the total exterior

* Ps. cxxii. 3, R.V.

circuit of the walls, which, on a donkey, can be done in about an hour. Starting outside the Jaffa Gate, as one proceeds south, east, north, and west, describing an irregular circle round the city, the name of each hill, valley, village, brook, garden, pool, well, as it is pointed out, comes home like a household word familiar from childhood. It will be a fitting *finale* to this tour to enter the city, perhaps by the Damascus Gate, and, proceeding to the Turkish barracks near the house of Pontius Pilate, to ascend to the top of that building, whence the whole of modern Jerusalem will be seen mapped out below, with its boundary-hills visible above the level of the walls; the eye will instinctively fix itself on the spot, "over against the Mount of Olives," where once stood God's Holy Temple. Recalling the former splendour of Jerusalem, how fully can one enter here into the psalmist's words, "The hill of Zion is a fair place, and the joy of the whole earth"!

I cannot say that I was dwelling *within* Jerusalem, for most of the hotels lie at some minutes' walk outside the Jaffa Gate, by far the healthiest position. When I arrived, it was the height of the tourist season. As my big, ugly vehicle drew up at the door of Howard's Hotel, it looked as if I were approaching a vast overflowing human beehive, many of its inmates being *settled* on benches outside the house, amid the *buzz* of conversation in my own mother-tongue. At sight of me some kind Americans, whom I had met in Egypt, came forward to greet me, expressing surprise that I was not "frightened to death arriving in this country all alone!" As a rule, *they* travel in a decidedly gregarious fashion; so *my* plan of tour generally afforded them some surprise. I met many Americans both in Egypt and Syria, and always found them most kind, intelligent, and sympathizing.

After passing one somewhat uncomfortable night, I was, thanks to Mr. Howard's kind arrangement, shifted to a pleasant upper room, which looked straight toward the Mount of Olives. I had felt some inward trepidation on seeing the crowded state of affairs, and thus the more appreciated this haven; its appropriation to me caused, I fear, some chagrin to an old lady, who imagined she had a prior claim to it.

The arrangements of the house were of a rough and "scratch" character, but there was no stint of food, such as it was; and the "waiters," though insufficient in number for the momentary demand, were most active and obliging.

A curious phenomenon here was a woman—the only one I ever saw in the East in the capacity of a domestic. She was supposed to be a housemaid, but, I am obliged to confess, fulfilled her duties in a far less satisfactory manner than does the usual house-*man*. She dawned on me like an apparition, as, small and low of stature, she entered my room entirely veiled in her dark hair, which flowed loose all round her, reaching far below her waist. It can be imagined that this appendage interfered considerably with the performance of her work, and portions of these locks had a knack of depositing themselves where not required. Understanding not a word of anything but Arabic, and being apparently very timid, she looked terrified whenever I tried by gesture to make her understand my wants, and my opinion too, that cleanliness was *not* her forte. We had some semi-tragic and semi-comic bedchamber scenes, into which Solomon had often to be introduced as interpreter. On one or two occasions he emphasized his words by giving the poor girl a good shaking.

Solomon was my true and efficient body-guard during the enjoyable month which I passed, exploring in and round Jerusalem. A Syrian by birth, owning Arabic as his mother-tongue, yet speaking German even better than he did English (for he had been brought up in a German Protestant school here), by creed a Roman Catholic, and by trade something of a soldier,—having served for a while in the Soudan cavalry under one of our generals,—he might be called a many-sided individual. He seemed proud, one day, to tell me, on our return from an excursion, that he had been taken for a Turkish soldier appointed as my escort. His riding top-boots, short military and medal-bedecked jacket, and red fez may have encouraged this idea.

Turkish soldiers are a brave, fine set of fellows, well behaved and respectful towards strangers, and wonderfully patient and contented under the ill-treatment and neglect which they often have to suffer from those set over them. They are not well fed, and seldom get a new uniform; thus they are compelled too often to present a poor appearance; were they better treated and better generalled, they would be a credit to any nation. I cannot say that Solomon impressed me with *his* valour; indeed, his advice to me was always of a most timid character, and one which I had constantly to combat. Doubtless this timidity was prompted by the sense of his responsible position towards me.

I had now cause to rejoice that the horses which I tried in Jaffa had not given me a sufficiently high opinion of their good qualities to induce me to hire one of them for a lengthened period. Herein I effected a great saving, as it is far the pleasanter way to explore Jerusalem on foot; the best alternative would be a donkey; no vehicle can enter within the gates. The town is traversed everywhere either by rough steps, or by very rude, narrow, and stony roadways; so it can be imagined that riding a donkey—let alone a horse—in such a place, and through the midst of a jostling, busy crowd, is not a delightful experience; one trial of it sufficed me. Horses can be hired by the day when wanted. For the hilly excursions round Jerusalem I generally preferred a donkey; it was thus easier to alight, which I constantly wished to do, in order to explore ruins, gather flowers, etc.

The two points in Jerusalem most familiar by name to all, are the parallel ridges of Mount Moriah to the east, and Mount Zion to the south-west, the latter being a hundred and twenty feet higher than the former. On these two ridges stands all that we can still trace of the most important edifices connected with Bible history. Each time I passed through the Jaffa Gate, I had on my right Mount Zion, where stood once the "City of David;" the only Jewish vestiges remaining of this famous place are some massive, finely bevelled stones, built into the great square tower, which still bears the name of Hippicus, and forms part of the present citadel. This Tower of Hippicus, with those—now vanished—of Phasaelis and Mariamne, formed part of the strong Jewish fortifications of this quarter. On famous Mount Zion, which is elevated at En-Rogel, about three hundred feet above the Kedron Valley, are supposed to have stood, in succession, the "Salem" of Melchisedec, the "Jebus" of the Jebusites, and the "City of David." Here, too, was the "upper market" of Josephus; and from here the last brave defence was made against the overpowering Roman hosts.

In the south-west corner of the English cemetery, which is situated outside and below this portion of the town, some very ancient, narrow, and steep steps have been discovered, hewn in the solid rock; and these must, without doubt, have formed the difficult path by which David's valiant men gained access to this "strong-hold."* It was discovered, during the excavation work, that the steps descend deep down to the valley beneath. I looked with intense interest on the few still left visible, which seemed to bring me into such close contact with the old Bible story. The palace of Herod and the house of Caiaphas also stood on Zion.

But the thoughtful traveller in modern Jerusalem finds his central interest fixed on Mount Moriah,— the spot selected by God for special communion with His people, from the very beginning of their history, when He first called them "in Abraham" to be His chosen ones, until the sad era when His Holy Altar was finally desecrated by the pagan Roman conqueror.

The foundation of the mount is a remarkable natural rock of uneven surface, and traversed, at some depth below, by subterranean water-springs. The surface has been made level by vast artificial labour, so that now the whole presents the appearance of a huge oblong platform. Near its centre the highest point of the natural rock protrudes, slanting irregularly above the level pavement, at an angle of four feet nine inches at its highest point. This rock, the "Sakhra" of the Moslem, has been by long tradition

---

* 2 Sam. v. 8.

considered a most holy spot. Close to it, Abraham, in will, offered up Isaac; later, Araunah, on the same high position, had his threshing-floor; and after the acquisition of it by David, arose here in succession the splendid Temples of Solomon, Zerubbabel, and Herod. The Palace of Solomon was also situated at the south-east corner of the raised enclosure, and most of the massive artificial work of the platform must be attributed to his time; the enormous supporting exterior walls measure, at one point, a hundred and eighty feet in height, and, in their restored condition, still form the eastern boundary of Jerusalem, embodying, as I have already said, many of the grand old Jewish stones.

Of the gates which remain, I will mention only one, that called the "Golden;" it is of peculiar interest to the Christian, as being the one through which our Lord passed in the midst of that strange procession, when He "in lowly pomp rode on to die." This gate is now strongly walled up and guarded, since Moslems have a tradition, that on the day when it shall be reopened their rule will come to an end. From various facts gained in travel, one learns that the followers of Islam have a private conviction of the insecurity of their sway. Thus, at Constantinople, all the vast Mohammedan cemeteries are situated at Scutari, on the Asiatic side. The reason is, that the votaries of that creed anticipate a time when they shall be driven forth from Europe;

and they hope, by laying the remains of their loved ones in Asiatic soil, to secure them from future disturbance.

"Kubbet-es-Sakhra," or "dome of the rock," is the name of the magnificent mosque which now encloses the "Sacred Rock" which I have described; for splendour it ranks second only to the Mosque of Cordova, and is esteemed by Moslems the most holy place after Mecca. Till late years all strangers were rigorously excluded from it, and they must still pay a heavy fee to gain admission. This grand structure probably comprises the site of an early Christian church, for the spot has ever been holy, both to Jew and Christian. When Omar conquered Jerusalem, 637 A.D., he showed leniency to the Christians, permitting them to retain the churches they already had, though forbidding them to erect new ones. Thus the Crescent may not have supplanted the Cross here till the tenth century, when the Fatima Khalîfs took Jerusalem and persecuted the Christians, burning their churches. If the Arabs erected the present mosque, they were probably aided by Byzantine workmen.

In the eleventh century the Christians were further maltreated by the Turks, who then got possession of the Holy City;—one Christian who escaped thence, full of righteous indignation, was Peter the Hermit, who by his burning words first kindled the crusading zeal of Europe. In 1099 the triumphant Crusaders entered this splendid shrine barefoot, singing their hymns of praise and exultation. They adorned the interior with Latin inscriptions and Christian symbols, which were all too soon to be obliterated; for, after eighty years of Christian sway, Saladin reconquered Jerusalem, and caused the interior dome to be decorated with the rich Cufic scrolls and designs, which remain there—as, alas! does also the Islam faith—unto this day.

The finely proportioned dome, ninety feet in height and sixty-six in diameter, rests on a grand octagonal structure; everything rich and costly has been lavished both within and without in excellent taste. Passing from the glowing daylight into the solemn grandeur of this interior, you seem to be transported at once to another world, and to breathe another atmosphere—one of awe and mystery, which is enhanced by the mellow effects of subdued light and colour all around. Stained glass of richest tints, mosaics, marbles, arabesques, beautiful antique pillars, many of them relics saved from the great Jewish temple, —all this, combined with exquisite proportion everywhere, produces a sense almost of bewilderment. Yet, most mysterious and touching sight of all, is the portion of bare natural rock, emerging from the beautiful central pavement, and enclosed by handsome railings; above it rises the grand dome of this temple, which has been erected expressly in order to enshrine the hallowed stone; one looks on it with true satisfaction, for it is a real and tangible portion of the great Jerusalem of the past. At the time when our Lord Himself was in His temple, it must have still been a hallowed object, and our reverence for it is even increased if we accept the idea that on this rock was reared the great Altar of Burnt Offering, which stood before the main entrance of the temple, and on which the daily sacrifice was offered.

Everything points to the fact that this altar must have stood, if not exactly here, very near this spot; for under the rock is found a cave-chamber six feet high, approached by steps from outside, and pierced in its rock-roof by a circular hole extending to the outer surface. It is thought probable that the offal and blood flowing from the slain victims were conducted, by means of this aperture, into the subterranean chamber (the ground of which sounds hollow under one's feet); hence they might be conveyed by sluices to a point in connection with the flowing water, which has always existed under this remarkable mount; thus all would be carried off underground without any visible trace.

The only real spring existing in Jerusalem is that of En-rogel, or the "Virgin's Spring." The discovery of the Siloam inscription, in 1880, brought to light the fact that its waters were long ago (probably in the time of Hezekiah) conveyed by an artificial channel, seventeen hundred feet long and two feet wide, to the Pool of Siloam, into which they still flow.

The whole construction of the platform on Mount Moriah evinces much scientific skill; besides its great internal supports, it possesses an enormous network of cisterns and reservoirs, so planned as to steer quite clear of the natural underflowing waters. Some of these cisterns, which are excavated mostly in the limestone rock, are from twenty-five to fifty feet in depth, and capable of holding enormous quantities of water. They are fed by the great reservoirs called "Solomon's Pools," which are situated miles away on the road to Hebron. These pools, constructed by the great king, admirably fulfil to this day their intended purpose; had we nothing else, they alone would suffice to witness to the wisdom of Solomon, and the splendid workmanship of his day.

But all this work of human labour would be profitless without "the former and the latter rain," on which this whole land, and Jerusalem above all, depends for salubrity—nay, even for existence. The glorious weather which had accompanied me to Jaffa, had favoured me ever since. I had planned to arrive in Palestine somewhat later than is usual, in the hope of thus evading the very necessary but, for my purpose, undesirable, spring rains; the sight of everything so bright and beautiful buoyed me up in this hope. However, I had not been long in Jerusalem before I was undeceived. I learnt that no considerable amount of rain had yet fallen; the inhabitants were becoming anxious at its unusual delay; and a drought in the city must be anticipated unless the precious rain soon arrived, for which prayers were being universally offered. I had but to enjoy the present, and trust that, if the anticipated deluge had to come, it might arrive while I was still enjoying the comfort of a water-tight roof.

Palm Sunday was the first I passed in the Holy City. On inquiring, the day after my arrival, as to Anglican services for Holy Week, I was sorry to find that, though there would be daily prayer with address, there would be, after Sunday, no Holy Communion (excepting on one evening) till the morn of Easter Day. It was strange to realize a dearth of the kind in this place above all others.

The church available for English Church-people is an ugly whitewashed building belonging to the "Society for the Promotion of Christianity among the Jews;" it is one from which all external beauty and symbolism have been carefully excluded. Even the sign of our redemption is absent, both inside and outside the building; I understand that the purpose of this omission is, lest the sight of a cross should prove a stumbling-block to the Jews, whose conversion is desired. But can such a policy be the right one to adopt in the very spot where Jesus hung for us upon the Cross of shame? How would it have approved itself to the greatest of missionary apostles? (see Gal. vi. 14).*

* "It may well be doubted if the severe and nude sim-

The services of Christ-Church are duly and reverently performed, and I found the chaplain kind and courteous ; he was good enough to add an early Celebration to the Holy Week services when he knew of the disappointment of some of us at its absence. I did not regret having to miss the Greek observance of Easter, which was to fall that year a month later than the Easter of the Western Churches ; for I felt that all the superstition and deception in connection with the famous " Greek fire " would be repugnant to me ; it is indeed an institution quite unworthy of the venerable orthodox Church, which occupies so influential a position in Jerusalem.

There is plenty of interesting human life, as also of religious devotion, to be viewed and studied at Easter-tide, when pilgrims from all parts of the world come flocking to the Holy City. Besides the cosmopolitan representatives of the Latin Church, are seen

plicity of a modern English service in Palestine, with its studied abnegation of ornament, is really attractive to the Jew, whose tradition, like a very memory, connects him with the simple, majestic, and gorgeous ritual of the temple, its music and its beauty. If the Jew is to be taught that Christianity is Judaism perfected—the antitype of the ancient type— if the lesson of the Epistle of the Hebrews is to be followed out, and the services of to-day shown in their fulfilment of the types of the ancient Church of God, then a somewhat different service might be discreetly presented from that now sanctioned. His friends in London may think that he ought not to desire it, nevertheless *he does;* and we must deal with facts, and not with the theories of fifty years ago." (From the " Primary Charge " of Bishop Blyth, p. 25.)

Russians, Armenians, Copts, Abyssinians, etc. Many of them, belonging to a very humble class, have only by long effort and self-denial been able to find their way hither.

I had a special opportunity of observing the Russian pilgrims, as a large hospice with adjoining chapel has been built for their accommodation at some little distance outside the Jaffa Gate; there they provide their own food, but have a free lodging granted to them. A great many of these pilgrims are weather-beaten old men and women—women more especially—who, with wonderful endurance, often trudge on foot for many a weary mile, in order to visit the holy localities of Palestine, sleeping by the bare roadside, and living on the most scanty food.

As I passed in and out of my hotel I frequently met groups of these interesting old people, who, in the coarsest of clothing, were carrying home the simple victuals they had purchased in the city; many of them were hobbling along with the aid of a staff. Their devotion seems most earnest, and one cannot but be touched by it, however much one may deplore the superstition which mingles with it. To kiss the sacred stone, placed near what they believe to have been the Tomb of Christ, will, they imagine, bring them nearer to heaven. On my remarking one day to Solomon that I saw no young women among these pilgrims, he drily replied that only the old and ugly ones are allowed to undertake such a journey, and to face the hardships to which these old saints cheerfully submit!

What shall I say about the Jews, who, flocking to Jerusalem at this season in great numbers, form so painfully interesting a feature in the moving scene? They scrupulously keep their seven days' feast, during which all shops are closed; and the Jew being, *par excellence, the* shopkeeper at Jerusalem, this arrangement is very inconvenient to strangers. The closing began immediately after my arrival, so I had to wait more than eight days before I could purchase a few requisites.

The Passover meal continues to be partaken of by Jewish families, but in an imperfect and fragmentary kind of manner; they retain only a shell, the kernel of which they have lost. I fear that many modern Jews are becoming sceptics—indeed, in Germany, rationalism is being taught to Jewish children instead of the Bible; and so low has Rabbinical learning fallen there, that Rabbis have to be sought for in Poland and Russia. The chief anxiety of the Jew is to get rich quickly, and in many parts of Europe he is gradually giving up his sabbatical observances; a return to Mosaic Judaism would seem to be now impossible for him. May his darkness be but that which precedes the dawn!

Of late, many Jews have been moved by the perusal of the New Testament as translated by Delitzsch into Hebrew; it has been, and is being, much read among them. We may be sure that, in leading His people back in such numbers to their old land, God has His purpose of love for them. I hear that the number that have lately arrived exceeds the total of those who returned under Ezra. One of the features of modern Jerusalem is the multitude of houses which have been erected for Jewish families outside the walls; mainly through the generosity of Messrs. Rothschild, who admit Jewish tenants into them at nominal rents, and some free of all charge.

We cannot but rejoice that, after groaning for three hundred years under Turkish misrule, the Jews resident in this land are obtaining now so much more favourable a footing. Formerly it was death to a Jew found daring to intrude into a Turkish quarter; he was restricted to close, unwholesome limits, and compelled to wear a specified Eastern dress; now he is left pretty well to himself, and permitted to erect his own hospital, schools for women and children, etc. However, Mohammedan, Christian, and Jew each still prefer to keep to their own quarter. Jews are accustomed to crowd much together, sometimes living five in one room.

Many of the Jews now residing in Jerusalem are of a fair type, with red hair, being either of Polish, German, or Russian nationality; the latter deserted the land of their adoption chiefly on account of the new law passed there in 1874, when, by introduction of the German system, all the men of twenty-one years of age had to be enrolled as soldiers; thus every Jew would be compelled to fight for Russia or for Poland, which would not be to his taste. In Palestine, by paying a small poll-tax, both Jew and Christian are exempted from military service.

The Jerusalem Jews may be classed as (1) Spanish; (2) Poles and Germans; (3) a mixed nationality who do not believe in the Talmud. The first, Sephardim, are of a superior order to the rest; they claim to have been settled in Spain before the Crucifixion of our Lord, and so to have had no voice in His death. They were turned out of Spain in 1492.

It can well be imagined that in the Jewish quarter there reigns a confusion of tongues, which often leads to quarrels. I was told that at the Rothschild Hospital twelve languages are in constant requisition.

The costumes at Passover-tide are striking and varied; as the Jews, with their families, then constantly parade the streets, one has full opportunity of observing them. Many of the men are attired in very costly garments; over a tight-fitting tunic of bright silk or satin, is worn a long loose coat or gabardine, often of rich-coloured velvet, trimmed with ermine or other fur; while on the head is worn a cap of velvet and fur. The long "love-lock" plaistered down on the side of each cheek adds to the peculiarity of their appearance. The women present a general aspect of gaudiness and absence of taste; their silk gowns are often surmounted by richly embroidered aprons and scarves, and all colours are heaped together promiscuously—"the brighter the better," seems their motto; across the head they throw loosely a veil of soft silk or embroidered gauze.

While I was preparing to enter into Easter joy, I felt that I was entering into the forfeited inheritance of these poor people. The countenances of many of them were haughty and disdainful as they swept along; yet how can any Christian feel indifference or lack of interest towards the Jews? Was not our Lord Himself a Jew, likewise all His apostles? Do not we owe to Jews all we hold most precious—both the Old and the New Testaments, the Psalms which we daily recite, the Canticles (excepting one) which we love to chant together?

I happened to be passing a synagogue one day towards sunset; a few Jews were sauntering forth after their evening service, while some still lingered within. I ventured to enter, and, finding they spoke German, had a few words of conversation with one or two. A point of meeting between us was the beauty of those Psalms, which they, as we, daily repeat. While they told me how they loved them, it was forcibly borne in upon my mind how all-pervading and heartfelt, as well as ceremonial, must have been the religion of those Jews of long ago, who, while all the world was wrapped in heathen darkness, were divinely inspired to pour forth and hand down to future generations prayers, praises, and aspirations which it has been *our* high privilege to appropriate in these latter days of fuller light and knowledge. Like us, "day by day" the Jews still "magnify God;" with their *lips*, they continue further to say, "The memorial of Thine abundant kindness shall be showed;"* but, alas! the sweeter, fuller meaning of those words is, as yet, "hid from their eyes."

How did I long then,—as so many other English travellers must do,—to see, reared in or near Jerusalem, a Church more worthy of England than is at present to be found;—one which, in the fulness of apostolic doctrine and the dignity of a simple and solemn ritual, might be, to the many nations and Churches there gathered together, a daily witness for our own dear Mother Church, which yearns to attract into her fold both Jew and Gentile.

Into the vexed question of the site of the Holy Sepulchre, or into a description of that famous building, or of the varied functions which take place in it, it is not my purpose to enter. As the rallying-point of all the Churches (excepting our own) which call themselves Catholic, this building must be fraught with an abiding interest, which is increased by the memory of its early history and associations down to, and including, Crusading times. Though one must deeply deplore the existing divisions in Christendom, and also the superstitions, etc., which find

* Ps. cxlv. 1, 2, 7.

expression here, it gave me a sense of isolation to know that we Anglicans alone have no altar among the many which stand side by side within the Holy Sepulchre.

I gladly availed myself, on Easter Day, of the opportunity offered by an English priest with whom I had made pleasant acquaintance at our hotel; he had obtained for Anglican use on that day the Chapel of Abraham,* which belongs to a large Greek monastery adjoining the Holy Sepulchre, and overlooking it. Here, in the presence of the Archimandrite, a few of us joined together in thankfully keeping our Paschal Festival.

Concerning the most probable scene of the Crucifixion, I prefer to hold to the idea, in common with many moderns, that the "Golgotha" of the Gospels is not the spot within the city, whereon stands the Church of the Holy Sepulchre, but that it is situated outside the present walls of Jerusalem, at the place still known as the "Skull Hill," from its likeness to a skull, when viewed from a certain position. The only geographical Scripture clue which we possess as to the locality is, that it was outside

* "This shrine has been assigned for the celebration of the service of the English Church by the present Patriarch of Jerusalem, who, while welcoming the revival of the Anglican Bishopric in Jerusalem, expressed the desire that its headquarters should be there, on the ground—that all *other* Churches had representatives in the Holy City." (Quoted from Bishop Blyth's "Primary Charge.")

the city, and called "Golgotha;" this word "Golgotha," meaning in Hebrew "a skull," is expressed in Greek by *cranion*, and in Latin by *calvaria*, which we render "Calvary." It is no wild fancy, then, that this peaceful little hill *may* be the spot where took place the greatest of all earthly events! Formerly, it was the place of stoning or public execution. A Moslem cemetery now occupies the hill, thus insuring its future undisturbedness. A little garden below the slightly raised cliff, and in which an old Jewish tomb has recently been discovered, helps the imagination to form her picture here ; while, close by, grows the prickly bush, which yielded the material for the cruel crown ; my man wove me one in a few minutes, just such as is seen in the picture of Carlo Dolce. My quiet Good Friday afternoon was spent at this place. I remember, with pleasure, how strikingly the position of the Skull Hill corresponds with the description given by Mrs. Alexander, in those sweet and simple verses, which we teach our little ones at home to sing—

> " There is a green hill far away,
> Without a city wall,
> Where the dear Lord was crucified,
> Who died to save us all."

JERUSALEM. (N. E. Corner.)
Showing the Kedron Valley and Gethsemane (left)

CHAPTER XI.

THE GREAT DESCENT.

Walks outside Jerusalem—Christian miscreants—Native alertness—The khan—Need of a Samaritan—In an oasis—Arab wedding—A strange night—A salt bath—Beth-Abâra.

EXCURSIONS in endless variety and of unwearying interest can be made round Jerusalem. The stranger is first intuitively attracted to the Mount of Olives, which, as viewed from the Eastern city wall or from S. Stephen's Gate, appears very easy of access. But, although only separated from both by the narrow Kedron Valley, it will be found a fatiguing walk—as, indeed, are all those hereabouts—so rough and stony are the roads, and so precipitate the ascents and descents.

After having twice explored these sacred slopes on donkey-back, I much wished to pass an occasional quiet morning there, alone with my thoughts. This I could only once succeed in doing; for Solomon seemed to regard the idea as impracticable, not to say preposterous. If I proposed dismissing donkey and boy, while he remained somewhere in my vicinity, he would say that I should never see my saddle again! If, on the other hand, I suggested his return with them to Jerusalem, he would draw a picture of ill-conditioned Arabs coming down from a cluster of neighbouring hovels to molest my solitude! Solomon was certainly a nervous man. I must admit, that on the one occasion when I made a solitary return from the mount on foot, I found the walk very fatiguing and irksome, under the burning sun.

One longs to get rid of those large intruding buildings—three or four in number, belonging to Greek and Latin Churches—which mar the simple outline of the Mount of Olives. One regrets, too, that the fig and olive trees, once so abundant there, are now but sparsely scattered in the stony soil. Nevertheless it *is* good to be on the hill, which the Feet of our Lord and His disciples so often traversed, and to stand on that white rocky path, so graphically described by Dean Stanley, whence bursts on the beholder the view which so moved the Heart of Jesus.

"The hills" still "stand about Jerusalem,"—but it is another city which now meets the traveller's eye. *What* a walk it is, from beginning to end! How full of Bible memories! From the S. Stephen's Gate down to the Brook Kedron, past the Garden of Gethsemane, up the steep stony ascent towards Bethphage and Bethany, thence returning down another road, by the grand old Jewish tombs, the village and the Pools of Siloam, up to Mount Zion, and, through the Jaffa Gate, into Jerusalem.

There can be no doubt that "the town of Mary and her sister Martha" occupied the same site as does the present village of Bethany. It lies, nestling peacefully in a sheltered fig-grown nook about a mile beyond the highest slope of Olivet, where the road has begun to descend a little towards Jericho. We are shown ruins of the so-called "House of Lazarus," retaining some traces of Roman masonry; also an old Jewish tomb, to which access is gained by dark and tortuous steps. I stood in the sombre sepulchral chamber with a strange sense of awe; for if not in this ancient tomb, in one very similar to it, and close by, the resurrection miracle must have taken place!

It is sweet to wander over the brown, undulating, thyme-scented hills near Bethany. I spent a happy hour on one of the most isolated heights; as I reclined there, on that bright spring afternoon, musing, and gazing up into the azure vault above, I knew that close by must have once hovered the "soft cloud" which drew its

"Bright veil across the heavenly way,
My Saviour's pathway to His home above."

The large Church of the Ascension (containing altars for Greeks, Armenians, Syrians, and Copts), which almost overpoweringly crowns the summit of Olivet, cannot have been the scene of our Lord's

Ascension; its position does not correspond with the scriptural account, as it stands in full view of the Holy City.

Easter was ushered in by brilliant and delightful weather. I thought it wise to profit by it to visit the almost tropical region, which is to be found only fifteen miles from Jerusalem. The excursion would be very dreary in bad weather, and unbearably hot if the temperature should rise much higher than it then was; so, on April 3, I set off for Jericho. A small hotel now stands in the modern village of this name, and therefore the carriage of tents is not essential. I engaged three horses for three days, the third animal being for the baggage and its keeper. It is made imperative on travellers to hire an armed Bedâwy as escort; but I fancy this is now done more for the benefit of those who own the monopoly of this lucrative business, than from any real necessity. Desolate as the road is, after the one solitary village a little below Bethany has been passed, there is now such constant traffic in this direction, that robbers would have a poor chance of doing a thriving trade. One passes many of their old cavernous haunts, but they are a deserted.

It is curious that the ancient ecclesiastical tradition in connection with this road continues to this very hour. Upon it prophet and Levite used to pass, in their journeys to and from the Holy City to the " School of the Prophets," then situated in the Jordan Valley;

and *now*, Greek ecclesiastics continue to traverse the same dreary defile, owing to the fact that their Patriarch in Jerusalem has lately restored a monastery near the banks of the Jordan for his own residence.

Judging by events which came under my immediate notice, I fear that injury may now be expected rather from treachery and ill-will lurking within the fold, than from robbers without. The following circumstance, of which I was an eye-witness, will exemplify this. One evening during Holy Week, the Franciscans, headed by their Superior, were celebrating a special service in the Church of the Holy Sepulchre. After an impassioned sermon had been delivered from the steps of the Latin Chapel, a procession marched round the ambulatory, which lies behind the Greek choir, halting at altars belonging to the various nationalities in communion with Rome. I was standing with a friend close to the steps of the Greek Chapel, when the solemn procession, headed by chanting monks, stopped in front of it. Suddenly came a pause, then a short disturbance. A Greek orthodox priest, who had been viewing the scene from the upper arcade of the choir, had thrown a bottle of ink straight at the head of the mitred Franciscan Superior! Fortunately it missed its mark, falling on the foot of a deacon. A Turkish soldier was at once in requisition, and, after some little confusion, order was restored. In this childish fashion did the Greek monk vent his ill-will upon his Latin co-worshippers ; probably he was annoyed that a Franciscan should be preaching in *his* tongue, at a schismatic (*Uniat*) Greek altar.

Though it may be difficult to avoid an occasional *fracas*, where many Christian communities are in close contact, still a scene like this is a disgrace, and must tend to lower Christianity in the eyes of Moslems. It teaches one, too, that there may be adequate reason for the presence of that Mohammedan unbeliever, who sits within this Christian temple as keeper of its keys ; reason also, for the concourse of Moslems who, in the shape of Turkish soldiers, are numerously stationed outside the church throughout Holy Week. This deplorable state of things is painful, and it ought to be also very humbling, to the Christian mind.

Another fact, of a similar kind, came under my notice ; this time in connection with the Greek Patriarch of Jerusalem. He had proceeded beyond Jericho, in order to consecrate a convent in the valley, when he was shot at by an ill-grained monk, who had been sent into retirement there as an outlaw ; his Beatitude had to be conveyed, in much suffering, back to his house near Jerusalem, for treatment of serious wounds in the fleshy part of the arm. It seems that some misunderstanding about money endowments, etc., had occurred recently, so that things were not just then quite happy in the neighbourhood of the patriarchate.

At half-past eight, on the morning of April 5, I left Jerusalem; my armed Arab was in waiting at the small village just below Bethany, the only one on this lonely route. To my surprise, he was unmounted; but he was so fleet of foot that he was always ahead of my cavalcade—often beyond sight of us altogether, and awaiting our arrival, perched upon some sharp, rocky crag. Certainly, had there been danger, *he* would not have been at hand in time of need!

I was constantly reminded, while pursuing this laborious road, how great must have been the bodily strength and enduring power of our Lord and His disciples. Their *physique* may have been somewhat akin to that of the natives of to-day, who are very muscular and agile. Not only must they have walked long distances at a stretch, but also upon the roughest and most tiring of roads. One such, especially is that from Jerusalem to Jericho. For thousands of years past it has been the sole access from the Holy City to the Jordan Valley, and we may be sure, therefore, that it was frequently pressed by the feet of that holy company.

How difficult and precipitate the descent is, may be gathered from the fact that it takes an equestrian nearly six hours to accomplish the short distance of fifteen miles; the total fall, as far as to Jericho, is three thousand six hundred feet (that is, in a proportion of one foot to every twenty), and there is a further incline of four hundred feet toward the Dead Sea. One often wonders how the animals can keep their footing on this rocky track, which is enclosed on both sides by lofty savage-looking heights totally destitute of verdure.

During the latter half of the journey, the Valley of Achor is passed on the right; and, indeed, Nature could nowhere have furnished a more fitting scene for that awful execution of Divine punishment which took place here, as related in Josh. vii. 24. In the descent, the heat grows more and more intense, the dazzling white chalk rocks reflecting back the burning rays of the sun in a blinding manner. By-and-by a deep narrow ravine is visible on the left, at the bottom of which rushes an angry torrent, called the Wady Kelt. The ibex and coney still linger in the neighbouring rocks—this region marking the northernmost limit of their habitation. The Wady Kelt is one of the very few streams existing in this part of Judæa. The guide tells you that here Elijah was fed by the ravens; certainly any one, finding himself, unhappily, in such a situation, could obtain food only by miraculous means. The scene of that event, however, did not lie here.

The only vestige of human habitation throughout this route is the solitary half-way khan, where all travellers halt for refreshment, and which, from time immemorial, has been the sole site of a khan (inn) on this road. We may conclude, therefore, that our Lord's most graphic story alludes to this very spot, and that here He and His followers must often have rested in their weary journeyings.

Khans—with which one grows so familiar in the East—are usually nothing more than a paved and covered-in shed, fronted by open arches; there man and beast find shade, repose, and refreshment together in a somewhat promiscuous fashion. It was in a khan, though a cavernous one, so not quite akin to this, that the Lord of glory first drew mortal breath :—

"Guests rudely went and came, where slept the royal Child."

During my ride to Jericho, I passed innumerable spots where the "certain man" of the parable might easily have been "left half-dead;" many, too, were the lurking dens whence the "thieves" might have issued.

By a strange coincidence it chanced that, while waiting at the khan, which I had reached about 11.30 a.m., I myself was asked to perform a Samaritan-like act. As each successive party came in, it appeared to be quite the correct thing that its members should sit down at once in a business-like manner, to consume food brought from Jerusalem—for nothing of the kind can now be obtained here. Much to the dissatisfaction of Solomon, I did not incline to a repast thus early in the day, nor did I wish to pass the conventional period of time, in this unrestful place, seated upon a hard chair, and surrounded by feeding creatures, both biped and quadruped. So I decided that, as soon as my animals should be sufficiently refreshed, I would be again *en route* for Jericho. Much of my comfort would depend on securing a suitable room there; and as to avoiding the heat, *that* could only be done by a halt of many long hours.

While things were preparing for the start, there arrived three ladies, whom I had met and conversed with when steaming through the Suez Canal. The *old* lady seemed to be the most alive of the trio; for the two younger ones, her nieces, speedily laid themselves down full-length on impromptu couches, which their attentive dragoman had arranged on the ground in one corner of the khan. They looked deplorably tired; in fact, one of them seemed almost past noticing her surroundings, and in a fainting condition. Thus far they had but accomplished one-half, and that the easier half, of the ride, so it appeared a doubtful question how they would succeed in reaching their final destination. The anxious aunt turned to me and asked eagerly if I could provide her with a stimulant; I much regretted, for the sake of the poor invalids, that I had neither wine nor brandy with me.

I was the first among the travellers to forsake the khan, and it was lucky for me that I did so; for when I reached the little "Jordan Hotel," it was empty, and I had a choice of rooms. I asked in vain for a single one, but found always two beds, or more, crowded into a small area. The only thing I could do was to engage one of the double rooms, under protest that I *could not* admit other inmates; mine host at the same time reiterating his protest that, in the event of a crowd of tourists arriving later on—as seemed probable—I should have to give in. Under the circumstances, I felt that to secure immediate possession was the only course. So, well locked in, I was beginning to refresh myself by a bath and change of toilette, when, lo! a sound of many voices was heard below; then came a thundering knock at my door, coupled with a forcible intimation that I must open at once to admit an inmate, as the hotel was full to overflowing! Dreading what might be done next, I promptly sent an answer through the key-hole, that I was ready to pay whatever was necessary for the second bed; and here ended the matter so far as *I* was concerned. I believe the landlord became the victim, having to turn out of his own room.

This little episode over, I was able, as far as the intense heat would permit, to enjoy a couple of hours' repose; then, about 5 p.m., sallied forth with servant and Arab to explore the vicinity on foot.

The Jericho of our Lord's day stood just where the Jerusalem road opens into the plain, rather to the left of *modern* Jericho (which is known as Er-Riha), where the present hotel is placed. I passed many mounds and ruins,—the only remaining traces of the original city which was favoured by the Saviour's Presence. The first peep one gets of the Jericho sites presents an aspect of green brightness, as contrasted with the barrenness lately traversed. Indeed, here is a veritable oasis in that sandy desert of the Jordan district, which is called "The Ghôr." Copious streams descend from the hills into the plain, so that the region formerly proverbial for its fertility possesses still a rich soil, and a rank vegetation which has deteriorated only through long neglect. The water-supply is miserably husbanded, soon losing itself in neighbouring sand ; and as you approach the Jordan,—three miles beyond Er-Riha,—all is utter desert once more. The only "trees" which I could discover near Jericho were of a very stunted and thorny character.

The chief interest now centres round a fount of beautiful, refreshing water, called in Arabic "Aîn-es-Sultân," which springs forth close to the site of the Jericho of Joshua's time, and which is said to be that made sweet by Elisha.* Close behind, rises a high mound, thought to cover part of the ancient city, the walls of which were miraculously shattered to the ground. Fragments of broken glass, potsherds, etc., have been found here, and they are the sole indications of the existence of the great city, once "rich in gold, silver, and vessels of brass and iron," but upon which the curse of God afterwards rested,

* 2 Kings ii.

so that no enduring foundation could ever again be laid there. After its destruction, however, the surrounding land continued to be well cultivated. In the time of Pompey it was noted for its roses and balsams, and, long after the Christian era, palms and sugar-canes throve here. In the early days of the Church, the "School of the Prophets" had been replaced by an Episcopal See; numerous monasteries sprang up, and were visited, among others, by Origen and Jerome.

My way to Ain-es-Sultân lay through a profusion of greenery and brushwood, and so freely did water flow, that sometimes I had to be carried across a stream too wide for a jump. To feel moisture underfoot, and to look upon tender spring verdure, were new and pleasant sensations after the glaring whiteness of the day's ride. It seemed at first as if no living creature were there to share the quiet solitude of the oasis with us, except the birds, which, having gone to roost as the sun began to sink, were frightened by our presence from their nightly shelters.

Suddenly I was startled by loud incongruous sounds, evidently proceeding from the throats of human beings; no doubt a musical cadence was *intended*, but if so, it partook of the harsh, inharmonious character with which one has to grow familiar in the East. In a very short time I found myself close to a strange, excited group of women, attired in gayest array, and decked with gaudiest

O

jewels; they were all shouting and dancing round a young maiden, who was mounted blindfold on the back of a camel. This was an Arab wedding; the girl was being thus escorted by her friends to the tent of her future lord, of whom as yet she probably knew nothing; for marriage is quite a commercial transaction among Arabs. The intended bride is allowed previously to spend three days of retirement in the seclusion of the mountains, or of her father's tent; is it in order that she may there bewail her contemplated loss of freedom?

On my appearance, I, instead of the bride, became for a moment the centre of the demonstration! The wild creatures joined hands and made a circle round me, performing a kind of dance to the music of harsh yells, among which the word "bakshish" was easily distinguishable. Their appearance was not prepossessing, nor their expression amiable; the natives about Jericho are said to belong to a very vicious, low type. I was secretly rejoicing in the good luck which had led me into this novel scene, when cautious Solomon came up, whispering that I had better get out at once, before the *cordon* became too tight round me! The move did seem a desirable one, as I had no intention of giving them anything, even supposing I had coins enough to satisfy all; so, making a rush, I broke through the ranks.

After this delay we hastened our steps through the tangle, as I was longing to get a view from the

hill behind the springs before sunset. Arrived at
the fountain of waters, my men at once began to
quench their thirst, evidently intending no further
exertion; so I climbed the hill alone, and as fast
as the steep, slippery way would permit, reaching
the summit just in time to catch the sun's last ray.
My panting form must have been a surprise to a
solitary Moslem, who was seated at the top, tucked
up on the ground, with his eyes fixed upon the dying
orb. He had doubtless just ended his evening devotions,—and what more fitting spot could he have
chosen for them? The whole Jordan plain lay
stretched at our feet, bounded to the east by the
Moab chain, on which the sun's reflection still lingered. The deep river-bed could only be traced by
a far-distant and narrow line of vegetation. To the
right I could, with the aid of my glass, obtain a faint
indication of the Dead Sea. And at its southern
extremity rose one grand solitary peak, above the
level line of the Moab mountains, which loomed cold
and stern in the fast-waning light. This was Mount
Nebo, where that holy man whose sepulchre "no
man knoweth unto this day" lay down to die. As I
stood gazing on it with eager eye, Mrs. Alexander's
lines on the " Burial of Moses" came floating through
my memory—

> "By Nebo's lonely mountain,
> On this side Jordan's wave,
> In a vale in the land of Moab,
> There lies a lonely grave;

And no man knows that sepulchre,
    And no man saw it e'er,
For the angels of God upturned the sod,
    And laid the dead man there.

. . . . . .

"And had he not high honour?—
    The hillside for a pall;
To lie in state, while angels wait,
    With stars for tapers tall;
And the dark rock pines, like tossing plumes,
    Over his bier to wave;
And God's own Hand, in that lonely land,
    To lay him in the grave!

. . . . . .

"O lonely grave in Moab's land!
    O dark Beth-peor's hill!
Speak to these curious hearts of ours,
    And teach them to be still.
God hath His mysteries of grace,
    Ways that *we* cannot tell;
He hides them deep, like the hidden sleep
    Of him He loved so well."

The followers of Islam profess to know that which God's Word tells us that "man knoweth *not;*" for about Easter-time they make a pilgrimage, with noise and ostentation, to the pretended tomb of Moses, on the Judæan hills which lie west of the Moab range. Perhaps this is intended to serve as a counterpoise to the attractions of the Christian Easter Festival.

By the time I had descended the hill all was hushed into silence, and it was nearly dark; with some little difficulty, I and my attendants made our way back to the hotel. Being tired, and in anticipation of a long day's ride on the morrow, I should have been glad of a good night's repose; but sleep was impossible. The heat of the place was stifling; in fact, it was a tropical climate, without those appliances which usually render such endurable. The thin walls and light roof of my upper chamber had been baked through and through by the sun's power, and though there were three windows, looking various ways, not a breath of air entered.

A night of wakefulness in such a place would have been a trifle, could any degree of quiet have been found. But of this there was small chance. As soon as it was quite dark, native women began to perform noisy vagaries outside the house, dancing and gesticulating wildly round a large gipsy fire, and making the most hideous sounds. I think they must have been in some way connected with the wedding-party. After they had been encouraged and tangibly rewarded, and the last embers of their fire had burnt out, they rapidly disappeared, and slumber soon reigned in the wide valley. But, alas! not in our inn! It takes much to silence *some* European tongues, and a party of French and Italian travellers made themselves audible in the courtyard beneath my window, talking and laughing loudly till long past midnight, and cruelly dissipating the mystic charm of that lovely night.

The moon had risen in peerless beauty from behind the Moab hills, casting a soft glamour over the valley, and lighting up the rocky promontories of the massive Quarantania Mountain, which towered like a black giant to the height of fifteen hundred feet behind the house. Most rugged in form, and quite devoid of vegetation, its cavernous shadows presented a sharp and solemn contrast to its moonlit peaks. According to tradition, it was here that our Lord passed those mysterious forty days and nights—

"Prowling beasts about His way ;
Stones His pillow, earth His bed."

At any rate, if not on this mountain, it must have been very near to it; and the thought seemed almost too much to grasp. Its numerous caves were once the abodes of devout ascetics, who yearned to taste somewhat of their Master's sufferings. Many of the cells contain frescoes and inscriptions dating as early as the fourth and fifth centuries. They are now neglected by the Greek Church, but Coptic and Abyssinian pilgrims visit them assiduously.

In the monasteries of the remarkable Abyssinian Communion, each devotee lives a solitary life. To such, therefore, these old ascetic haunts would possess a special interest. When in Jerusalem, I had visited a cluster of isolated huts, which they term a monastery, and very meagre were the comforts contained in each hut. The Abyssinians are a fanatical and superstitious race of Christians; they believe that to kiss the stones of Jerusalem will obtain forgiveness of sin ; and have thought fit to exalt Pontius Pilate to the dignity of a saint in their calendar! The dark-skinned faces of these sons of Africa often look very handsome when lit up by the fire of devotion. I used to watch them, and thought they seemed thoroughly in earnest.

Soon after 3 a.m. work-a-day turmoil began in our busy little house; a party next door to me were preparing, in the noisiest possible manner, for an early start to Jerusalem in order to escape the meridian heat. The tramp of feet, moving of luggage, clatter of tongues, cups, and plates, resounded through the darkness. These travellers, with a not uncommon concentration on their own affairs, had perhaps forgotten that everybody else in the hotel was not wishing to be up and doing at quite so early an hour.

About 4 a.m. I looked out into the plain, now steeped in the misty dimness which precedes the dawn. There also I descried signs of movement, yet of *how* different a character from that lately experienced within-doors! From lowly and scattered hovels, tall, lithe figures, wrapped in long cloaks, were seen silently emerging, and moving along with light, noiseless tread upon the dewy earth. "Man goeth forth to his work and to his labour until the evening." Sheep and oxen too were being led out from their nightly shelters into the day-pasturage by boys and girls. Yet no sound either of man or beast broke that stillness—"the hush and whisperings" of nature; I stood, joining breathlessly in the mute concert, till the spell was gradually broken, when at last the sun rose in majesty above the Moab hills; then soon the world was "up, and every swarm abroad."

It was already very hot at 8 a.m., when I started for the Dead Sea. The road thither being very uneven, careful riding was required; it took me quite two hours to reach that sea—the deepest and most remarkable depression on the surface of our earth. It lies thirteen hundred feet below the Mediterranean, varying considerably in depth; towards the east, where it is bounded by the sheer rock of the Moab mountains, the depth is as much as two hundred fathoms. The Dead Sea, which is forty-six miles long and ten wide, receives every day the total inflow of the river Jordan, which rushes down tumultuously into it, bearing much *débris* accumulated during its rapid seventy-mile descent from the Sea of Galilee; other smaller streams also empty themselves here from the south, and it is computed that a total accession of six million tons of water is made daily to the Dead Sea. There being no outlet whatever to it, the work of evaporation unceasingly going on is a noteworthy phenomenon. Its waters, shallow towards the southern end, are there marked by a curious salt-rock, thirty-five feet high, the deposition from which contributes to the saline character of the lake. Apart from this, its best-known feature, the water contains a considerable quantity of chloride and bromide of calcium and magnesium; in fact, solid matter exists in a proportion of 25 per cent. It will be understood, then, that this sea is unfit to sustain life, though it is false to say that creatures cannot live in its vicinity. Birds, including storks and cranes, constantly fly across it.

As I approached the Dead Sea, its placid surface glowed like sapphire in the sunshine, and it seemed to me to possess a beauty all its own. Of verdure there was but little trace, yet no lack of colour, for the golden sand was strewn with glistening salt and rich-hued patches of sulphur, while here and there, on the white shore, lay bleached boughs of fantastic form, deposited there from the Jordan. The mountains on the eastern side, with their ever-changing shadows, made a dark feature in the landscape, and away to the south-west, in the soft distant haze, were seen the undulating hills of the wilderness of Judæa.

To modern times alone does this sea owe its present dismal name. It was known to the Jews as the "Salt Sea," and to the Arabs as the "Sea of Lot." Various considerations have induced the now almost universal opinion that Sodom and Gomorrah were situate at the *north* instead of the south end of the sea, as was formerly supposed. The neighbourhood possesses now, as in ancient days, elements of combustion, which serve to explain or illustrate the awful destruction which once took place there. The "slime-pits" of Gen. xiv. 10 are represented by petroleum wells, which still exist in abundance, and which, if coming into contact with other igneous substances, would produce a very serious explosion. An analysis of the strange geological character of this region helps to explain the story of Lot's poor lingering wife, fatally enshrouded in what was probably a shower of liquid salt.

As I sat quietly on the beach, waiting to get cool before betaking myself to the inviting waters, I distinguished, about half a mile to the right, a host of "Cook's" people, halting on the shore. The gentlemen were swimming away to their hearts' content, but the poor ladies had to be satisfied with a saunter on land. How I *did* rejoice that there was nobody near enough to hinder *me* from taking the anticipated bath! Solomon had already disappeared, leaving me and the horses under the charge of the armed Arab, who sat at a respectful distance; after a waving gesture from me he vanished out of sight like magic.

Shall I ever forget the buoyancy of those waters, or the refreshment of that bath? It invigorated me for the whole of the long after-ride. One of the bleached boughs, before mentioned, was my *garderobe*, and, in conjunction with an umbrella, it was also my *salon de toilette*. After the bath I hung up my improvised bathing-garments on the bleached pegs which nature provided; and they soon assumed such a rock-salt substantiality that I scarcely knew where to stow them away when the time for departure came; it took long days of fresh-water soaking before they would part with the solidity they had acquired.

At 12.30 (noon) we made a fresh start, and, turning northward, reached that wide stretch of the Jordan known as "the pilgrim's bathing-place." It is also the feeding-ground of travelling-parties. Yes, here they were! the same company whom we had lately seen by the sea, now already busy with knives, forks, and I know not what besides. I resisted all Solomon's persuasions, that *I* should, according to custom, make this noisy spot my resting-place. Proceeding about half a mile further on, I pitched upon a nice shady nook by the river-bank, where no incongruous sound jarred with the soft murmur of the waters and the sweet song of the birds; here I enjoyed my little repast in peace.

The river was narrower than I had expected to see it. One must descend from the barren desert above to a terrace below, thick with tangled bushes, before its brown waters can be seen. It has a very rapid current, and is bordered on either side by a variety of trees and shrubs, the boughs of which bend down gracefully from the steep bank, kissing the stream.

When I was on the 'move again, there came a tug of war! It was only one o'clock, and I knew that we could easily accomplish the next six miles further north, which would bring us to the chief Jordan ford of ancient times. I was anxious to do this, it being quite the most interesting point of the valley, and opposite to Beth-Nimrah, or Beth-Abâra, now called Beit-Nimrim — the supposed scene of our Lord's baptism. The ordinary traveller is seldom taken to this spot, and when I now spoke of my intention both my men appeared scandalized. All manner of difficulties were brought forward: I should be benighted if I attempted to go so far that day; there would be risk in taking the lonely road seldom frequented by Europeans; caravans of Bedawîn tribes were continually passing through it on their way from the east country to Jerusalem, and some of them were noted for treachery! It was not till I had made my Arab understand that I meant to go back to Jericho, and there exchange him for another and a braver one, who *would* conduct me to Beit-Nimrim, that I gained my point.

I had much hoped for a canter across the sand, but it was too uneven and full of holes; the slow ride, therefore, took two hours. After skirting the Jordan banks, and then bearing leftwards, we once more entered a totally desert region.

Jericho, with its background of hills, was discernable in the west as we pursued our lonely way while the sun poured down on us with scorching power. About a mile and a half to the east of Jericho we came near to the site of Gilgal—the first camping-ground of those sons of Israel who, after long training in the pure and healthy desert, had entered so miraculously into their land of promise, headed by the faithful Joshua, and full of hope and vigour. The "forty thousand prepared for war," who passed over, must have crossed this very track in their march from Jordan to Jericho, bearing with them the stones which they were to set up for a memorial in Gilgal. There they obeyed God's Law in the ordinances of Circumcision and the Passover Feast; and there, at last, their miraculous food ceased, when they first tasted of "the fruit of the land"—not a barren one as now, but "a goodly land" indeed. To this region also the people from Jerusalem must have flocked when attracted by the voice of the Baptist, whose "cry" resounded in this wilderness.

The latter part of the ride took us through some very remarkable sandy elevations, at one time rising about us in hillocks of every conceivable shape, at others taking the form of gigantic fortresses, such as children love to build in miniature on the sea-shore. We were now approaching the caravan highway, and Solomon hastened to inform me that he could see a long line of camels coming towards us from the east. As my retinue was very unpretending, this gave me no alarm; the only precaution that I could take was to tuck my gold eye-glass and watch-chain out of sight. We saluted the cavalcade amicably as we passed, and all went well.

Presently a huge black cloud appeared most unexpectedly from the direction of the Moab hills, moving rapidly towards us across that sky but now so blue and cloudless. Then a loud peal of thunder was heard, and enormous rain-drops refreshingly bespattered my heated face. No shelter was at hand, so there was nothing to do but wrap myself well round in my mackintosh and ride to meet the storm. Luckily our destination was not far to seek. As we drew near to the green margin which conceals the Jordan waters, the storm-cloud vanished, the sun shone out as brilliantly as before, while a sweet bulbul warbled its melodious greeting. Those two voices— the one of thunder, the other of sweetness—thus succeeding each other, seemed strikingly appropriate in this sacred place where once the Divine Voice had audibly spoken to man.

> "The dread
> Soul-giving voice of God, that spoke of old,
> Speaks *still*; and he who hears is crowned with gold."

I was thankful to alight, and sought out a cool secluded spot on the river-bank, where I requested to be left undisturbed for an hour at least. Poor Solomon was again very uneasy; I fear he thought that I was contemplating suicide! I had previously spoken about bathing in the Jordan, and here its banks looked certainly very steep and dangerous! I made the attempt; but the steepness and the slippery mud prevented my being able to do more than stand up to my knees in the sacred stream. This done, and having drunk copiously of its refreshing water, I laid me down to reflect upon all the wondrous events which had happened hereabouts ;—the crossing of the Israelites ; the translation of the great Elijah to heaven in a chariot of fire ; his greater antitype baptizing at this ford the spotless Lamb of God ; the Feet of that same Jesus treading this way as, with His disciples, He took the long last walk to Jerusalem !—With a store of memories such as these to ponder over, one was alone, but it did not seem to be solitude.

Over a newly erected wooden bridge, I crossed to the Plain of Shittim opposite, after which, at about 4.30 p.m., we made the homeward start ; I reached the hotel very tired, but after having spent a most enjoyable day. The surroundings of the house would not allow of much sleep, therefore I got up early, and we were off at 6.30 a.m. on the return journey to Jerusalem ; and none too soon, for before eight o'clock the sun's power became almost unbearable. I shall never forget the fiery force with which it poured down during the long glaring ascent through the defile, where no fresh breath of air seemed to penetrate. At the top of the pass, near Bethany, I was conscious for the first time of a faint reviving breeze. On reaching Howard's Hotel, a thorough rest was gratefully welcome, after the fatigue of the last three happy days.

CHAPTER XII.

PROCEEDING NORTHWARDS.

Change of weather—A new cure—Hill-country of Judæa—
Pastoral scenes—The watch-tower—Stoning of tourists—
Haifa—Ride to Akka—Syrian temper—Historic episodes—
" Place of Burning "—Ascent to Nazareth.

THE day after my return from Jericho came a total change of weather—cloudy sky, violent wind, and cold temperature. In the course of a year one can experience in Palestine every conceivable climate, from bitter cold to tropical heat. Under the burning sun of April or May, it is difficult to imagine the frost and snow so often alluded to by the psalmist; nevertheless they are a reality in winter, and one the harder to bear because the houses are ill provided with the comforts needed in severe weather.

Dwellers in Jerusalem were rejoicing at the sudden change, which portended the arrival of the much-desired rain. In two days it came, in violent showers, with a hurricane of cold wind. I certainly had an opportunity of seeing the Holy City under very different aspects. Now, huge black storm-clouds flew across the angry sky—thunder, lightning, and hail accompanying a deluge of rain, while the wind shrieked wildly around. That this exceeded the worst of English spring weather, was the conclusion I came to, as I recalled the stormy skies at home, which I had almost forgotten during my stay in a balmy and brilliant atmosphere.

It was not surprising that, after the recent heat at Jericho, I took cold. Fearing a bronchial attack, I had to nurse myself a little, and alarmed Solomon by the announcement that, if he did not soon get me all right again, I should have to give up my riding-tour and return to Europe. Jerusalem is not a favourable place to be laid up in at any time, especially in such weather. I found an English chemist, but when I asked him for remedies, was told, in a tantalizing manner, that nothing could be sold to *me*, as the pharmacy was only in connection with a local missionary institution. The sole alternative was a little German shop, where I tried to make a young boy understand what I wanted, and purchased a few doubtful nostrums.

Fortunately, I hit upon a cure of my own, which I am glad to make known, for the sake of any who may suffer from bronchial cough or chest irritation, only—it may not *always* be attainable! I had brought back from the Dead Sea a quart bottle full of its wonderful water; in this I soaked a linen compress, and laid it on the affected part for a few consecutive nights, accompanied by occasional water-rubbings. In a week a cure was achieved, and it was a cheap one!

The weather was not uninterruptedly stormy; there came intervals of sweet brightness and freshness, when explorations were most enjoyable, amid the renewed verdure of Mother Earth, and in the absence of dust. This last, however, is only troublesome on the well-beaten track, for Judæa is essentially a land of stones and rocks; "stony places" are everywhere. Large stones, ranged at intervals, form the only boundaries of cultivated fields. These landmarks being easy of removal, one can understand the force of the old Levitical curse on this subject.*

During my rides, I continually came across large natural amphitheatres, in which could be traced successive terraces hewn by the hand of man. Here had once flourished the vine, the olive, and the fig tree, which all need watchful culture; so, in its protracted absence, the supporting walls of the terraces have long ago given way, while pouring rains have washed down every scrap of the rich soil which once fostered such goodly fruits; nought but bare rock now remains.

From the results obtained in a few neighbouring localities, where careful cultivation is still carried on, as at Bethlehem and Ain Karîm, one can form some idea of the former fruitfulness of this land.

* Deut. xxvii. 17.

The last-named place is a small village, picturesquely nestled among hills, on whose sunny slopes the vine still grows in great luxuriance. Tradition has it that here stood the summer residence of "Zacharias the priest;" the birthplace of John Baptist is commemorated by the erection of a Franciscan convent. Here, then, must have been poured forth the sublimest of all Christian hymns; and here, too, must that happy father have uttered his exultant "Benedictus."

As I rode slowly thither, by the most direct route from Jerusalem, across a mountain track, which for difficulty and roughness exceeded any I had yet traversed, I recalled the laborious journey once taken this same way by the Blessed Maiden who left her native Nazareth, and "arose in those days, and went into the hill country with haste, into a city of Judah." After reaching the mountain brow, a steep descent has to be made to Ain Karîm. The smiling valley into which I looked seemed to offer a fitting framework for the scene of the "Visitation," which the artist Albertinelli has made to glow so tenderly on the canvas of his picture in Florence.

I descended from the convent to the one old well of the village, which bears the name "Spring of Our Lady Mary." There the blessed Elisabeth, with her yet more blessed young kinswoman and visitor, must have often resorted among the other women of the place. *I* found a somewhat different group there.

Mohammedan men, young and old, were diligently preparing for their midday devotions; some washing at the fountain, others seated in the shade in preparatory meditation ; a few of them had books open, and it looked as though they were assembled for some kind of united service.

The excursion of six miles to Bethlehem is easily accomplished, as a road,—a rough one,—goes past it, and has been from time immemorial the only highway from Jerusalem to Hebron and the south country. King Solomon caused a fine, well-paved road to be constructed, traces of which are still visible. Along it he must have constantly driven in his chariot, as his royal gardens were situated three or four miles beyond Bethlehem, on the way to Hebron, and near to the large reservoirs known as " Solomon's Pools."

After passing outside the Jaffa Gate on my way to Bethlehem, I was importuned by many of the poor lepers, who still hover about near the city. A leper hospital has now been provided for them on a height above the village of Siloam. We passed the scene of David's victory over Goliath in the Rephaim Valley, also the tomb of Rachel—these two forming the chief points of interest on the way. And now, the vision of fields and vineyards, tethered goats, grazing cattle, and a general appearance of industry and prosperity, announced that we were approaching Christian Bethlehem. No Jew ever sets foot either in it or in Nazareth ; he instinctively shuns both places, even were he not excluded from them by common consent of Moslem and Christian, as he is to this day, as he was all through the mediæval ages.

Ancient Bethlehem doubtless occupied nearly the same site as the present town, which stands pleasantly in a shallow undulating valley, its neat whitewashed houses having flat roofs, reached by an outside staircase, just as they must have had in our Lord's day. Its women are remarkable for their good looks, picturesque costumes, and industrious habits.

The lack of natural springs has always been a great drawback to the place. Water can only be obtained by storing it in cisterns after rain; and such is the character of "David's Well," which I visited soon after entering the village. It was for the waters of this well that David so yearned when forced to concealment in the cave of Adullam.* The natives still look to this deep ancient cistern for their chief water-supply.

On the hill now facing me, stood a grey Franciscan convent, and adjacent to it, the church which covers one of the holiest spots on earth; for in the cave beneath it, the native ruggedness of which is now nearly hidden by elaborate ecclesiastical ornamentation, there can be little doubt that the Saviour of the world was born.

The Church of the Nativity is the oldest and

* 2 Sam. xxiii. 15.

most interesting in existence. Built in A.D. 327 by the Empress Helena, it has been for more than fifteen hundred and sixty years uninterruptedly devoted to Christian worship, which can be said of no other church. The large nave is separated from its two aisles by handsome ancient pillars, said to have belonged to the Jewish Temple, and on its walls hang some mosaics quite black with age. It is interesting to the British traveller to learn that the roof is of British oak, the gift of our Edward IV., as was also its lead, now all stolen by the Moslems. A plain wall separates the nave from the sanctuary, which is appropriated by the Latin, Greek, and Armenian Churches, each having its own altar there.

No visitors were in the Holy Place when I entered, but I was surprised to see one solitary Turkish soldier, who stood on the pavement between the Greek and Latin altars. Looking to Solomon for an explanation, I learnt, with a sad revulsion of feeling, that it is thought necessary to station a soldier there, in case of quarrels which are apt to break out between the respective members of those two Communions. How great is human depravity, that such a thing should be possible at the place where, in the Person of the Incarnate Son, mercy and truth met together, righteousness and peace kissed each other!

After descending to the Holy Grotto, which is in the hands of the Franciscans, I passed to an adjoining cave, where S. Jerome lived for more than thirty years, where he made his valuable Latin translation of the Scriptures, and where he breathed his last. I was only just in time to catch sight of the bare natural walls of this interesting spot, which, after remaining intact for long centuries, were then in the very act of being converted into a chapel by busy workmen. Truly, this *is* a cruel age of bricks and mortar; it tries to put out of evidence all visible trace of holy sites and associations.

After leaving the convent I descended eastward, towards a gentle upland, smiling with corn-fields, vineyards, and varied greenery, most refreshing to the eye. Looking a little to the left, through a spreading valley, a distant vista opened before me; for there, straight and dark, above the line of haze indicating the Dead Sea, stood the Moab range—now, in midday heat, seeming far away, but towards evening looking much nearer; whilst in the early morning before sunrise, this chain presents a cold, grey, frontier-like aspect. How dear to *one* individual, once present in those fields, must have been that distant mountain-peep towards the land of her birth, and of so many happy youthful associations, as viewed from this, the land of her adoption, in the mellow happiness of her maturer years!

The spot I have described offers all the indications which would mark it as having been the scene of the sweet story of Ruth; but tradition, and the guide, point you here to a small olive-yard enclosure which they designate as "the field of the shepherds," though I should say quite incorrectly; for a night-watch would scarcely be necessary within a mile of the town, neither does the fertile appearance of the land suggest that it was ever given up to pasturage. But —looking straight ahead—gentle undulating hills rise in constant succession, till their outline is lost in the hazy distance of the wilderness of Judæa. These hills, in summer quite bare, would, during spring, autumn, and perhaps in early winter, offer a wide area of dainty thyme-scented herbage, over which flocks could freely range; at night they would need defence from the attack of the wolf and the jackal, which still frequent the locality, as also did formerly the lion and the bear of which we read in David's day.

Many a solitary night must that youthful Bethlehemite have passed on those rugged hillsides, where, while faithfully fulfilling his worldly calling, he could freely pour out his fresh heart's devotion to his God, and muse adoringly on His wondrous works. Dear to David was Nature's nocturnal solitude, wherein his poetic soul could hear and see

"The silence that is in the starry sky,
The sleep that is among the lonely hills."

Tuned to the same key, and "bow'd untaught to Nature's sway," were the souls of those other shepherds, who, hundreds of years later, were also here "keeping watch over their flocks by night."

To those simple-minded men were vouchsafed such sounds and sights as had hitherto been hid from mortal man, since to them *first* was given to hear the great angelic anthem which, with

> "Sudden blaze of song,
> Spread o'er the expanse of heaven;"

and afterwards—

> "With lowly hearts
> T' approach the Babe Divine."

One hill-peak is conspicuous in all the views around Jerusalem; it is that called in Arabic "Nebby Samwil," which rises above the high surrounding table-land to an elevation of six hundred feet. This is the Mizpeh of the Book of Samuel. The ride to its historic summit is delightful, and full of ancient associations. After traversing the usual amount of loose stones and rocky steeps, one finds at the top only a dilapidated mosque and a few humble houses, into which handsome old bits of masonry have been heterogeneously introduced.

This quiet, deserted hill formed once the stage of some of the most stirring incidents of Israel's history. At many critical periods Samuel made Mizpeh his rallying-point for the people. Here the Jews first raised the shout of "God save the king!" and here, in turn with Gilgal and Bethel, Samuel had his seat of judgment. It was well called "watch-tower," as thence a very commanding view is obtained; but its tenderest association comes to us from the fact that, near by, Samuel rolled the great stone of witness, called "Eben-ezer," which, as interpreted, has become throughout Christendom a motto of confidence and friendship. On the ascent I gathered some handsome dark red everlastings which specially grow there; they seemed to speak symbolically of God's everlasting protection of His people.

On arriving at the top, an extensive panorama was before me. Turning to the left, I traced the silver line of the Mediterranean Sea; then, the soft outline of the Plain of Sharon, leading toward Beth-Horon; while, in the wide expanse in front, rose a number of rounded hills, probably such as are intended by the "little hills" of the Psalms. They are now crowned only by heaps of stones; but formerly each was the site of a town, possessing a little world and history of its own. There, ranged in succession, and all within easy reach of Mizpeh, I could see—Gibeon, Gibeah, Ramah, Anathoth—places which recall such names as Samuel, Abner, Joab, Saul, Solomon, Abiathar, and Jeremiah.

What varied scenes have taken place on those hillsides, situated so near together, yet once so separated by opposing claims and interests! Thus, side by side in the valley, are Gibeah and Ramah, near to which took place the memorable parting between Samuel and Saul. Never to meet again in this life, each of these remarkable men repaired to his own abode, in the town then crowning each of these two hill-tops, which stand now, as then, so closely staring at one another.* The record of all these ruinous mounds, could they speak, would be one of alternate trouble and prosperity, triumph and despair ; of deep degradation and sin, yet also of many a holy life and much-devoted service!

As I turned to look back, there lay the Holy City, and Mount Olivet towering a little above it on the east, while to the north stood Scopus, the land of Nob. Mizpeh is said to be the " Mount-joye " of the Crusaders, whence they first descried Jerusalem ; if it be so, it was here that our valiant and zealous King Richard I., hiding his eyes with his hands, and casting himself on his knees, uttered the prayer that he might not set eyes on the Holy City unless he should be permitted to deliver it out of the enemy's hand.

The many hill-tops on every side reminded one sadly of the "groves" which used to abound in the "high places," and in which the Israelites of later days offended God so grievously by their persistent idolatrous worship. Where are *now* to be found, " upon the tops of the mountains and on the hills," " the oaks, the poplars, and the elms, under which they sacrificed and burnt incense " ? † Truly, Nature herself seems to have shared in the punishment of the rebellious people!

By the middle of April I found a great diminu-

* 1 Sam. xv. 34. † Hos. iv. 13.

tion in the numbers at Howard's Hotel; the last large company of tourists had passed on its way, some of its members having tried hard at Jerusalem, but without success, to free themselves from its "meshes," and to take to *my* line of travelling. However, arrangements of this kind are difficult to make off-hand. After the last influx of visitors belonging to a huge yachting-party had left, I became, with the exception of one lady and her invalided son, the sole inmate at Howard's.

One of my desires remained still ungratified; it was, to make from Jerusalem a visit to Hebron— that ancient city, which is seven years older even than Zoan in Egypt. I knew that the cave of Machpelah would be closed to me, for the hated Christian has been only four times permitted by its present owners to pass within the sacred precincts; the favoured ones were—the Prince of Wales, the late Crown Prince Frederick of Germany, the Marquis of Bute, and lastly, the sons of our Heir-apparent.

I felt that *I* should be quite content to wander undisturbed among those quiet *rural* haunts, where Abraham and Isaac had been privileged to live in such close communion with their God. I would view the remains of the old wells which they had caused to be dug, and would seek traces of the rich olive-yards and vineyards which they had caused to be planted; I would see the reputed trees under which they had sat for shelter from the heat, and the hill whereon Abraham had stood pleading for the doomed cities of the plain.

My wish for the excursion was heightened by the following account, which I heard direct from an American family, who had lately gone there. They had started, a large party, with tents, litters, dragomen, etc., and accompanied moreover by the American consul; yet all had suffered the indignity of stoning at the hands of the fanatic Mussulmans, while quietly riding through the streets of Hebron! The attack, though not severe, was unpleasant; the consul was naturally indignant about the affair, and afterwards obtained some *amende* from the ruling power.

I flattered myself that, with my humble little retinue, I should probably meet with better treatment—or, rather, no notice at all—from these ill-behaved people; so, in spite of advice to the contrary, I eagerly hastened preparations for the trip. As there is no hotel at Hebron, and I had no tents, I could only obtain a night's shelter there in the Hospice, built for the reception of Russian pilgrims, where nothing more than a bed is provided. To gain this boon, an introduction was needed from our consul to the Russian consul. I had obtained every requisite when, after all, I was obliged, alas! on account of persistent bad weather, to give up the excursion; and also, from the same cause, compelled to relinquish my intention of riding through Shechem and Samaria. The season was getting advanced, and, did I linger further in Jerusalem, I might be unable to accomplish satisfactorily the remainder of my intended travels. So, very reluctantly, I decided to return to Jaffa, and steam thence to Haifa.

I could describe many other objects of interest near Jerusalem: Mar-Saba, Scopus, Emmaus, Anathoth, Aceldama, the Pools of Gihon, the Tombs of the Kings, the hill composed entirely of the ashes formerly carted outside the city from the fire of the holy sacrifices, the extensive quarries under Jerusalem whence came the material for its construction, etc.; such details, however, would be beyond my present scope.

I had been warned that the unsettled weather would continue much longer near Jerusalem than elsewhere, and I proved this to be correct, for at Jaffa it was perfect summer; the hedges of prickly pear were already white with dust, and I was glad to cast off the warm garments recently assumed. The same lovely weather accompanied me to Haifa, where I landed on April 22, and it continued during the remainder of my tour.

The little town of Haifa, which occupies the site of the ancient Achsaph,* stands in a narrow plain not more than from half to three quarters of a mile wide, between Mount Carmel and the sea. This strip is in connection with the maritime plain of Palestine, which ever formed the highway of con-

* Josh. xi. 1.

quering armies when passing to the north or south of the then-known world. Across this narrow stretch of land, therefore, has tramped many a marching host —Egyptian, Assyrian, Greek, Roman, Saracen, Crusading, Turkish, Napoleonic, and lastly, Khedivial.

Haifa now contains a population of more than five thousand, the majority being Christians and Jews. It has greatly benefited by the settlement in its vicinity of an extensive German "Temple" colony, which has erected for itself buildings, comprising a college, chapel, and reading-room; it has also opened up the neighbourhood by agriculture, rough roads, etc. I had to walk a mile through a straggling street of white, European-looking dwellings before reaching the neat little house called "Carmel Hotel;" it is essentially clean, and the German tongue reigns supreme there.

The serious business of finding suitable horses for my further journey had now to be arranged. My dragoman, who, since his removal from familiar home-surroundings and the eye of his patron, seemed more than ever to realize the responsibility of his charge, had received full instructions as to the kind of animal he was to look out for my own riding. It was to be neither a slug nor a runaway, neither a shier nor a stumbler! I had already met two ladies who were suffering from broken arms through horse-accidents. But, in such cases, the rider is probably more at fault than the animal, since persons who are quite unused to equestrian exercise at home expect, apparently, on arrival in Palestine, to be able to ride safely horses, of the habits of which they are ignorant, during six or seven hours at a stretch, through a rough and difficult country. My own experience has been that there are more *dawdlers* than *runaways*. Some of the horses are of a skittish, uncertain temper, and during a heavy season their spirit, even if good in the beginning, usually dwindles to a minimum as time goes on. Whenever the rare chance of a good canter *did* occur, careful Solomon, from a long distance behind, could be heard shouting, "Hold him in tight, ma'am ; he is running away!"

At last, three horses were chosen and hired—in fact, we had four, as the owner elected to accompany us on his own steed, in order to take care of the animals. He professed to be always leading the baggage one, but more often than not it was left to follow its own sweet will, whereby my luggage had on some occasions a narrow escape of being rolled (together with the poor beast) down a considerable declivity.

The first trial of my new charger was made in the ride to Akka, a distance of about twelve miles along the bend of the beautiful bay, at the north end of which stands that once famous fortress and town. The transparent atmosphere made it look much nearer than it really was, and I fancied we were close to it when we had scarcely reached half-way. One

could get a delightful canter on those golden sands—
the blue sea to the left rippling close to the horses'
hoofs; to the right, distant hills bounded the horizon,
and in front stood the rocky promontory which shuts
off the view of Phœnicia. Behind rose the solid pile
of Carmel, separating this plain from that of Sharon.

The horse-proprietor, who had seen fit to accompany us on this ride, evidently thought that I was beginning my career in too Jehu-like a fashion for the well-being of his animal, so he became full of solicitude for *my* welfare, warning me against the danger of over-fatigue in the outset, etc.

We had another uninvited follower in the person of a second dragoman, who had just ended a tour with a German lady and gentleman. He was unable to speak English; but when he found that I could understand him in German, he became very communicative, relating to me the various difficulties he had gone through with his late party. The poor lady, whose horse had to be constantly led, had ridden on all day long in fear and trembling, and had spent her nights in tears at the prospect of what should come on the morrow;—while her husband's temper had been constantly ruffled by her needless timidity!

I did not notice at the time that during our conversation Solomon had turned sulky and retired well into the background, leaving me in the hands of my new friend, who, apparently, thought that I might prove a more hopeful customer than his late charge, though it never occurred to me then, as it evidently did to Solomon, that this man was trying to insinuate himself into my favour in the hope that I might take him on instead of my present attendant, who was, as the other mildly intimated, not well acquainted with the north country.

Next day Solomon expressed himself to me in no measured terms about this " rascal," who, he declared, should feel the full force of his indignation when they should meet again in Jerusalem ! I suggested the impropriety of a Christian, as he was, cherishing such vindictive sentiments ; also the desirability of his trying to keep in check his too impetuous temper. I fear, however, that my words failed to impress him, for he replied that he gloried in his temper, and that had he not " a good hot one " he should not consider himself " half a man " ! I was glad that *I* had not to experience its potency.

Before reaching Acre we forded two rivers—the historic Kishon and the ancient Belus, which latter is expressed in Hebrew as " glass river." Old tradition says that some Phœnician sailors had kindled a fire of seaweed on the banks of this stream, when they observed a vitreous substance—now known to be *glass*—coming from the fusion of the sand with contiguous flint.

Acre (the ancient Accho, and the Arabic Akka) has been the coveted possession of all great conquerors, and the scene, therefore, of untold woes. It offers the only practicable access to the fertile plains of Central Palestine. Of Phœnician origin, it had already become a great city in the days of Alexander, many of whose handsome coins have been discovered here. At his death Acre fell to the possession of his Egyptian general Ptolemy, whence it derived the new name of Ptolemais, which it retained after the Roman occupation, and by which it was known at the period of S. Paul's visit there.*

It early became an Episcopal See ; and its bishop was present at the Council of Neo-Cæsarea, A.D. 314. The Saracens got possession of Ptolemais in 638, and named it Akka, after its old name Accho ; but in 1104 they were forced to yield it to the Crusaders, under King Baldwin. They in their turn surrendered it to the victorious Saladin in 1187, after the battle of Hattîn.

Crushed though the Christian cause was, the zeal of its followers did not flag. All Europe burned with indignation that the Holy Land should be again in the hand of the Moslem. Thus from the fierce contact between Islamism and Christianity, was engendered that great Crusading movement, which exerted so mighty an influence, socially, morally, and politically, throughout the Middle Ages, and the reactionary effects of which are felt to this very day.

In 1191 our lion-hearted King Richard, aided by Philip Augustus of France, recovered Acre, which, from 1121 to 1191, became the seat of Christian rule

* Acts xxi. 7.

under the King of Jerusalem. Then came the final blow; the Sultan of Egypt, with an enormous force, besieged and took the town. Its Christian inhabitants, including the Knights Templars—of whom but two or three escaped to Cyprus—were almost exterminated. Of the old place scarcely a vestige was left, and a death-like solitude reigned in the spot, once famous as a centre of life and activity.

In 1517 Akka again changed masters, falling into the hands of the Moslem Turks. How strong the dismay of all Christendom was at the powerful aggressions of these new unbelievers, may be realized by an examination of our English Book of Common Prayer. Among changes made in it at the Reformation, the word "Turks" was, for the first time, inserted in the third Collect for Good Friday, which had long formed a portion of our Liturgy. Surely the time has now arrived when "Turks" might reasonably be replaced by "Mohammedans," since the followers of the false prophet are of *many* races, and are permitted, in God's inscrutable Providence, to hold sway, not only in those spots which we deem the most sacred, but also over a large portion of two vast continents, including our Indian Empire. Would that this charitable Collect were offered in our churches, not on Good Friday only, but on many other occasions also! Are not "infidels" needing our intercession to be found now everywhere, at our very door—nay, even within the visible Fold?

But I have not yet done with the woes of Akka. In 1799 the insatiable ambition of Napoleon I., who laid siege to the town, was checked by a small English fleet under Sir Sidney Smith, who, aiding the Turks, compelled the French forces to leave the country. Finally, the Egyptian, Ibrahim Pacha, attacked it both by land and sea, and took it after a six months' siege; but only to be driven out from it by our English fleet, in alliance with Austria and Turkey.

The miseries of Akka, during this last desperate resistance and warfare, were much aggravated by the accidental explosion of a large powder magazine, causing the death of thousands.

The modern town contains a population exceeding nine thousand, of whom two-thirds are Moslems, and the rest belong to the Latin or Greek Church. There are good bazaars and much traffic in grain; also in heavy millstones, conveyed hither by camel-caravans for exportation. The old forts of Acre tell their own pathetic tale, crumbling, as they gradually are, into the blue, pellucid waters at their base. I much wished to mount the ruin of the one formerly captured by our King Richard in his own person. It looked tolerably solid, but I was warned against it, as being too rotten to bear human tread.

Next morning I left Haifa for Nazareth, *viâ* Carmel. This mountain, which forms a conspicuous feature in the scenery of Central Palestine, presents the aspect of a straight uniform ridge, eighteen miles long, extending in a north-westerly direction. The eastern extremity is higher than the western, reaching an altitude of sixteen hundred feet, but the highest point of all measures seventeen hundred and fifty feet. Its chief interest centres about the east end, where, in a hollow, stands an isolated natural amphitheatre, surrounded on two sides by fine trees; in the midst lies a shapeless heap of ruins, which has for centuries given to this spot its name, " Place of Burning," expressed in Arabic as " Mohrakah." Near by is a deep well, which has never been known to fail; a fact which would account for Elijah being able to obtain water to pour on the sacrifice which he offered here, when, owing to a three years' drought, nearly all other water-supplies had been dried up.

The place, " Mohrakah," would seem eminently suited for the large and remarkable gathering which once assembled there. A steep path thence down the mountain-side leads to the brook Kishon, and close by is a rounded knoll, still known in Arabic as " the Mount of the Priests," where no doubt took place the slaughter of the idolatrous worshippers of Baal. The stream (Kishon) is still called in Arabic " River of Slaughter," so pertinaciously do the old names cling to this interesting locality.

Carmel was ever held to be a holy mountain, even by distant heathen nations, to whose ears the fame of Elijah's sacrifice may have reached. It is said that Pythagoras remained there in meditative seclusion on his way to Egypt, and the Emperor Vespasian also halted to offer sacrifice at the traditionary "Place of Burning." The Carmel caves early became the haunts of Christian hermits, who, in the thirteenth century, had developed into the Order of Carmelites, or "bare-footed friars," founded by Louis IX., who himself was once here; Edward I. of England was a lay-brother of this Order. Though they formerly experienced serious opposition from their Mohammedan neighbours, the Carmelites still retain their hold on "Mar-Elyas," as the mount is now called. Their monastery, on the western side, rebuilt in 1828, is inhabited by a few monks, who keep beds ready for the use of travellers.

Carmel means "Park;" we are told in the Bible that this place formerly rejoiced in an exuberant vegetation,* and such is, in a great measure, still the case. Within its glades such trees as the oak and chestnut flourish, though they are gradually being cleared away for fuel; sweet-scented, blossoming shrubs abound, and during the short spring this is a perfect garden of lovely flowers.

After skirting the base of the mountain for some time, I crossed a level, cultivated plain, forded the Kishon once more, and then began a gradual ascent through park-like scenery adorned by small evergreen oaks and other trees; it was quite different from

* Isa. xxxv. 2.

anything I had yet seen in the East—indeed, I was often reminded of our English uplands.

When we had made a considerable ascent, a lovely view opened over the Plain of Buttauf, or Zebulon; then, after some pretty, varied riding on high ground, came a grand peep into the Vale of Esdraelon, its hills ranging right and left far away towards Nablous; while Mount Gilboa and Little Hermon were seen more and more distinctly in the foreground as we proceeded.

After passing the village of Yâfa, we descended a little for two miles, towards the high mountain basin in which Nazareth lies; I rejoiced for many reasons to see it before me. The scattered little town lies on a steep slope; its streets are winding, precipitate, and slippery, and it was thought best that the horses should be led. So I alighted, and proceeded on foot, as it was most fitting that I should on entering this, the early home of Jesus.

It was a very long ascending mile to the orphanage of the "Society for the Promotion of Female Education in the East," which stands at the highest part of the town. Here I met with a most kind and hospitable English welcome, and was installed in a cosy little room approached by its own special staircase, and familiarly called the "pilgrim's chamber."

CHAPTER XIII.

FROM TABOR TO TIBERIAS.

The well and the hillside—Domestic details—A mountain fortress—The Great Plain—Freebooters—Tiberias—My quarters there.

I AROSE next morning to find myself positively in the clouds. The temperature was considerably lower than what I had lately experienced; indeed, it felt quite chilly in the spacious, airy halls of the orphanage. Nazareth stands so high, that it partakes of the same uncertain climate as Jerusalem, and its hills attract many a storm which passes tranquilly over the plains below. I was told that the extremes of winter cold and summer heat are experienced here, and the former would be felt the more severely within doors on account of the absence of European heating appliances. The mountain basin in which the little town is situated, is a feature somewhat peculiar to Galilæan scenery; thus, though Nazareth stands very high, it is almost lost to the sight of the outer world; yet close by it lies the chief highway from the sea to Upper Galilee and the eastern plain.

The town, which formerly had a considerable population, was never walled—an exceptional fact in the East. But Nature provided her own immutable barrier of bare limestone hills to hedge round the mountain-nook, wherein was to be reared the fairest Flower of humankind—the "altogether Lovely One."

The modern straggling village, which is gradually extending in a lower direction, has but a population of five thousand. Its prosperous air contrasts strikingly with the "ruinous heaps," which alone indicate the sites of some of the forty busy Galilæan cities mentioned by Josephus as existing in his day. Little Nazareth is now the chief business centre of the whole region; the wild Bedawin tribes east of Jordan, whose main wealth, as was Abraham's of old, is in flocks and herds, find this a convenient place for exchanging their goods, it being on the most ready line of access to the sea-coast.

Knowing that all the present buildings are modern, one pays little heed to the mythical sites so confidently pointed out to the stranger, such as —the workshop of S. Joseph, the synagogue frequented by our Lord, the exact spot of the Angelic Salutation, and the "Hill of Precipitation;" this last, a considerable distance off, has been selected, in direct opposition to the precise record of S. Luke, which says that they "led Him unto the brow of the *hill, whereon their city was built.*" *

* S. Luke iv. 29.

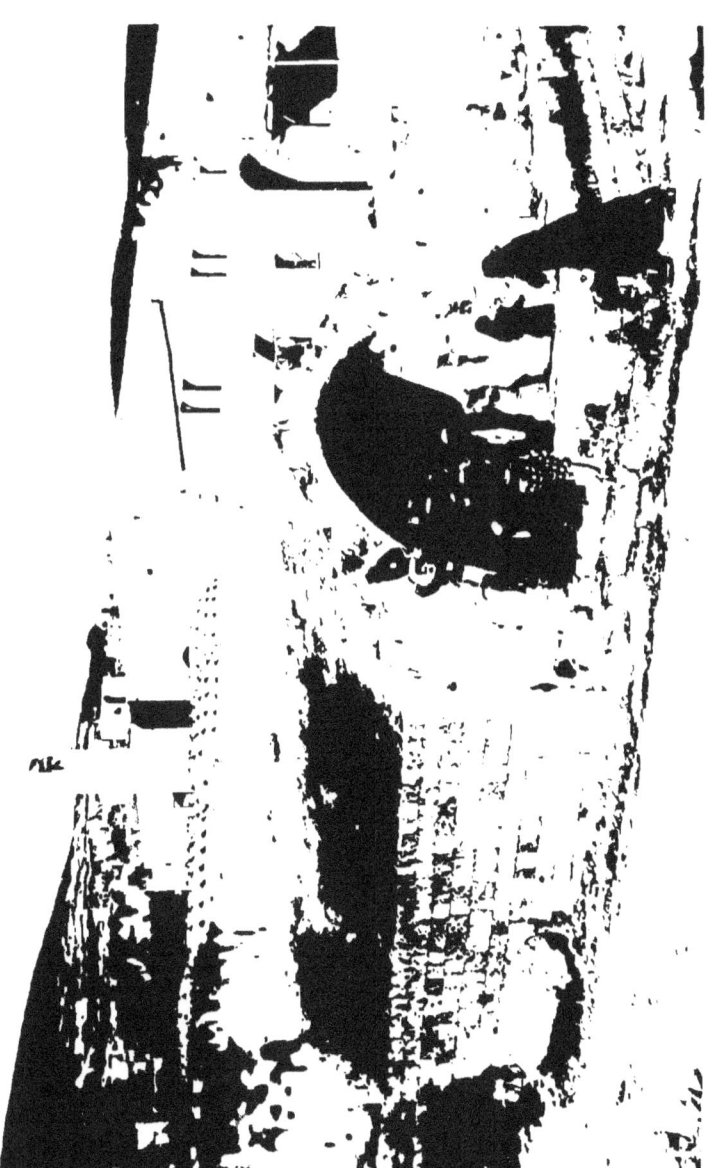

THE FOUNTAIN AT NAZARETH.

Recent discoveries have made it certain that the old site was in the upper part of the valley, round which are found many precipitate bluffs, from any one of which the atrocious act might have been attempted.

The public well or fountain will generally be the oldest reliable feature of a vanished city. So thoroughly and so skilfully did the ancients understand how to dig wells and to arrange the water-channels for their reservoirs, that these are constantly found intact for the benefit of a later posterity. So it is at Nazareth; the old fountain must always have been, as now, situated a little outside the lower part of the town—it is fed by very ancient artificial channels, which never fail in their supply. A modern structure has been built for the convenience of the water-drawers, who constantly frequent the place, and have done so from time immemorial. The women, often accompanied by their little ones, poise the well-filled jars adroitly on their heads, and bear them homeward up the most steep ascents. We may be sure that the Blessed Mary, with her Holy Child, must have been of those who, in that day, often visited the well.

In the absence of a city-gate, this spot forms the chief *rendezvous* where gossips meet together. The fountain had a great attraction for me; it was interesting to note there the quiet, modest demeanour and costume of the Christian girls in contrast with that of their Mohammedan sisters. My man seemed also quite content to be there, and, at a glance, could indicate to me the particular creed of each woman. They have, from early ages, been remarkable in Nazareth for their beauty, which they still retain; their dress also is picturesque, and their head-gear quite distinctive. It is composed of small silver coins, fixed on a cushion round the face; these coins form the special property of the wife, and are passed on by her, as an heirloom, to her daughters. What force does this little fact give to our Lord's familiar parable! Great would be the loss of one piece to the poor woman who owned altogether but the modest number of ten. It is to be regretted that this style of adornment is less in vogue than formerly.

I am sorry to know that there are six different sets of Christians—orthodox and unorthodox—now in Nazareth. Moslem converts, it is said, are very rarely made, and this is not to be wondered at, for a house, alas! so divided must be weakened in its power of attracting outsiders; and those who have any leaning towards Christianity will be puzzled to know which is the right communion for them to join. Islam converts, moreover, besides being cast off by their own people, often have literally to carry their life in their hand, for a bigoted Mohammedan would be ready to kill his own son or daughter who had openly professed Christianity.

My favourite haunt was the high hill called Nebby Sa'in, north-west of the town, and easily accessible from the orphanage, as no doubt it was also from the old quarter, which, as I before said, stood on the height. Here the grass, especially in early spring, is bright with varied flowers. As I reclined there, far away from the world's din, the scent of wild thyme and other odoriferous plants came wafted on the pure mountain air, while before me was spread, on both sides, a grand panorama, embracing hill and plain for many a long mile. This fine view is remarkable, as comprising in one glance the three chief mountains of Palestine—the snowy, majestic Hermon, the rounded, foliage-covered Tabor, and the long, rugged line of Carmel. May we not be sure that He Who, during His busy, brief life of ministry, so gladly sought intervals of mountain solitude, would often repair to this hill-top, during those mysterious years of waiting Manhood which He passed in seclusion at Nazareth? He, "by Whom all things were made," and Who yet, for our sakes, "was found in fashion as a man," could here, with thoughts unutterable filling His Human Breast, gaze undisturbed on this fair sight of nature—" the living, visible garment " of the Infinite One.

I had fallen into excellent quarters at the orphanage, and was most hospitably entertained. Two of the senior girls waited on me; they spoke English with a good accent, and were exceedingly gentle and pleasant in their manners. The whole establishment is admirably conducted, and the boarders, as a rule, appeared to be very happy and intelligent. The three ladies who manage the school work indefatigably, and with loving interest, each in her own special department, and are—as they ought to be—much beloved.

The climate must be rather trying to an English constitution; the diet, too, has to be of a somewhat monotonous character. I was surprised to find that sheep or goats' milk is the only kind that can be obtained, as the pasturage is not sufficient to support cows. The ladies told me that they can only get butter (made from sheep's milk) in the spring months, so that through the summer they must eat dry bread more frequently than is agreeable. The process of butter-making is a very primitive one, the milk being just shaken up in a goat's skin. The natives are very fond of curdled milk, which was also an ancient dish; my man generally took some of it with him on our journeys, and ate it with his bread, finding it a sustaining as well as a refreshing and cooling food. I tasted it sometimes, and should soon grow to like it, I think, in hot weather. The native bread was a trial, being tough and unpalatable; I therefore generally contrived to carry a stock of bread somewhat more European in quality, from the last place where it had been obtainable. The water-supply is also sometimes a difficulty, as there is a risk in drinking chance water; I always carried a large bottle, which was filled from any dependable source within reach.

Poor Solomon was rather "out in the cold" while I was at the orphanage, as he was not allowed to pass within the entrance gates. I was rather inconvenienced thereby, as I had to descend an enormous flight of stone steps whenever I wanted to parley with him. The horse-proprietor, too, had betaken himself and the animals to some far-removed quarter; thus altogether I had a difficulty in collecting my small *suite*.

After a day or two of rest for us all, another move had to be initiated. By a delightful arrangement, my kind hostesses allowed me to make the school my head-quarters, whence to proceed to various excursions in the neighbourhood. Of these, the one to the Sea of Galilee is the most extensive; it was to cover three days.

I was off at nine one lovely April morning for Tiberias *viâ* Mount Tabor, which is about six miles distant from Nazareth. After a sharp descent into the Plain of Esdraelon, we found the famous mountain facing us. It rises abruptly to a height of fourteen hundred feet, and has a comfortable, cheery aspect, being covered with trees and bushes up to its rounded summit. Herein it differs from all the hills about, which are more or less barren. Clouds frequently settle on Tabor, which thus serves as a good weather-glass to the natives; in summer, dew also lies heavy upon it. The precipitate upward path is rough and stony enough ; but it was delightful to find some occasional shade during the ascent, which took me nearly an hour.

It is now a generally received fact that Tabor was *not* the scene of our Lord's Transfiguration, but rather some point of the Hermon pile, which, from Tabor, is seen rising in snowy majesty from behind the Galilæan hills. Tabor was always a thickly populated and strongly fortified position, and must certainly have been so in the time of our Saviour, when the whole region of Galilee was densely peopled. Now nothing remains at the summit except a Greek and a Latin convent and some stone ruins.

Its commanding position has always made the mount an important possession. It has seen many vicissitudes during long Jewish history—from the time of the Judges, when Barak there massed his forces, ten thousand strong, against the Canaanites under Sisera, with his nine hundred chariots ; then later, under the *régime* of the Maccabees, when it was held by Antiochus,—till finally the Romans made it their strong fortress. To come down to modern times, Napoleon I., in 1799, on the plain at its base, and within view of peaceful Nazareth, fought the battle of Mount Tabor, one of his most brilliant engagements.

Standing, as Tabor does, quite isolated, a delightful and extensive view is obtained from its summit. The point which most fascinated me was that towards the north-east, where, between the Galilæan and Bashan hills, shone a distant silver speck; it was a corner of the sacred Lake of Gennesareth, which I now saw for the first time, sparkling far away in the sunlight. Looking south, all the geographical points of the Plain of Esdraelon could be clearly made out.

That famous plain, one of the world's great battlefields—once teeming with the life of flourishing cities, and bounded by verdant and peopled hills—now lies, calm and silent, in Nature's solitude, and nearly devoid of all save vegetable life. The undulating chain which constitutes its eastern border, gradually contracts in the far distance, till, when met by the corresponding offshoots of the Carmel pile on the west, a central gorge is formed; in front of this stands Nablous, though not visible from Tabor. Each of the eastern hills in the foreground has a familiar biblical name. First comes the "Hill of Moreh," now better known as "Little Hermon," on the north slope of which stands Nain, and, on the hinder part, Endor; then, further back, the more imposing pile of Mount Gilboa, on whose slopes a royal father and son fell, united in the bonds of a common death; on it still rests the curse invoked there by their royal mourner, King David;[*] for rugged, dry, and desert is Mount Gilboa to-day; its extensive spurs gradually sloping southward towards Gerizim.

[*] 1 Sam. i. 21.

Yet, from the hard rocks at the foot of this Gilboa, flows the spring which forms the famous "Fountain of Jezreel," or "Pool of Gilboa," formerly often called "The Pool of Trembling." It was here that Gideon, more than three thousand years ago, selected his three hundred picked men—"Every one that lappeth of the water with his tongue as a dog lappeth" —from among the rest of the people, "who bowed down on their knees to drink." * With his small band he proceeded, under Divine direction, towards the hosts of Midian encamped beneath him in the valley; panic-stricken, those thousands fled at the blast of the trumpets and the breaking of the pitchers containing the lighted torches. I had an opportunity of noticing that the natives still resort to both fashions of drinking described in that history, for my men were constantly lapping in one way or the other at any good water they passed; they seemed possessed by an insatiable thirst.

Jezreel, the sometime handsome capital of Israel, which stood below a spur of Gilboa, is now represented only by a ruinous village, called Zerîn, perched picturesquely on the slope. A few handsomely carved sarcophagi, at present used as watering-troughs, alone tell of the former splendour of this place; while the form of a crescent moon, visible on one or two of them, helps to remind us that here once an important worship was rendered to the

* See Judg. vii.

goddess Ashtoreth, "the abomination of the Zidonians," under the patronage of the wicked Phœnician and Israelitish Queen, Jezebel. Close by must have been situated the field of Naboth, wherein was cast the corpse of Jehoram, son of that unhappy woman.

Only one flourishing little town is visible from Tabor, smiling in the plain below, and that is Jenin, formerly En-gannim, surrounded by well-watered and well-cultivated soil, in which luxuriate the orange and the palm. This splendid Esdraelon Plain is dowered with such great natural fertility, that, without the use of manure, its soil yields abundantly under only slight cultivation. Much of it is possessed and worked by certain wealthy Syrian bankers, but a part also by Jews, who have lately taken successfully to farming.

I have already alluded to the recent return of these people in considerable numbers to the land of their affection. The Ordnance Survey of 1872 helped to prepare their way; they have been further aided by the Syrian Colonization Society; while the passing of a new land-law in 1867 has made it now easy for them to buy land in their own names. Previously it was impossible for them to acquire any, unless they would consent to become Turkish subjects, or "rayahs," a condition which would be most repugnant to them. I may here mention that Russia, Germany, and France have, of late years, vied with one another in acquiring land in Palestine, with the view of strengthening their footing there. I have not yet heard of the British Government doing much in the way of acquisition, either here or in Jerusalem. Are we not, as a nation, rather supine in this matter?

Prodigal as Nature is in the Esdraelon Plain, her benefits cannot be always enjoyed by those rightfully entitled to them ; for the nomadic hosts of " Midianites and Amalekites," which, in Gideon's time, " lay along the valley like grasshoppers for multitude, and their camels without number," still have their representatives in wild "children of the East," who, from their haunts beyond Jordan, make frequent raids into this fertile region, terrifying its sparse inhabitants, and carrying off indiscriminately all within their reach. On account of this insecure state of things, Christian dwellers in the plain have been more and more deserting it, to find greater safety in the distant and mountain-guarded town of Nazareth. Almost everybody living in Palestine deems it necessary to carry a weapon, and I fear that such a precaution will not be superfluous so long as the imbecile *laisser aller* of Turkish misrule continues. Whilst the higher Bedawîn tribes have their own peculiar code of honour, some of the neighbouring nomads—a hybrid of Turcoman, Kurd, Egyptian, and Canaanite—are as morally depraved as they are meanly born, cruelty and treachery being their too frequent characteristics; these speak the Arabic tongue common to all, but they cannot rightly be called " Arabs."

I halted in the Greek convent on Mount Tabor for about an hour, which was as great an interval as I could usually allow myself during my long days of riding. There was a soothing, not to say sleepy, atmosphere about the place, which seemed inhabited only by two or three monks. I ate my luncheon in a room on the ground-floor, looking into the square of the monastery. It was not very restful, for, there being neither blinds nor curtains to the windows, the brethren indulged their evident curiosity by watching me as they sauntered up and down outside.

In Latin convents I usually made myself understood in French or Italian, but here I could find no tongue wherein to communicate with my hosts; so when it became time to resume the journey, I had some difficulty in collecting my retinue. It appeared that the men with the animals had betaken themselves quite outside the precincts—where, I knew not. My gesticulations to the monks availed nothing; so I had to go outside and shout until Mount Tabor re-echoed to my call. The men had (for *me*) an unfortunate facility for sleeping soundly at inconvenient times; punctuality, too, is a virtue generally unknown to Easterns; so I should more than once have been benighted during my travels had I not kept myself constantly alert and on the watch.

I was out nine hours this day, there being seven hours of riding besides the halts. After descending the hill, we passed on through a somewhat monotonous but pleasant country, consisting of slightly ascending ridges, alternating with small plains. At last, just before sunset, the long-desired view of the Sea of Galilee burst full on my sight. There it lay, spread out beneath, at a depth of a thousand feet, encircled by its bare, mountainous walls, now gradually becoming wrapt in evening gloom. I was glad to have arrived on the scene while the higher points were still crimson and golden with the reflection of the setting sun. Below, in dark shadow, close to the water's brink, was nestled Tiberias, apparently just at my feet. It was, therefore, with some surprise and disappointment that I found I had to descend wearily for another hour in the growing darkness before I could reach the little town.

There was always some uncertainty about my night-quarters, there being no means of securing any beforehand. The Franciscan Convent here, for which I was bound, contains only three or four rooms available for strangers; I was, therefore, all the more thankful to find a good-sized one at my disposal. Indeed, I was especially fortunate on this occasion, for, later that evening, there arrived a distinguished ecclesiastical party, who had to be crowded uncomfortably into two rooms, as the "padre" was too courteous to derange me. He was a dear, kind old man, and we were able to converse freely in Italian. I was allowed the luxury of dining in a small refectory, together with an English artist staying in the house; whereas, in most monasteries, I had to be content to feed in my uninviting bedroom. The details of the bed-chamber, in such an Eastern establishment, should not be too minutely inspected; in fact, very near-sightedness is, under a few special circumstances, a desirable infirmity.

Tiberias stands close to the site of the "Chinneroth" of Joshua's time; it was a new town in the days of our Lord, having then been lately founded by Herod Antipas, the murderer of John the Baptist, and was named by him after the Emperor Tiberias Cæsar. At first it had only Gentile inhabitants, being deemed by Jews ceremonially unclean, because built over an ancient burial-ground. Herod had to people it in the beginning, by forcing slaves to dwell there, and by his persevering efforts he succeeded at length in making it a fine Roman city. There is no mention in the New Testament of our Saviour ever having entered this, among the many great towns which He frequented on the borders of Gennesareth. His avoidance of Tiberias may perhaps be accounted for by the above-mentioned circumstances. It is strange that this city, once essentially Gentile, should now be essentially Jewish. After the destruction of Jerusalem, it became, in the second century, during three hundred years the seat of the Sanhedrim, and the centre of rabbinical learning. It still retains its ancient university, and is now one of the four holy

Jewish cities,—the others being Jerusalem, Hebron, and Safed.

The existing town is modern, yet it presents a ruinous appearance, having suffered severely in the earthquake of 1837—a calamity to which this whole region has always more or less been subject. Its shattered walls and fallen towers, some of them crumbling into the clear waters of the lake, give the place an air of sadness and desolation. It formerly extended up the steep hill by which I had descended, now peopled only by hyenas, foxes, and jackals, which inhabit its numerous caves; it also contains the sepulchres of many illustrious rabbis. Near the base of the hill, a ruinous castle forms a picturesque feature, and its tower affords a good view.

I had again come into an almost tropical climate; the level of this deep little valley is seven hundred feet below that of the Mediterranean, and its hills encircle it in such way as to exclude keen blasts; and snow and frost are unknown. This sacred lake, through which the Jordan flows, has for its bed the crater of an extinct volcano. It measures twelve and a half miles long, and six and a half miles wide, though at first sight it hardly appears so large. At a casual glance, it reminded me rather of that other still more depressed sea, into which the Jordan finally empties itself—the same calm-looking crystal waters (only here teeming with life), bounded by mountain slopes; but here they much more continuously enclose "the liquid plain;" the same character of climate is also experienced. However, on closer inspection, one decided contrast is observable; while, near the Dead Sea, Mother Earth derives her colour almost exclusively from the sand, salt, mineral or chemical substances on her surface, *here*, in the sweet springtime especially, she is wont to deck herself in gorgeous flowery array, in "order wild"— "a fragrant maze"—lavishly strewing the verdant plain, wherein meander sparkling streams, which shed freshness and fertility over the teeming soil as they flow towards the lake.

Just a month had elapsed since my trip to the Jordan Valley; then I had been able to enjoy the beauty of the Paschal moon as it rose in glory above the Moab hills; now I was equally privileged in being able to watch the queen of night, emerging peerless from behind the precipitate rock-plateau of the Bashan chain which walls in the sea to the east; —anon, she cast her pure rays upon "the lake's still face," sleeping "sweetly in the embrace of terraced mountains."

As I stood enjoying the lovely and peaceful scene from my window, I was attracted by the sound of slow, monotonous chanting, produced by the mingled voices of men and women. It proceeded from a neighbouring house, which I had already noticed as being closed early for the night on this Friday evening; now I could see that it was fully lighted up within. It was evidently some kind of Jewish meeting-house, where the solemn sabbatical observance had already begun. Many of the Jews residing at Tiberias are strict and devout as well as learned ; they believe that their long-expected Messiah will manifest Himself near Gennesareth, and initiate His kingly rule in the holy and elevated town of Safed near by.

As the thought of their now, alas ! aimless and denuded worship was thus brought before the mind, how one longed that those stubborn hearts might be opened to admit the life-giving rays of the Sun of Righteousness ! How piteous seemed Jewish unbelief—*here*, above all ! in this region so pregnant with precious gospel memories—calls, teachings, miracles, mercies, warnings, promises, prayers ; and all once centred round the gracious bodily Presence of the " Incarnate Maker " of all things ! The Christian, as he gazes, with a vague sense of pain and loss, at the present desolateness and forsakenness of this locality, recalls with thankfulness, for his comfort, those precious words of the Master, " Blessed are they that have not seen, and yet have believed."

> " Thrice bless'd is he to whom is given
> The instinct that can tell
> That God is on the field, when He
> Is most invisible."

I made my preparations for the night with some misgivings ; the heat was oppressive, and I knew that my Levinge-bag and mosquito-net would have to be in full requisition, so that I should feel more stifled than ever. The small nocturnal co-occupants, which one has to put up with to a great extent at Tiberias, have gained a far-famed reputation for their activity and audacity. One needs not only a quiet conscience, but also a very thick skin, to be able to sleep in their proximity. I hope I have in a measure the former, but certainly not the latter; so I should have fared ill but for my calico defences, which proved satisfactory. Under the soothing influence of the nasal Jewish monotone, which was prolonged late into the night—for ought I know, all through it—I passed into the land of dreams.

CHAPTER XIV.

GENNESARETH SCENES.

The ride along the shore—Haunt of the pigeon and the vulture—Safed—Arab treachery—Vanished cities—Tell Hûm—A row on the lake—Sunday at Nazareth.

THE morrow dawned bright and beautiful; I was able, for the first time, to view the Sea of Galilee glowing in early morning sunlight. Towards the north, too, in the background, the snowy mass of Hermon was now revealed to me in unclouded majesty. This mountain adds infinitely to the beauty of the Galilæan Sea, redeeming its scenery from a certain monotony, which would otherwise be produced by the uniform outline of its eastern and northern boundary hills. Though clouds frequently conceal Hermon, when free of them, its outline, as seen from the lake, is so distinct that one realizes with difficulty that it is forty miles distant; its height is about ten thousand feet. It reminded me, in some respects, of Etna, which is nearly the same height, and which rises similarly, massive and solitary, like a stern giant, among much less important elevations, and appears to dominate the whole of the surrounding country.

I started early on one of the most interesting rides that can be taken—that through the Plain of Gennesareth and skirting its lake. In an hour we reached the few squalid hovels of a wretched-looking village called "Mejdel," formerly Magdala—the home of Mary, whence she was called "the Magdalene." Of all the great and "exalted" cities which once crowned the borders of the lake, and to which our Lord vouchsafed His earthly Presence, no portion or remnant remains, save only of this Magdala, the name of which is, and will be, perpetuated through all time.

This place, now so degraded, was formerly a centre of art and industry, as were most of the neighbouring cities. Commerce had developed rapidly in Galilee shortly before the birth of our Lord, and in His day its inhabitants are reputed to have possessed a higher moral and religious tone than the dwellers in Judæa, who regarded the Galilæans with a feigned contempt born of envy. In the neighbouring fields—now swamps—flourished the indigo plant, whence the name given to Magdala in the Talmud, "the city of colour;" its women were skilled in weaving linen, and producing fine cloth.

Near here lies the old road, which was, in gospel days, the main thoroughfare leading past Nazareth and Capernaum towards Damascus, and which is still often used by camel-caravans. It passes through the rocky, savage defile called Wady-el-Hamâm, that is, "of pigeons," which forms the south-west boundary of the Plain of Gennesareth. The gentle birds, which once found their homes in thousands in the holes of its cliffs, formed a valuable commercial item, and three hundred shops in Magdala were devoted to the sale of these pigeons, for purposes of sacrifice. They have long since been supplanted by the fierce vulture, which now reigns supreme amid these fastnesses, the caverns of which are the abodes of various wild animals.

But the Wady once had other inhabitants than bird or beast. In the stormy times of the Maccabees, it had become a haunt of robbers, who, unassailable in the elevated caves of the precipitate rocks, were a terror to the whole of Galilee. About A.D. 39, King Herod gained much favour among the Jews by extirpating these wretches, which he did with boldness and cunning. His soldiers, being unable to reach their impregnable dens, were let down by chains from the top of the mountain in strong wooden boxes; they were armed with long iron hooks, by means of which they dragged out and precipitated into the abyss below all who would not at once submit themselves. It must have been subsequent to this that the pigeons took possession, and also that the neighbouring towns rose to such prosperity. The caves were afterwards, for a time, the abodes of hermits.

On leaving Magdala, I found myself in the Plain of

Gennesareth, which is three miles long and one wide; —small, yet precious stage, whereon were revealed to man some of the greatest of Divine mysteries. Once full of corn-fields, vineyards, and olive-yards,—each yielding after its kind richest produce,—the Gennesareth Plain is now devoid of cultivation; it is a wilderness, but a green one, being fertilized by its perennial springs. I was too late for the gorgeous array of tulips, anemones, narcissus, and iris, each of which, in great variety, with many other flowers, helps to deck the plain in spring. It is probable that the "lilies" which attracted our Lord's notice were either of the narcissus or iris species.

The genial climate and rich soil of this favoured region have been proverbial. Josephus informs us that, in his day, all "rival fruits" were drawn together here. A considerable trade was carried on in olive-oil, which was of the best quality, and greatly in demand, since oil was then among the Jews a common remedy in sickness; King Herod, when seriously ill at Jericho, was nearly killed by being immersed in too hot an oil-bath.

The hills which bound this side of the lake are far more broken and picturesque than those on the eastern side, where "Kersa" marks the ancient Gergesa. 'Mid bare, precipitate cliffs, the eye detects, in this clear atmosphere, one green sward * only which

---

* Mr. Macgregor remarks: "a verdant sward is here, with bulbous roots on which swine might feed. And on this I

has a steep, even slope towards the water's edge; here it is thought that possibly the "whole herd of swine ran violently down into the sea."

The mountain, called Kurûn Hattîn, had already, at some distance, been pointed out to me. After forming one side of the Wady Hamâm, it becomes here the partial boundary of the plain. Its flat summit is surmounted at each end by a curious elevation, resembling a horn, whence its name. It is generally believed that the "Sermon on the Mount" was delivered on one of the lower green plateaux; it may also have been the scene of one of the occasions of miraculous feeding. However, this can be only a matter for conjecture. The stern voice of later history speaks with no uncertainty of one terrible scene which took place on this hill— the battle of Hattîn, in 1137—when the Crusaders received from Saladin their last and most crushing overthrow. Brave as was their resistance, the difficulties of their position were overwhelming, and the Saracen conqueror,—who had already taken Tiberias, —after nearly annihilating his Christian foes, marched on to the victorious conquest of Acre, which was the final blow to the Crusading cause.

Our path often lay close to the translucent waters of the lake; we had to ford several wide streams which, fringed with oleander-blossoms, poured them-

observed—what is an unusual sight—a very large herd of oxen, horses, camels, sheep, asses, and goats, all feeding together."

selves into it. The Sea of Galilee, as in olden times, swarms with fish; but the many ships which formerly sailed on its busy waters, are now represented only by one or two small boats brought here from Beirût. The once famous ship-building trade of Tarichæa has disappeared together with the existence of that town.

From all parts of the plain Safed is conspicuous, mounted on a rocky, northerly eminence, two thousand eight hundred feet high, and embracing towards Tiberias a vast panorama. This is supposed to be "the city set on an hill" of our Lord's discourse. Strongly as it appears to be fortified by nature, it has experienced some terrible episodes, not only from the horrors of war, but also from the cruel ravages of earthquakes; that of 1837 nearly annihilated the town; previously it had been a nucleus of Jewish learning, and had contained considerable schools, printing-press, etc.

Safed has a long past history, having become the refuge of the Jews when driven from Jerusalem by the Edict of Hadrian in A.D. 132. Here also was the centre of the Sanhedrim till its removal to Tiberias. Of late, Jews have been persistently streaming back to this their holy city, and, in their zeal to find residences, have been known to continue building operations all through the night.

There always existed a short cut of two hours thence to Tyre and Sidon; so we may believe that the "great multitude" travelled this way, who, as S. Luke records, "came from the sea-coast of Tyre and Sidon to hear Jesus, and to be healed of their diseases."

The first considerable stream we crossed was that of Aîn-el-Tîn, or "The Fig Tree," so called from the fig trees growing near. Where its waters pour into the lake a marsh is formed, in which the papyrus flourishes among other aquatic plants, and where the sportsman can find plenty of wild birds.

Near a fountain of beautiful water is a solitary and primitive halting-place called Khan Minyeh. We paused here to water our animals, and I noticed some Arabs doing the same thing. Two days after my return to Nazareth I was shocked to hear that a murder had taken place in this peaceable-looking spot. Very soon after my visit a party of French pilgrims, whom I had left encamped at Nazareth, had followed on my track towards Gennesareth. A lady and her son among the party, attracted by the sweet calmness and freshness of Aîn-el-Tîn, had requested to remain there quietly while the rest proceeded further. Their dragoman ought never to have consented to this, as treacherous Bedawîn lurk in most unsuspected quarters, and one or two Europeans, if alone, are never safe from their attack. When the company returned to pick up the two lingerers, they could nowhere be found. Their bodies were afterwards discovered in the waters of the marsh, where they had been placed for concealment after they had been murdered and robbed.

Having ascended, by a bridle-path, up a steep white rock, which stands abruptly close to the seaside, another mile brought me to the site of Bethsaida (now Ain-el-Tabigha), so full of Gospel memories. Scarcely any trace of the city has been found; but the gently sloping white beach, which here shelves into the lake, would be well adapted for fishing-boats. It is thickly scattered with tiny broken shells, and the water is exquisitely clear and blue. There seems never to have been any regular harbour; however, the piles of stones which still remain in the water would have afforded shelter for little ships in the times of sudden storm, to which this tranquil-looking sea is subject. At Bethsaida one solitary dwelling now exists, in connection with a mill, which is turned by the abundant water-supply, and where the maiden-hair fern luxuriates.

I passed, a little further, the "Round Fountain" of Capernaum, one of the largest in Galilee. I had already observed traces of the old aqueduct which formerly supplied it. The fountain still contains good water for drinking, though of a peculiar flavour. All the streams hereabouts are slightly warm and brackish, but wholesome.

Sir C. Wilson, having identified this well as the "Fountain of Capernaum," to which Josephus especially alludes, was able further to fix pretty definitely the much-discussed site of Capernaum at Tell-Hûm, which lies north-west, forty minutes further on, and close to the head of the lake. Here fragments of every description lie strewn over a considerable area. Some are of limestone, but the majority of black basalt, which abounds in this volcanic region. And this is all that remains of proud Capernaum, once an emporium of commerce, a military garrison, a religious nucleus, a busy world-centre in every sense! How literally has the "exalted" been "cast down"! Not a stone now remains in position; though, thanks to the Palestine Exploration Fund, broken columns belonging to some of the many synagogues of the town have been disencumbered from the rubbish, and, as far as possible, sorted and placed together.

Very near the sea-margin lie the extensive white limestone remains which are supposed to have formed part of the synagogue built by the believing centurion, and if so, of one probably often frequented by our blessed Lord. The pot of manna, discovered in relief on the stone lintel of a doorway, has excited great interest, it being imagined that this may have served for a visible illustration during our Lord's mysterious discourse upon the Bread of Life. It seemed to me wonderful to realize, that in this now desolate spot of the tiny Gennesareth valley, which at first sight appears shut off by nature from all the world, should have been spoken those precious words which, gradually spreading from pole to pole,

CAPERNAUM.

have ever since been bearing fruit unto eternal life! I made out, among the ruins, other ornamental devices, such as the holy candlestick, a palm tree, a bunch of grapes, sacred utensils, and an apparent representation of the ark; pillars and decoration alike were on a miniature scale.

The kind Franciscan abbot had, before my start, offered me fish fresh caught in the lake, to take as an addition to the bread of my midday repast. I gladly accepted this most fitting food—the very same as that which the Divine Master shared with His disciples at that strange post-resurrection dinner on this shore.

I searched in vain for a shady resting-place. On the ruin-covered beach the sun glared fiercely; no "great rock" was near to cast a friendly shadow, nor was a tree anywhere to be seen. The vegetation around was of the rankest description; nothing but huge thistles, nettles, and other noxious weeds, springing up to the height of large bushes among the stony ruins, and through which it was difficult to make one's way. Scorpions lurked near, and venomous insects hovered in the air; their vicious buzzing alone broke the silence of the heavy atmosphere. Truly a blight seemed to rest upon the place!

I rose early on the following morning (Saturday), in order to be rowed on the sacred lake before returning to Nazareth. It was most enjoyable, in the fresh early morning, to glide along those calm waters, which are pleasant to the taste as well as to the eye. I visited the Baths of Tiberias, about a mile beyond the town of that name, which have been for centuries in high reputation as a cure for rheumatic affections. The springs are salt, sulphurous, and hot, their temperature being 144° Fahr. A city existed here long ago, but only the baths now remain; there are both public and private ones, but not so well arranged nor so cleanly in appearance as we English should desire. Many poor sufferers were being conveyed thither in litters as I was returning to Tiberias.

Though I had directed my men to have all in readiness for an immediate start, I found them in a most dawdling mood, and nothing prepared. Their tardiness was often a trial of patience, when I was wishing to get through my journey before the meridian heat. On this occasion I had, up the steep ascent, to endure the full force of the sun's rays, unmodified by any refreshing breeze, till I gained the summit. We returned by a different route from that previously taken; this one led through Kefr Kenna, the most probable site of Cana of Galilee, though another village makes the same claim. This Cana is a pleasant, healthy spot, lying high among the hills, four miles from Nazareth. A small day-school is conducted there by one of the ladies from the orphanage. I did not care to visit the little Roman Church, which professes to contain the waterpots whose contents were once changed at the word of our Lord.

I had noticed a marked decrease in the temperature since gaining the high ground, and on reaching Nazareth it was positively chilly. I was looking forward to a bright and refreshing Sunday; but, alas! the morrow dawned wet and misty, and rain continued off and on throughout the day. The English Church at Nazareth is of good style and proportion, which can hardly be said of any other in Palestine. My disappointment at having to spend the morning indoors was somewhat lessened when I found that, until the evening, there would only be an Arabic service in the church. In the afternoon it cleared a little, and I sallied forth to visit the reputed "synagogue" of Gospel story; the slimy soil of the precipitous path had become so slippery since the rain, that I could hardly keep my footing, and should have fallen more than once but for Solomon's assistance. After this experience, I did not venture to take the long walk to the church in the dark evening, but contented myself with watching the departure of the children of the orphanage, as they marched off in procession with their teachers, each carrying a lighted torch; they are doubtless well acquainted with the turns of the circuitous route.

CHAPTER XV.

FROM NAZARETH TO TYRE.

Nain and Endor—A dangerous road—Arab encampment—A bargain struck—Protestant or Catholic?—Shelter in a khan—Approach to Tyre—Its history and modern condition.

BEFORE leaving Nazareth, I descended again into the Plain of Esdraelon, in order to visit Nain and Endor, which I had only as yet seen from afar. It was disappointing that a hazy distance shut out the majestic form of Hermon, which, from a point on the road to Endor, is visible in clear weather standing in a line with Tabor, and forming that beautiful view which must have been familiar to the psalmist: "Tabor and Hermon shall rejoice together."

Endor is a remarkable place: perched on the bare eastern shoulder of the Hill of Moreh, it possesses, strange to say, a perennial spring (whence its name) flowing from a fissure in the barren rock. Large caverns abound, extending some distance into the back of the hill, and any one of which might have formed a fitting scene for the dread vision of

King Saul. At Endor we have true cave-dwellings, such as, in early days, were in use among the Amalekites, Horites, and other races; indeed, the dwellers in Southern Palestine did not abandon these abodes till scared from them by the depredations of the Saracens. The wretched mud hovels which compose modern "Ain-Dûr" are literally clinging to the bare hillside, and sometimes form only a frontage to the cavern behind, which in many cases still constitutes part of the dwelling. Not a scrap of vegetation exists at Endor; a more miserable-looking village I never beheld.

Skirting the base of the hill, another two miles brought me to Nain, which is situated on its northern side, about four miles distant from Nazareth. This interesting spot is one of the most reliable of Gospel sites, and its name continues unchanged. A few flat-roofed Moslem huts, scattered here and there on the steep, rocky slope, are all that is left to remind one of the walled Jewish city, whence issued that mournful procession which moved the heart, and called forth the resurrection power, of the Son of God. The present burying-ground extends east and west, under the shallow cliff, which bounds the upper portion of Nain. On one side some old Jewish tombs exist, and probably it was in this direction that the mourning mother was met by the Lord of Life. I descended the hill to the one ancient cistern of the place, which must always have been *in situ*.

On May 1st I took leave regretfully of peaceful Nazareth, and of my kind hostess and comfortable quarters at the orphanage. I knew that I should not find the like again for many days. A cut of six and a half hours was to be made to Akka by a rather unfrequented and solitary route, but a pleasant one withal. During the whole ride I only passed one place which could be called a village, and that was Sepphoris (Sefurieh), four miles beyond Nazareth. Once a Roman city, it has been in turn a Roman, Jewish, and Christian centre, and is now but a collection of Moslem huts, among which are scattered the ruins of a Christian church, an old fortress, sarcophagi, prostrate pillars, etc.

Every Mohammedan village has its sacred place, however humble, where the Moslem can rest, meditate in peace, and deposit his valuables without fear—even though there be no door to the building. Such is the good faith among themselves of these followers of the false prophet! In spots far from any human habitation, one often comes upon a tiny whitewashed and domed structure, which is the tomb of some saint, and considered a holy shrine. The trees or bushes near it will be seen festooned with rags and shreds of every description, which have been brought here from the bodies of the sick, in the hope that they may derive healing power from proximity with the holy dead. Many nomads who never enter a mosque, confine their devotions to superstitious worship at these lowly wayside shrines. The Jews have also their own rural holy spots scattered throughout Palestine, where it is their wont to burn costly articles, such as shawls, scarves, kerchiefs, etc.,—I imagine, with some idea of obtaining propitiation thereby.

As we wandered along through sweet, varied nooks, bright with wild flowers and rich with spontaneous vegetation, I could scarcely believe that I was in an Eastern land; the surroundings reminded me rather of some blooming upland in Devon. However, I was soon recalled to my whereabouts by the sight of a stray native, who, as he met us, uttered his " salame "—the greeting of " peace "—while he passed his hand rapidly to his heart, lips, and forehead—the sign of Oriental salutation. The agricultural natives are for the most part a harmless set, somewhat resembling in character the Egyptian fellahîn, to whom they are partially allied by original descent. Intelligent over their work, they are sometimes forced to do it under oppressive circumstances; thus, for instance, the Turkish owner will oblige the peasant to provide, for the labour of irrigation, the animal which he ought himself to find.

It is wearisome to ride for hours consecutively at a uniformly slow pace over very rough roads; so when we did come to a tolerably even piece of ground, I was always anxious for the change of a trot or a canter; but Solomon seemed loath to keep pace with me, and this sometimes led to words between us. On the present day's ride I noticed especially that we were all the time creeping alongside the baggage-animal, which of course could not be hurried. After one of my very short canters, there was an animated Arabic interlude quite unintelligible to me; but I observed that the owner of the horses looked very cross. Solomon informed me afterwards that we were passing through a dangerous, unfrequented region, in which acts of treachery were not uncommon; and the bagbage-man had protested that he would not consent to be left behind at any time with the goods, lest some one should fall upon him suddenly, and murder him for the sake of the baggage! Of course, after that I was silent, and had to submit to the crawling pace.

Before descending to the level near Akka, we came to sterner and more mountainous scenery. I had the pleasure of riding close by several black Arab tents, made of goats' hair, which were clustered together among the lonely hills. Spread out wide on the ground, they were of such slight elevation, that it seemed impossible for a full-grown person to stand up inside of one. I passed a tent which was partially raised on one side, so that I could see its interior occupants. I suppose they can only obtain air and light in this manner. How I longed to enter! But Solomon forbade;—I should probably have got there more than I wished for!

What a strange, free life this must be! The means of the family subsistence were visible near the tents, in the shape of flocks and herds, browsing under the charge of the elder children; the fathers make distant raids on their horses, bringing back whatever comes to hand, while the mothers cook the meat in a primitive fashion in the common cauldron outside the tent-door.

The cattle in this part are red, shaggy, and very tiny, reminding one of the small breeds seen in North Britain. They have often to be led long distances for watering; the level plain near Akka, as also that near Jaffa, may be seen thickly studded with these queer little herds, which have descended from their pastoral heights in order to drink of the fresh springs which pour themselves into the Mediterranean. I had expected to skirt the shore, as previously when riding to Akka from Haifa; but the present cut took me continuously through hill-country, and I did not descend to the level till shortly before reaching the town.

There was a long parley in Arabic at the convent gate before I was admitted, and I was beginning to be exercised in my mind as to what my next move would be if refused a night's shelter; the private houses of Akka did not look at all inviting. However, Solomon at last came back to relieve me by the news that I could sleep at the monastery on condition that next morning, before starting, I paid the abbot "with my own hand" the specified equivalent for my night's lodging. This arrangement had rather a "worldly" ring about it; but it appeared that the religious community had, a few days before, been cheated by an Englishman's dragoman, who had got his master away early in the morning without paying a farthing to the monks. I presume that he had paid *himself* instead!

I cannot say that either my quarters or fare at the monastery were first-rate. The meat was too hard to be eaten, and there was nothing else except eggs, very nasty bread, olives and black coffee—neither milk nor butter. The "padre," too, kept marching up and down my bedroom while I was dining, an attention I did not appreciate; he kindly wished me "buon appetito," at the same time embarrassing me by the question, "How did I like the fare?" I found it difficult to answer him honestly, yet politely! There seemed a sad torpor over the establishment; the only sounds of animated life proceeded from the kitchen, where the tongues of the menservants, chattering with my men, never ceased.

I did not know till afterwards that I had gained admittance to this convent under false pretences, for I was not aware that the Pope had recently issued a decree, forbidding the reception of "Protestants" into Roman religious houses. Considering the shoals of persons of all creeds who now visit foreign lands, it is not astonishing that his Holiness should wish these houses reserved for the convenience of the "faithful." It turned out that my lucky admittance had been due to a former conversation with Solomon on Church matters. As already mentioned, he was a Roman Catholic, and one who had the courage of his convictions. He was wont sometimes to speak slightingly of " Protestantism," in the ranks of which he imagined that most English people were to be classed. Certainly the line taken by some Protestant teachers in the East is not quite the one calculated to inspire the full respect of strangers. I did my best to convince Solomon that I belonged to an old historic Church, which at home was not represented in the same stinted, meagre manner as it is abroad.

I wonder *when* English Church-people will discard that narrow, negative, limiting term " Protestant," which tends sadly to mislead foreign nations concerning our national creed, and also to place us in a false position in the eyes of Eastern sister Churches! Would that more and more teachers went forth in the grand *affirmative* spirit of the great missionary S. Paul.* While rejoicing that, as a Church, we Anglicans have been enabled to throw off the mediæval incrustations of Romish error, shall we not beware of seeming to limit her historic existence to that period of reform? Shall we not the rather strive, both by word and deed, to uphold before all the world our continuity with the primitive Church universal, whence we originally derived the deposit of eternal truth—a deposit which, though at times

* 2 Cor. i. 18, 19.

obscured, has ever been the precious heritage of the Church of England?

Leaving Akka at 8.30 a.m., I had in anticipation a day of more than eight hours' riding before reaching Tyre, my next destination. The way seemed the longer, because in parts dreary and monotonous, often skirting the sea-shore, or the bare rocks near its margin ; while as we approached Tyre, sight and smell gave evidence that we were passing through a land which, though now so desolate, had once teemed with human life.

About eight miles beyond the Promontory of Akka, we came to the famous " Ladder of Tyre," known in Arabic as the " White Cape," from its bare white rock. The bridle-path, which here leads unpleasantly near the edge of the cliff, brings you, at its summit, to a dizzy point, whence you look down a sheer descent of three hundred feet into the chafing depths of ocean beneath. There was no protection of any kind along the edge of this dangerous and uneven road, where many small landslips have already occurred ; one felt that a false step or start of one's horse might have dreadful results. The baggage-man, who acted as guide, *kindly* seized this moment of perilous situation to point out to me the exact spot whence a horse and his rider had, a few days previously, been hurled into the abyss ! I think that the landing at Jaffa, and this ride over the " Ladder of Tyre," had been the two points of my

Palestine trip which I had really dreaded in anticipation; so I was glad—this last peril over—to find myself in a sandy plain, with Tyre already visible in the distance, though it proved to be a very *long* distance.

I was overtaken by a violent storm of wind and rain, the first encountered since leaving Jerusalem. It was grand to hear the angry waves roaring against the shore, and to see the black storm-clouds flying across the wild expanse of sky; but I was getting wet through, so gladly alighted at the first available shelter which offered on this bare coast. It was that of a rough khan, where I found a crowd of men and animals huddled closely together in refuge from the storm. For an hour, I had to form one of the promiscuous party, thankful to find a roof over my head; and here I ate, as best I could, my long-delayed luncheon.

All trace of the storm cleared away in the afternoon; and it was

"A beauteous evening, calm and free,
. . . . . the broad sun
Sinking down in its tranquillity;
The gentleness of heaven o'er the sea."

We entered modern Tyre, now called Sûr, while its walls still glowed with the borrowed hues of the tender sunset; but it is a miserable place, built up among the ruins of departed grandeur. I was thankful that the lady in charge of the "British Syrian Mission" was able and willing to offer me a bed, for it was very doubtful where else I could have slept. One of the party generously gave up her own room, where, amidst English comforts, I was able to rest my weary limbs.

The establishment was very small; its "workers" deplored to me the activity of the Roman Church here, from which, and from the Greek Church also, it seemed that their few "converts" were alone made! Next morning, before my start, the mission ladies most kindly escorted me round the place, to see what remains of this painfully interesting old Phœnician city—the greater daughter of great Zidon.

The vast resources of ancient Tyre first came prominently into notice during the reign of King David, when his Phœnician friend and neighbour, Hiram, King of Tyre, "who was ever a lover of David," contributed in many ways towards the erection of his royal palace at Jerusalem. In the reign of Solomon his son, Hiram aided yet more extensively in the building of the great temple.* In all branches of art and trade, Tyre at that time excelled; her ships sailed to every part of the world, bringing back raw materials to be wrought into strength and beauty by her cunning workmen; and her neighbouring forests were rich in all manner of costly wood—so that she surpassed all in riches and commerce.

Tyre had a special monopoly in glass, which, as

* 1 Kings v.; 2 Chron. ii.

I have said, was a Phœnician discovery, and, in the ninth century A.D., its secret was conveyed to the north of England, probably in some commercial connection. Tyrian dyes, too, were universally famous. I was interested to see, outside the town, a large heap of the broken shells belonging to the "murex purpura," whence the beautiful purple dye used to be obtained. Alas! the secret of this trade has perished with the nation.

The histories of Tyre and Zidon can hardly be separated till the time of the Minor Prophets, when we learn, from such passages as Amos i. and Joel iii., that Tyre, which had long taken precedence of Zidon, had already begun to develop those national sins for which she was to suffer the Divine retribution. However, it was long in coming. Strong in the pride of her insular position, Tyre withstood the attack of the Assyrian Shalmaneser, who had taken captive the tribes of Israel.

In later history she alone, of all the Phœnician cities, defied the great world-conqueror Alexander; after seven months' siege he could only effect an entrance by the construction of a huge causeway, by means of which he joined Tyre to the mainland, converting it from an island into a peninsula. The mole made by him still remains, though covered with driftsand, which, having extended to the mainland, at present forms a barren sand-ridge disconnecting Tyre from her cultivated inland plain.

Under Roman sway, she continued to be a flourishing and privileged city; and to this period must be dated the ruins which are yet visible. The Crusaders took Tyre in 1124, but in 1291 she surrendered to the Saracens, and after that gradually declined. A hundred years ago only a dozen fishermen composed the population. "It shall be a place for the spreading of nets in the midst of the sea." *

Wandering along the irregular cliffs, and looking over them, I could see below, tranquilly reposing in the clear blue depths of ocean, architectural remains of every description—witnesses to the former greatness of Tyre, and to the truth of God's Holy Word; for here the remarkable prophecies of Ezekiel (chs. xxvi. and xxviii.) were literally fulfilled before my eyes: "What city is like Tyrus, like the destroyed in the midst of the sea?" "I shall make thee a desolate city, like the cities that are not inhabited; when I shall bring up the deep upon thee, and great waters shall cover thee." The sea has encroached considerably, and the rough hillside is full of holes and ruins, now the abode of jackals. The remains of the old harbour are nearly choked with sand; a few small ships and fishing-boats are seen, but little goes on in the weak, unwalled Tyre of to-day.

The most interesting and recognizable ruin is that of the cathedral, once the finest in Syria, and conspicuous in ecclesiastical history; the oration

* Ezek. xxvi. 5.

which Eusebius delivered at its consecration is still extant. Here repose the bones of Origen, also those of the famous Frederick Barbarossa, which were conveyed from Tarsus to this holy spot. The Crusaders rebuilt the cathedral, and the historian, William of Tyre, became its bishop. Hardly any portion of its structural form can now be distinguished, earthquakes having aided time and war in the work of destruction.

The massive Phœnician tomb, reputed to be that of King Hiram, lies two miles inland, and near it have been discovered other curious old tombs, some containing fine specimens in glass, such as wine-flasks and cups, also various funereal vessels, dishes, etc.

Deep old wells are found close to the sea-shore, testifying to the fact that a great city once existed in their vicinity. As I rode along the yellow sands, I could vividly recall that touching scene of parting,* when S. Paul, after a stay of seven days in Tyre, "kneeled down on the shore and prayed" with his disciples previous to his departure for Jerusalem. Doubtless the flourishing early Church of Tyre sprang from those few faithful ones.

* Acts xxi. 3-6.

CHAPTER XVI.

THROUGH PHŒNICIA.

Between Tyre and Zidon—Zidon past and present—Druses and Maronites—Novel experiences in the house of a priest—The start for Beirût—Flaying a camel—Return to city life.

AFTER reconnoitring Tyre, I started about 9 a.m. on the long ride to Zidon. We skirted a splendid bay, and for the most part kept near the sea-shore. The sand was heavy and uneven, so it took more than eight hours to accomplish the distance of twenty miles. At every step I was passing through a classic territory, the fame and the trade of whose primæval possessors had once extended over the whole world, —even as far as to our own little Cornwall. This Phœnician plain, now so solitary and desolate, would afford the preacher a good text on the vanity of human greatness. The only indications of former populousness are fresh-water wells deep dug in the sand, and old tombs and cave-sepulchres visible on the right in the distant cliffs. Such traces speak to us of the past,—as does also the great Egyptian necropolis,—more forcibly than the voices of history.

We forded some considerable streams, flowing

here into the Mediterranean; the largest is the Litâny, the ancient Leontes, crossed by a well-made and well-preserved bridge—a rare phenomenon in this country! It is, next to the Jordan, the largest river in Syria, and, like it, derives its source from the Lebanon Mountains. Broken Roman arches and portions of Roman road could often be distinguished; but not a human habitation of any kind did we pass for many miles, and scarcely a tree. So, on alighting to eat my midday meal, I perched myself on a sea-rock, my feet dangling in near proximity to the heavenly blue ocean waters. Hot as the sun was, it was tempered by the soft sea-breeze; I noticed curious flowers growing in the sand close to the water's edge.

One familiar old place alone remains on the lonely route between Tyre and Zidon. It is Surafend—the biblical Zarephath—"which belongeth to Zidon." Its modern inhabitants have transplanted it from its old site in the plain to the top of a hill more distant from the sea, hoping on this height to find better security from Bedawîn depredations. They have removed thither, for building purposes, all available stones; so the old well near the shore, and a few tombs, are all that remain of the Zarephath (or Sarepta) in which Elijah lodged with the widow woman, and where also it is thought probable that our Lord met that other woman of Canaan, great in faith, when He passed "through the coasts of Tyre and Sidon."

As I drew near modern Saîda I was also approaching the grand Lebanon Hills, which now added their charm to the glory of the sunset view. Luxuriant gardens, extensive mulberry and orange groves, indicated the vicinity of a place of some little standing, and one evidently possessing a fertile *entourage*.

Zidon, now called Saîda, or " the place of fishing," is beautifully situated, with one foot on the sea, and the other on her wide, productive plain, which is backed by the Lebanon Mountains. A walled city, of about nine thousand inhabitants, Zidon has a certain amount of trade in silk, fruit, and copper, though lately much of it has been absorbed by the more prosperous Beirût. The oranges grown here deserve the highest commendation for size, sweetness, and thinness of skin. They are much superior to those of Jaffa, or any others which I tasted.

A considerable number of the inhabitants are Christians and Jews ; the Jesuits are busy, and so are the American teachers, who have excellent schools both for boys and girls. At the latter school I gratefully took refuge for the night ; the superintending lady most kindly and cleverly, by a few magic touches, transformed her pretty sitting-room into a bedroom for me. The only drawback was, that I could not repose my weary limbs there till late in the evening, when its day-occupants had retired.

As I rode next morning among the tall white modern houses, and through the narrow built-over streets, it was hard to believe that I was really on the site of great, ancient Zidon, mother of cities— that Zidon which, we learn from Gen. x. 15, 19, was founded by the great-grandson of Noah, and was therefore first cousin * to that other famous old city, Memphis in Egypt. This Zidon had become, by her religion, her wealth, her commerce, her products, her artificers, her ships, her sailors, weavers, and architects, hewers of wood and hewers of stone, and what-not,— famous far and wide among the surrounding nations, many of which had not at that time emerged from the darkness of barbarism. The biblical allusions to the advanced civilization of Zidon are corroborated by the poet Homer, who makes special mention of her fine art, her work in brass, gold, and silver, and of the beautiful weaving produced from her looms.

The false dual worship of Baal and Ashtoreth, which emanated from Zidon, spread thence later to the great world-centres of Greece, Carthage, and Italy; whilst in Palestine, the worship of one or other of these divinities became the constant snare and idolatrous sin of the children of Israel, who, on entering their land of promise, did not attempt, either at that time or afterwards, to subdue the powerful Zidonians among the other Canaanite inhabitants.

This old-world Venice cared little for inland conquest or acquisition, and left her neighbours in peace, her whole national energy and ambition being cen-

* See p. 22.

tred in her maritime and commercial life. The natural harbour of Zidon, formed by detached rocks, would be thought small nowadays, but it sufficed to shelter from tempest the ships of the ancients. If its picturesque ruined outworks be examined from a boat, there will be seen in calm weather, lying clearly visible under the crystal waters, ample evidence of the masonic and architectural skill of this gifted people. Traces of the ancient landing-place remain, the same on which S. Paul must have landed during his short stay at Zidon.* That the Christian faith took good root here is evidenced by the fact that its bishop was present at the great Council of Nicæa.

A crumbling mediæval castle, standing on an islet in the sea, and approached by a fine bridge, added to the charm of the landscape as I looked back soon after leaving the gate of the city. The "many-twinkling smile" of ocean, the golden sands, the white town with its irregular walls, the old harbour-ruins, the green gardens, the mountain background,— all, together, formed a fair picture as it glowed in the radiancy of that Eastern morning.

I had already had two consecutive long days of riding, and that from Zidon to Beirût would be longer than either of these, being a ride of over nine hours ; so I determined to break the journey at a little half-way village, where I was told that I could be received into native quarters in the house of an orthodox priest.

* Acts xxvii. 3.

Not long after leaving Zidon, we lost sight of the sea, and passed into the interior of the well-cultivated plain, where we found ourselves in the refreshing shade of all kinds of fruit trees, while clear mountain-streams gurgled beneath our horses' feet. The mulberry tree is much cultivated on account of the silkworm, which is largely reared by the natives of Northern Palestine.

The character of the inhabitants, too, becomes somewhat changed here; for the fanatic Moslems, in a measure, give place to the more amenable Druses, who dwell in considerable numbers between Zidon and Beirût.

This mysterious race keep their religion so entirely to themselves, that it is hard to ascertain what they really believe, as they worship together in their houses with barred doors. It appears that they mingle modern politics with a certain phase of the Islam creed, but their views are much broader than those of Mussulmans. Banded together by strong political and religious ties, they have the character of being brave, courteous, and industrious; indeed, I was told by a lady residing in the Lebanon that the Druses are far pleasanter to deal with than the Maronites— very numerous in the north—who are Christians in communion with Rome.

The Syrian Church, which is the oldest of all Christian Churches, contains two well-defined divisions: (1) Jacobites or Monophysites, and (2) Maronites. The patriarchate of the former is at Antioch, and each of its long line of patriarchs has ever held the same name, "Ignatius." The Maronite sect, which is now the predominating one in the Lebanon, arose in the fifth century, deriving its name from its founder, a hermit of the Buka'a. Condemned as heretics at the Council of Constantinople, A.D. 681, the Maronites, through contact with the Crusaders, became, about five hundred years later, subject to the Pope, though retaining their own Patriarch under his Holiness. The Roman Church showed her astute spirit of compromise by allowing the priests to retain marriage, and also by permitting Syriac to be used in the churches, beside other privileges.

The Maronites have a great number of convents, but their people are often very ignorant, and not distinguished for high moral attainment. Nearly all the villages of this region contain a considerable sprinkling of Christians, who, it will be remembered, suffered severely (especially the Maronites) in the cruel massacre of 1860. After that sad occurrence, the Sultan, through the pressure of European powers, was forced to appoint a Christian governor over the Lebanon district, and under his sway things have since worked more harmoniously.

I found the village for which I was bound quite buried in mulberry trees and vegetation of all descriptions. I suppose the clatter of our horses' hoofs through the stony, narrow street had from afar excited the attention of the inhabitants; for, on alighting at the priest's house, a small crowd was immediately round me. His Reverence, in ample long cassock, and with flowing beard, came forth immediately to greet me, to be soon followed by his smiling, comely wife, nursing her infant. I was introduced to *the* room, which proved to be the only presentable one of the establishment; it was a spacious, lofty, whitewashed chamber, the main portion of it—as is customary in Oriental countries—being slightly raised above the part near the entrance door.

This room served the whole family for their reception, feeding, and sleeping room; rugs were scattered here and there on the floor, divans stood round the walls, while above, in the central wall, was a recess full of deep shelves, on which was stowed away the bed-furniture of the household. This was all that the room contained, except one tiny, low, circular table; on this, at meal-times, it is customary to place, on a tray, the one bowl out of which all share the family repast, seated on the ground.

When night approaches, the mattresses and blankets are dragged from their shelves and laid on the divans and on the ground, according to the requirements of the inmates. Thus, to "take up" one's bed is, in the East, a daily occurrence. I presume that the most important part of the toilette is performed outside the house, as there seemed to be no provision inside for any ablutions.

This simple home appeared to be open to all; as I sat in my riding-gear on the edge of the divan, two or three other pleasant-looking women joined my hostess, each holding an infant in her arms. Plenty of children also stood staring at me, and the lads were not excluded. All looked very amiable and sociable; but, in reply to their incomprehensible, chattering queries, I could only give incessant nods and smiles, for my few words of Egyptian Arabic did not appear to pass muster here.

Meanwhile Solomon, with an air of importance, had gone off to "prepare my room," aided by the only woman of the community who was unencumbered by a baby. She came bustling in and out, dragging a variety of things from off the public shelf. I began to feel curious as to what kind of room mine would be, and very desirous of escaping thither from the embarrassing scrutiny which I was undergoing; I inferred that an arrival such as mine was unusual in the village.

On being informed, after considerable delay, that all was ready, I was conducted to a room adjoining the one in which I had been waiting, and which appeared to be a kitchen, combining also the requirements of a bakehouse and a granary. A queer, weird-looking bedroom it made! The lofty roof of open beams seemed scarcely air-tight; there were *no* windows, and, half-way up the high, bare walls, yawned a succession of curious, hungry-looking bins, in which I presume the household provisions were stored. But the most conspicuous feature of all was an enormous chimney, up or down which two or three men could have easily climbed.

The "furniture" arranged for my night's lodging was just a few rugs laid upon the uneven stone floor, a mattress, on which one or two blankets were deposited—*et voilà tout!* not a vestige of chair, table, drawer, peg, or cupboard! I was somewhat taken aback; for this was certainly a "come-down" from the accommodation I had had in the monasteries. There was no alternative but to deposit my weary limbs on the floor, as it was too early to take to the bed, which, from the look of it, I judged would afford me a sufficiently hard experience during the coming night's "repose" upon it!

The few toilette comforts which I unpacked had to be tossed promiscuously on the ground—an arrangement which was terribly inconvenient to my shortsighted eyes. I began to wonder, too, how I should manage to eat, in my lap, the "dinner" which was being prepared; also whether my limbs would ever recover from the effects of their prolonged, cramped posture on the ground. At last my urgent appeals, through Solomon, were responded to by the production of one rickety old chair with three legs, which had been rummaged out of some far-away corner, and on which I managed to balance myself; also a tiny stool; on this were piled two small wooden boxes, and this impromptu erection formed my diningtable, my washstand, my everything.

The dinner, for which my appetite had for some time been sharpening, proved a disappointment; there were neither vegetables nor fruit, both of which I had been longing for and expecting in this green retreat; but only a greasy stew of hard meat—the joint production of Solomon and Madame—and a few fried eggs floating in oil.

The ponderous door of my chamber would not shut close; besides it was necessary also to keep it open, in order to obtain any light, so all my movements were fully *en évidence*, and a group of inquisitive children stood peeping in upon me all the while. When it became dark and chilly, the old door was tied up and drawn to as close as possible, while my darkness was illuminated by a monstrous, patriarchal-looking oil-lamp, which, of course, had to be stationed on the ground. It stood quite high, and its light soon drew forth from the hidden recesses of this strange chamber a queer collection of nocturnal creatures—bats, chafers, and other buzzing and flying things of various kinds,—till the cobwebbed walls and roof seemed sonorous with a subdued kind of life. It was evident that I was in a well-peopled, as also in a well-provisioned place.

I decided that, under my peculiar circumstances, it would be best to keep the great lamp burning all night, though it and I, being both upon the ground, should have to glare terribly at each other. Much sleep was not to be expected, for the mattress did feel *very* hard upon the stone floor, and it possessed some ticklish occupants. Moreover, there seemed to be a village conclave going on in the adjoining "salon;" in it were assembled, besides the priest and his wife and children, his sister and her family, and also a neighbouring couple, who had come in for an evening chat, and, in addition to all the rest, my two men. The volubility of the party was incessant till between 11 and 12 p.m.; then the visitors departed, and all the rest stowed themselves away in the one room; but it was long before silence prevailed.

Next morning I hailed for breakfast the luxury of some boiling goat's milk with my black coffee; but, disappointing fact! for lack of a jug, it had to be put in a large, flat-bottomed tin basin, and so soon got cold and nasty. There was a dearth of utensils of every description in this well-to-do house; nothing but large, ugly tin bowls, a coffee-pot, and a few plates, could be produced. I only escaped eating with my fingers by having, fortunately, my own knife and fork.

It was on May 5th, a very hot morning, that, amid many gestures, smiles, and hand-shakings, I took leave of my good-natured friends. Uncomfortable as my quarters had been, I had gained quite an uncommon experience. With a pang, too, I now remembered that I was leaving, probably for ever, the rural haunts full of holy and cherished associations which it had been my privilege to pass through during the last few weeks. I was next to be landed in great Beirût, which, beautiful city though it be, would speak of European civilization more than I cared to think of.

There was no monotony in the scenery of this day's ride, for, as I proceeded, peak after peak of the grand Lebanon chain came rising into view, some of them peering with dazzling snowy cap from behind the tree-clad hills of the foreground. Our road often lay near the sea, the beautiful sapphire tint of which contrasted well with the peculiarly rich hue of the red-coloured sand on its margin.

Suddenly I came upon a scene which recalled Bible words * to my memory. An Arab was leaning over his poor camel, which, worn out by age, and probably after long years of faithful service, had laid itself down to die, and had just breathed out its last breath. Instead of lingering in lamentation over his lost companion, this practical man was, in hot haste, busily tearing the hide from off the still warm corpse. It was a horrid sight; but Solomon told me that unless this be done at once after death, the hide, which is a valuable trade commodity, can never be removed. The poor carcase, after having been thus flayed, would be left to afford an ample meal to the vultures, which would speedily gather around it;

* Matt. xxiv. 28.

afterwards the perfect skeleton would remain to bleach in the sun till it became pure and white. A sight frequently met with in Eastern travel is this "ship of the desert," thus stranded on its own sandy sea, and forming its own eloquent cenotaph.

Before leaving the less-beaten track, we passed through several Druse villages, the houses of which, composed only of earth and stones, mostly present a cheerless aspect. The Druse makes a great point of keeping his mouth covered. As I passed along, I saw many women of handsome countenance, the whole of which was generally visible with the exception of the mouth, over which the head-veil was carefully drawn.*

Several fine groves of pines were skirted as we approached Beirût; its white houses had been in sight from afar, gleaming brightly in proximity to the blue sea. A dusty high-road soon conducted us into the town, where I alighted about one o'clock at the Victoria Hotel, kept by French people. My guide had taken me there by mistake, for it was not the one to which I had been recommended. However, it did very well, and had a good view over the lovely bay, being close to the sea.

As I should not need to ride again till after reaching Damascus, I dismissed the three horses, which had done good service ever since we had left Haifa. Then it was pleasant to get my budget of letters from the civilized-looking post-office, and to rest awhile.

* See Cover.

CHAPTER XVII.

ACROSS THE LEBANON.

Beirût—Thirteen hours in Turkish company—The Abana and Damascus—The Great Mosque—An heroic queen—Scenes during Ramadân—Trying a horse.

BEIRÛT (the Berothath of 2 Sam. viii. 8) is now rapidly developing into an important modern town ; it was formerly comprised in the kingdom of Phœnicia, which at one time extended far beyond it in a northerly direction. Rebuilt by Herod Agrippa, it became a favourite Roman city, rich in theatres, baths, law-schools, etc., though very few Roman remains now exist. However, in 1873, great interest was excited among archæologists by the discovery, at the mouth of Nahr-el-Kelb, *i.e.* "Dog-river," near Beirût, of wonderful subterranean caves and lakes ; also later, of some very ancient monuments cut in the solid rock and bearing Babylonian cuneiform inscriptions.

The drive to Nahr-el-Kelb is very charming, as a succession of varied views are obtained over the lovely bay. Before approaching the solemn, rocky defile whence issues the above-named river, Assyrian and Roman inscriptions and reliefs can be easily seen from the carriage road cut high in the cliffs above, and reminding one of the many conquerors who marched this way.

By the time of Justinian, Beirût had acquired celebrity for its literary attainments, especially in law; but in A.D. 551 its fine buildings were destroyed by earthquake. It afterwards declined in importance under Moslem rule, and did not come into prominence again till its bombardment by an English fleet in 1840, when Ibrahim Pacha was thwarted in his ambitious aims. Twenty years later, Beirût became a centre of sympathetic interest throughout Europe,—namely, at the time when its streets, as well as those of Damascus, and many other towns and villages in the Lebanon, were flowing with Christian blood shed by fanatical unbelievers. With the concurrence of the Allied Powers, France came forward to quell the rage of massacre and civil war, and, with six thousand troops, took and *pro tem.* occupied Beirût.

Since that terrible time, the city has been gradually improving in every way, and Mohammedan fanaticism dying out. Christians have flocked to Beirût as their central rallying-point, so that, out of its population of more than eighty thousand, the Christians now number two to one. Shipping and trade have rapidly increased, also the manufacture of such fabrics as silks, gold cloth, etc. Here is now the chief literary and philanthropic centre of Syria ; hospitals, libraries, churches, abound ; also a printing-press, which is kept in active use.

Though many European languages, as well as Syriac, are heard in its streets, English is much taught at Beirût, and a Presbyterian form of Christianity is being propagated in the American mission schools, where upwards of four thousand boys receive instruction, besides a large number of girls. Through the medium of their schools, printed literature, and trained teachers, the Americans are gaining considerable influence here, as also in other parts of the East. Their schools in Beirût are models of order and arrangement, exciting the admiration of travellers. The same may be said of the British Syrian schools, which have good success and outward prosperity ; but one cannot help regretting that they are not conducted on a sound Church basis.

Beirût, as viewed from the sea, looks a very queen of cities, planted on her splendid bay, and backed by the grand Lebanon Mountains, which form one vast encircling amphitheatre ; their sombre rocks were, even in May, at many points tipped with snow. Brilliant and varied colouring in earth, sea, sky, and rock, enhances the charm of the bright-looking town, while steamers and other crafts at anchor give life and interest to the foreground.

The bay is named after S. George, who is reputed to have slain, near by, the dread dragon of mythic story; he is the patron saint *par excellence* of Beirût, and the only one equally revered by Christian and Moslem. The climate here is more equable than in many parts of Syria; in fact, it may be called a very fine one. The numerous surrounding gardens and orchards produce a large amount of fruit; mulberry and apricot trees predominate, apricots being grown in large orchards as apples are in England, but they were hardly ripe when I was there.

The Syrians have a very sweet tooth and make a great quantity of apricot preserve, also of luscious marmalade, a mixture of sweet oranges and lemons. When you call at a native house, humble though its inmates may be, they will offer you, besides Turkish coffee, a spoonful of some such home-made preserve, which you are bound *par politesse* to swallow, however much you may dislike sweets, or they you! The last course offered is generally lemonade or iced water, with sweetmeats.

Having arrived at Beirût on a Saturday, I was able on Sunday to attend the Anglican services, which were held by Bishop Blyth's chaplain in a room at his residence set apart for that purpose. Simple as the accessories necessarily were, the services in that room were the most satisfying which I had met with in Palestine, where, as I have already intimated, religious privileges, for English Church-people, are few.

I fixed May 11th for the start to Damascus, and engaged places in the French diligence some days previously. However, that fair city would never have greeted my eyes had I not been fortunate enough to awake about 3 a.m. on the appointed day. The evening before, ample assurances had been given me by the hotel worthies that they would be up early to call me, and to procure a hot breakfast for me before the long coach journey of thirteen hours. But, on my chance awakening, no sound of movement was discernible in the house; in desperation I marched about, peering vaguely into many hitherto unknown quarters of the establishment, and knocking promiscuously at many doors in the hope of arousing somebody. For a good while this seemed a vain hope; loud snores alone greeted my ears; even Solomon was adding to the chorus!

It being a long drive to the diligence office, I had ordered a carriage to fetch me from the hotel at 3·45 a.m.; and there it was, waiting outside the house, long before I had succeeded in rousing its heavy inmates. Of course, the end of it was, that I had to go off *minus* my breakfast, tasting only a little cold coffee and some dry bread.

It was very chilly at this early morning hour, so I was congratulating myself that I had been prudent enough to engage an inside place; but on inquiring at the Bureau for my appointed seat, what was my annoyance on being told that I must take an *outside* place, as the whole of the interior had been bespoken by a Turkish family! I had a very hard fight with the French officials before obtaining my undoubted rights. It seemed that two Turkish ladies, wives of influential pachas, had applied, after me, for all the seats for themselves and servants, and to accommodate them I was to be ousted! So much for French justice! As I firmly declined to go outside, the male attendant of the Turkish party was at last turned out to make room for me inside the coach.

I cannot say that I much appreciated my companions' society in such close quarters; the ladies gave themselves great airs, and seemed bent only on their own comfort and convenience quite irrespective of any one else. They even tried to rest their feet on my knees, and spent the day mostly in taking their shoes off and on, lifting up and down their face-veils, eating sweets and other dainties which they were continually producing from their capacious under-pockets; and last, but not least, smoking cigarettes, which, together with matches, were being handed to them every half-hour or so by their women. They kept up a constant prattle, during which I was often accosted; but Turkish was even more unintelligible to me than Arabic, so I could only smilingly accept their proffered sweets, and give signs and nods.

The diligence started at 4.30 a.m. on this drive of seventy miles along the splendid macadamized road made by a French company after the sad events of 1860; it has been hitherto the only good one in Syria.* The toll, which has to be paid for its maintenance, is so heavy that the natives still prefer to travel with their laden camels along the old difficult road, which we could often recognize. During the long mount to the top of the pass, we were moving among magnificent scenes, though as yet hardly perceptible in the dim morning light now gradually and beautifully overcoming the darkness in which we had started. It was a grand opportunity for watching rosy-fingered dawn as she gently prepared the pathway of the sun, ere his

"Chariot roll'd
On wheels of amber and of gold."

When we had reached the summit of the pass, his rays had not even yet gained sufficient power to dissipate the thick mist in which we there found ourselves enshrouded; indeed, it felt extremely damp and chilly when I put my nose outside, so that I had good cause to be thankful for my escape of being hoisted aloft. The sun shone brightly as usual later in the day; but the violent wind and huge showers of dust, which attended us all the time, did not make the drive a very agreeable one. We were drawn by six fine horses, which had to be changed eleven times on the way; the passengers were allowed only one interval of twenty minutes for refreshment at the

* I hear, on good authority, that the arrangements for the construction of a railway from Haifa to Damascus are completed, and that the line will be made at once; it would have been begun earlier but for French opposition.

little inn of Schtora, situated in the plain, which we reached at 11.30.

Afterwards, another but less steep climb had to be made, before the gradual descent began into the fine scenery of the gorge which forms the entrance to the Damascus plain. The rushing waters of the river Barada, the ancient Abana, which here make their way through a rocky channel, accompanied us during the latter part of the journey, pouring themselves at last with mighty fertilizing power into the wide plain.

At 6 p.m. I was very glad to be released from my cramped position in the diligence, and to establish myself at the comfortable Hotel Victoria; close beneath its windows murmured, now more tranquilly, the same river Barada with which I had already made acquaintance.

Beautiful Damascus, supposed by the natives to have been the Garden of Eden, and called by the Arabs "The Eye of the Desert," is situated at the foot of the Anti-Lebanon chain, at an elevation of two thousand two hundred and sixty feet above the Mediterranean, from which it is fifty miles distant, and from Jerusalem a hundred and thirty-three miles. It has a population of a hundred and twenty thousand, of whom twelve thousand are Christians.

This is another of the few very ancient cities on the original site of which flourishes a large modern town; we know that it was a city in the time of Abraham. Grasped at by many conquerors, it became, 63 B.C., an important Roman centre, and later, an early Christian bishopric. The Saracens, on conquering it, made it the capital of their empire; and, though it lost this position under the Turks, it has ever since maintained its commercial importance in the East.

In some respects the rival of Cairo, Damascus must bear the palm for natural beauty of situation. Viewed from a distance, it looks like a bright emerald embowered in its fresh vegetation, and set in the wide plain bounded by bare brown mountains and, in the far East, by yellow desert. The white houses and domes of the city emerge from a perfect labyrinth of trees and gardens which surround it on all sides, and are watered by abundant perennial springs; these gurgled everywhere around as I rode through the pleasant shade outside the walls. Mud is greatly used for building purposes; nearly all the substantial-looking walls in the neighbourhood are constructed of huge cakes of sun-baked mud.

One finds near Damascus such a variety of trees, fruits, and vegetables, as are but rarely met with growing side by side in an Eastern country. Among trees may be mentioned—the poplar, cypress, palm, olive, walnut, myrtle; among fruits—citrons, oranges, pomegranates, figs, grapes, apricots, dates; among field produce—beans, artichokes, wheat, barley, and other grains. Few of these could be grown successfully without constant irrigation, for which the plentiful streams offer ample facilities. From the produce of the vines, raisin-brandy—a favourite drink—is made. The myrtle tree is heavily taxed, as it is customary to deck Moslem graves with its boughs, and the fruit is used medicinally.

The bazaars of Damascus are deservedly famous for their extent and variety; especially noteworthy are the rich stuffs in silk and in gold-cloth, the unique cutlery, and the delicate jewellery exhibited in them.

Of course, reputed sites are pointed out in connection with S. Paul's history, and a street called "Straight" still exists, though a brand-new one, which has supplanted the old, and takes the same tortuous course. A leper-refuge is erected on the supposed site of the house of Naaman, near the banks of the Abana. Outside the city, a large open space is reserved as the halting-place of the huge caravans which travel this way to and from Bagdad. The town has its separate Jewish, Christian, and Mohammedan quarters; in the Jewish one I was courteously allowed to visit the interior of a private house, the beauty of which would never have been suspected from its exterior approach.

Of the seventy large mosques which Damascus contains—besides double as many smaller ones—I will only allude to the so-called "Grand Moschee," which is exceedingly interesting and beautiful. The spot on which it stands has, from time immemorial, been devoted to religion, since it was on the site of a previous Roman temple that the Emperor Arcadius, in the fourth century, reared here a fine Byzantine basilica dedicated to S. John the Baptist, whose head is said to have been preserved in it and to be still carefully enshrined under Moslem keeping. When, in A.D. 634, the church became the property of the Saracens, they arrived at an amicable arrangement with the Christians, that each creed should retain one-half of the building; so for a century Christian and Mussulman worshipped under one roof. However, in the eighth century, this mild toleration came to an end, and the Saracens seized the whole church. In the "Dome of Treasures" are still kept, locked away from Christian eye, many precious Christian manuscripts and relics.

The Mussulman of Damascus has since developed a sternly fanatical spirit, and, a few years ago, it would have been death to the Christian who endeavoured to enter the sacred enclosure. But the love of gain has now so far conquered, that a golden key—and it alone—can win access through the ancient gates which guard this shrine;—the fourth holiest in the world, according to Mohammedan computation.

In company with an American lady and gentleman, a kawass, or consular attendant, and two dragomen, I entered with feelings of eager expectation through the massive iron gates of splendid workmanship, which must have belonged to the Christian basilica, since, distinctly traceable in relief upon them, are, among other devices, the Sacred Chalice, and the Triangle, symbol of the Holy Trinity. One can detect, 'mid the spacious, airy architecture of this grand building, many features of the ancient basilica form; also remnants of fine mosaics, and rich and rare bits of old coloured glass remaining in the windows.

After the destructive fire of 1069, the Saracens built the present elegant cloisters and fountains, and, with refined taste, enriched and added to the structure for their own purposes of worship. Besides its splendid marbles, stalactites, and arabesque adornments, the interior beauty is much enhanced by its elegant lamps, and exquisite glazed tiles, both formerly important branches of Damascus trade; the production of the latter, in their ancient splendour of colour, has now, alas! become a thing of the past. The exterior of the mosque is built in layers of yellow stone and black basalt, and one of its elegant minarets is the loftiest in all Syria.

From the one we ascended, a splendid view was obtained; we could see every portion of the large, compact city as we looked down on its flat or dome-shaped roofs, its long covered-in bazaars, its extensive ramparts, its citadel, and its numberless minarets and cupolas. Beyond the green gardens of the wide plain stretched out the brown Anti-Lebanon chain, redeemed from monotony at the point where beautiful Hermon reared his majestic head still capped with snow. South-east, could be dimly detected the hills and plain of the fertile Haurân; while, due east, was traceable the hazy outline of far-away hills in the vast eastern desert towards Palmyra (a hundred and twenty miles distant),—a name which calls up romantic memories.

Extensive ruins amid surrounding desolation are all that can now be seen of that once famous "City of Palms," the "Tadmor in the wilderness," which was built by the great King Solomon* half-way between the rivers Orontes and Euphrates. From it he derived many valuable products; but, after his time, nothing is known to us of this district till, when conquered by the Romans, it became a most flourishing province, and, under the Emperor Hadrian, arrived at great commercial importance.

For the ordinary traveller, the main interest of Palmyra will centre round the story of the noble Queen Zenobia who, seventeen centuries ago, having thrown off the hated yoke of conquest, heroically headed her people against the attacks of Roman legions. Forced at last to submit, she maintained to the end her queenly courage and fortitude. One cannot help feeling indignant that such grand qualities should have failed to save her from the cruel humiliation of being dragged in chains through the streets of Rome to adorn the triumph of the "enlightened" Emperor, Marcus Aurelius!

* 1 Kings ix. 18.

In the mosque of which I have been speaking, the most interesting point of all for us Christians is reached with difficulty; you have to ascend by a ladder to the top of the book-bazaar, after crossing the roof of which, and descending again, you can see a Greek inscription evidently cut here by the Christian architects of the basilica in an already existing Roman arch. The ground has now risen so much, as to conceal more than half the arch. In this out-of-the-way corner are recorded, in Greek words almost unknown to, and certainly uncomprehended by the Moslems, with slight interpolation, the grand text of Ps. cxlv. 13, "Thy kingdom, O Christ, is an everlasting kingdom, and Thy dominion endureth throughout all ages." Blessed prophetic words, which we trust may yet find their fulfilment in this great Mosque at Damascus, as also throughout all lands where Christian shrines are now painfully desecrated by the unbeliever!

I was fortunate enough to arrive in Damascus just before Ramadân began, so was able to observe the manner in which this great fast is initiated. Orientals usually terminate business at sunset; shops, bazaars, and mosques also, are then closed; indeed, the latter are not often lighted up, except during the fast. But now, all was changed; everywhere candles were lit, lamps trimmed, and the rich carpets removed from the mosques, leaving only plain matting on the ground.

X

This long fast of thirty days varies as to date, since the Moslem year is lunar; it varies also in its daily duration according to the season in which it falls, as total abstinence from food and drink must be maintained from before sunrise to sunset. When I was in Damascus, this interval was from 3.30 a.m. to 7 p.m.

On the first of the thirty days, I noticed that all the little stalls became void of edibles, excepting in the Jewish and Christian quarters, where they were tantalizingly displayed for sale. The poor Moslem, denied even the comfort of his friendly *narghileh*, looked like the veritable martyr that he was, as he sat patiently on the counter of his little shop, his grave face growing longer and longer as the day advanced. It can be imagined that he must suffer serious bodily pangs in the beginning of this arbitrary abstinence; let us hope that, after a few days' experience of it, his internal organs learn somewhat to accommodate themselves to their cruel new *régime*. The long exhaustion produced by hunger and thirst would naturally engender a sleepy, torpid state, such as cannot conduce to brisk business transactions; therefore many, who are able to do so, wisely stop business during Ramadân.

The longed-for evening hour when food and drink may at last be taken, is announced to the public by the firing of a large gun; but, after that happy sound has been heard, it is necessary that refreshment should be partaken of in a very gradual and scientifically regulated manner, in order to avoid the new pangs of indigestion. The first course is hot soup; in another half-hour something a little more solid; while a yet longer period should elapse before substantial food be eaten with impunity.

Shortly before the welcome public signal was given, busy servers could be seen in many street-corners, preparing to ladle out the steaming broth. In the large square opposite my hotel was a house outside which this process was actively going on, and it was amusing to me to watch the poor hungry men all hurrying *pêle-mêle*, eager to break their fast;—the driver left his coach-box, the pedlar his wares, the water-carrier his goat's-skin bag, the fellâh his well-laden donkey. Naturally the claims of the ill-used stomach would be—and they were—regarded now, by all, as supreme.

The nights at this season present an indescribable scene of noise, confusion, and rioting; but all must suddenly be checked at the one solemn and inexorable note which gives warning of the approaching dawn, and of renewed abstinence. I was told that the poorer classes observe this religious institution more scrupulously than their well-to-do neighbours, and I can quite believe it; indeed, I can testify, from facts which came under my own notice, as to the obedient compliance of the humbler class in this matter.

The season was now so far advanced, that European travellers were becoming scarce; I think I was the only one of my sex remaining in Damascus, and at last I and a Scotch peer were the sole inmates of the hotel. The fascinations of the city are so numerous that I should have been content to spend in it many more happy days under the escort of the sub-guide, whom Solomon had to provide, since he himself knew nothing of the locality. This man—George Nafâcha—was very serviceable in many ways, and most anxious that I should take him back to England as my servant, professing himself able to undertake cooking, house-work—indeed, to be competent as my factotum. Poor fellow! I might no doubt have found him a real boon, could I have made sure beforehand that, under our leaden skies and chilly atmosphere, he would not soon be pining for his own bright Damascus.

I had now to face the fact, that it would soon be getting too hot for the enjoyment of Eastern travel; also, that it was time I began to set about lessening the great distance which at present separated me from my native land. I was glad there was still in anticipation one bit more of unconventional travel amid some of nature's grand, solitary haunts. It was that through the region of Anti-Lebanon to Baalbek. For this excursion three horses had again to be provided, and Solomon was busy making inquiries for them whilst I was being escorted by George about Damascus.

When a suitable horse had at last been selected for me, I proceeded to the hotel balcony in order to watch the trial of his paces in front of it. The beginning of the trial was a ridiculous scene. The young stable-man who was riding the animal was just issuing from a side street towards the front of the house, when he came suddenly in contact with a carriage and pair proceeding straight along the great promenade. In the twinkling of an eye, horse, man, and saddle were all rolling on the ground, and the two first were as quickly up again; but the frail Eastern saddle-gear had quite given way, so a retreat had to be made for needful patching-up. I thought it certainly a good sign that the horse did not resent his unceremonious overthrow, but stood up again, though riderless and saddleless, yet quiet, and evincing no malicious tendencies.

When he returned re-caparisoned, I begged Solomon to make him canter before me, which he did in a very queer fashion; his style of riding did not betoken that he had served in the cavalry! Being anxious to find out if the horse shied, I was glad to notice another carriage coming at good speed towards him and his cantering horse. But what was my surprise and disappointment to see him, at its approach, pull up short at the side of the broad road, to stand ignominiously at the furthest possible point from imaginary danger, until the vehicle had well passed by!

I eventually engaged the horse—a beautiful chestnut—together with two others, and their owner who served as their groom and our country guide. I became quite fond of my animal, and could have bought him for a very modest sum ; but it would have been considerably exceeded by the cost of his transport to England.

CHAPTER XVIII.

EXCURSIONS BY LAND AND SEA.

District of Abilene—Lodging in a tower, its superfluities and deficiencies—Mount Hermon, its treasures and ruins—Grinding corn—Serio-comic results of a storm—Baalbek—Last rural dormitory—Coasting along Asia Minor—Farewell reflections.

ON May 15th, I took leave of Damascus and started on an eight hours' ride. For the first hour we had to follow the hard carriage-road; then turned into a defile of the mountain which led through glaring chalk rocks, and eventually into the pretty wooded glen of Ain Fijeh, surrounded by bald yet richly coloured and curiously shaped rocks, and abounding in walnut and poplar trees. But the special charm of this peaceful valley is the splendid stream of crystal water which, flowing at one bound and in vast volume from a rocky cavern, constitutes the chief source of the Barada, that great fertilizer of the Lebanon district.

After lunching in this cool retreat, I continued my journey through green and varied scenery, constantly going up and down hills and over rushing mountain-streams, till we entered another romantic gorge, called Wady Barada. Humble villages lay half concealed amid trees in the valley; among others, Sûk, the ancient Abila, capital of the former district of Abilene.* Here again I was in the midst of classic associations, and surrounded by traces of Roman workmanship. The very peculiar and richly tinted rocks are full of ancient tombs, some at a height of a hundred feet from the base of the cliff, and approached by high flights of well-worn steps. Roman tablets, and inscriptions too, abound—one of them announcing that the Roman road, which the modern one constantly touches, was made by command of the Emperor Marcus Aurelius, *at the cost of the natives of Abilene.* The same arbitrary method of road-making is frequently adopted by the Turks.

On emerging from the gorge, we found ourselves in the wide green plain of Zebedâny, and rode among its fruit trees and cultivated fields, for two hours before reaching the village of that name, which was to be my halting-place for the night. I was there received into another native house,—this time that of a Syrian layman, under whose roof I had some experiences quite amusing in the contrast they afforded to those previously met with. The kind genial people seemed to be in comfortable circum-

* See Luke iii. 1.

stances, as their house could boast of a special guest-chamber. This was built apart, over a room distinct from the family dwelling, and approached by its own outer staircase. After ascending it and crossing a flat stone terrace, I found myself in a spacious, lofty chamber, which actually possessed eight large windows, all quite innocent of either window-frame or glass! Should the light or air, therefore, be found excessive, the only alternative would be to close the rough wooden shutter with which each window was furnished—a proceeding which would involve an unpleasantly abrupt transition from light to darkness.

These paneless and comfortless-looking windows are quite in vogue in the Lebanon district. When, in bad weather, the shutters have to be kept closed, I should think the inmates must have a dull time of it! As I passed through the country, the numbers of these obscured and guarded windows gave a cheerless aspect to the straight, tall, whitewashed houses which it is the fashion to erect thereabouts.

The contrast between the eight windows of my present abode, and the no windows of the last native lodging, was equally remarkable as to the bedroom arrangements. The floor here, as there, was strewn with rugs, and a narrow divan extended round the walls; but whereas there it had been a case of *no* bed, here the bed was the prominent feature, indeed the only piece of furniture in that vast room! It was a huge gilt four-poster, surrounded by a ragged mosquito-curtain, and rejoicing in a gorgeous wadded quilt, or *duvet*, of crimson satin; but in nothing besides, except one mattress and a bolster;—not a vestige was there of either sheet or blanket! I pleaded hard, but in vain, for a sheet or two; they seemed to be an unknown article; so having at length obtained the favour of one blanket, I had therewith to be content.

Although the nights were chilly, the days were now intensely hot, and I was very tired; but, before resting, I thought it advisable to profit by the light streaming yet through the numerous windows, in order to open out my stores and rearrange my disordered toilette. To my dismay, on investigating fully this pretentious chamber, I could find nothing—not even a drop of water or a towel for use! Loud laughter and talking could be heard below in the distance. Solomon was evidently having fine fun with his Lebanon friends; but meantime, I was quite the "forlorn lady" in my lofty solitary tower, and had to clap my hands and shout on the terrace for some time before I could attract any notice.

When I did at last succeed, I got too much attention; for the whole family came trooping into my room—father, mother, sons and daughters, all brimful of smiles and gestures,—to find poor me and my room in considerable disorder. I had artfully to beguile them on to the terrace in order to get rid of the intruding party, having first, through my interpreter, obtained the promise of a small tin cooking-basin which, set on a diminutive stool, had to do duty for a washstand.

When it grew dark and chilly and I began to close all the heavy shutters, I discovered that they were by no means air-tight, but, on the contrary, contained large chinks through which plenty of nocturnal creatures could insinuate themselves,—not to mention draughts. So I had to be busy till bedtime in patching up, with all available material, the deficiencies of the shutters, especially of the one close to the head of my bed. It was with a sense of great relief that I awoke next morning to find myself without either stiff neck, sore throat, or venomous bite.

There was another ride of eight hours before I could reach Baalbek; it was a fatiguing day, for the sun burnt fiercely, and our bare, shadeless track now lay chiefly up and down rough mountain-sides. In front there was little of interest; but behind, grand Hermon raised his majestic, snowy head in calm sublimity: "a thing of beauty," which afforded me a new "joy" each time I turned back to gaze upon it.

This mountain is well called by the natives "Gebel-esh-Sheikh," or the *chief* mountain, for it is not only the most imposing summit of the Anti-Lebanon chain, but also a vast storehouse of internal riches. At its base, or in its immediate neighbourhood, are found bitumen, sulphur, rock-salt, lead, copper, iron, coal; but the Turks themselves are not active in exploring for these treasures, nor are they willing that others should do so.

In the volcanic strata of this region are plentiful the hard millstones so constantly in demand in the East, since by means of them the women grind their corn for daily use in baking and cooking. Two millstones, from eighteen to twenty-four feet in diameter, are placed on the top of one another; the lower and harder one* contains a small cavity into which descends, little by little, the grain, which is introduced through an aperture in the upper stone. By means of a wooden handle inserted between the inter-fitting stones, two women seated face to face keep turning the upper stone round and round; thus the corn is ground and made ready for use. I constantly saw women thus employed as they sat outside their huts, and was reminded of our Lord's solemn words concerning His second coming.†

Many ancient temples and inscriptions have been found in the vicinity of Mount Hermon, some of the latter as old as the Assyrian period. It seems probable that here was once the centre of Syrian Baal-worship, as other temples dedicated to Baal, which have been discovered, all face towards Hermon. Canon Tristram has suggested that the largest circular temple, now in ruins, may have been over-

* Job xli. 24.   † Matt. xxiv. 41.

thrown by the children of Israel after their entry into Canaan, in obedience to the Divine command.*

As we drew nearer Baalbek, the wide Plain of Buka'a came in sight. It separates the Lebanon and Anti-Lebanon Mountains, whence flow into this plain the two large rivers Orontes and Leontes, the former taking a northerly, the latter a southerly direction. As I descended towards the Plain of Buka'a, it was difficult to believe that, somewhere on this now treeless ridge extending for miles before me, had once grown in such abundance the splendid cedars famous throughout the world. To obtain some of them, King Solomon had employed eighty thousand hewers of wood; these trees had been used as material for some of earth's greatest and holiest edifices; they had also aided in the construction of ships for the maritime Phœnicians, and of idols for the surrounding heathen.

By making a whole day's journey east of Baalbek, the two hundred or so of the ancient cedars which survive can be seen in an interior glade of the mountain. Wantonly as they were formerly destroyed by the natives for fuel, the few yet remaining are, I am glad to say, carefully guarded by the Maronites, who claim their possession, and have a chapel amidst them.

Some American friends, whom I met afterwards in Europe, gave me a graphic account of their

* Deut. xii. 2.

experiences whilst near this locality. They had started northward from Judæa earlier than I did, and, while encamped on the Lebanon, had had to face the full fury of the same tempestuous weather which had visited Jerusalem during my stay there. Their tents had faithlessly deserted them, leaving them at night uncovered, and exposed to all the force of the storm. The ladies of the party suffered so much afterwards from the effects of this misfortune, that they had to remain for some days in their beds, under the roof of a primitive village domicile to which they had been conveyed on that dreadful night. I have already intimated that great freedom of access is permitted into these humble Syrian dwellings. In the present instance, the arrival of a large foreign party under such peculiar circumstances created a wide-spread sensation. So all the inhabitants of the village came flocking to the house, and could not be prevented from entering the chamber of the sick ladies. This constant intrusion became embarrassing; yet the kind Pater Familias was loath to use harshness in repelling the *naïve* and well-disposed Lebanon folk. Suddenly a happy thought struck him; through an interpreter, he informed them that by their presence there they were invading the sacred seclusion of his "harêm!" The effect of the words was instantaneous; all the self-invited visitors decamped at once, never again to disturb the repose of the invalids.

To return to my ride. During the last two days, the largest tombs I ever beheld had been pointed out to my notice. The Moslems hereabouts pretend to have a monopoly of the "dust and ashes" of all biblical and antediluvian patriarchs, though I have not heard any explanation as to how they became possessed of their relics. Adam, Abel, Seth, Noah, Ham, are each said to be buried not very far apart in North Palestine, and the size of each tomb has been made more or less enormous according to the imagined *status* of its occupant while in life; thus the tomb of Seth measures as much as a hundred feet in length!

As I descended into the Plain of Buka'a, the backward view of beautiful Hermon became lost to view, and the six stately columns of the "Jupiter" Temple grew clearly visible above the large area of ruins which mark the site of Baalbek's famous shrine. We had already passed the quarry whence the stone for its construction was obtained. There is ample evidence that this was worked, on the spot, into its smoothness of surface, and shaped into the grand forms of obelisk and pillar which once abounded in the sacred pile of Baalbek. All travellers view with special admiration one gigantic smooth-wrought stone weighing eleven hundred tons, which measures sixty-eight feet long, seventeen feet wide, and fourteen feet high, as it lies, detached all round from its native rock-bed, save at one underlying point;

evidently the hand of the workman was suddenly arrested.

It has long been an unsolved problem as to how the ancients could have transported such enormous masses as this stone to their destined place; but Sir A. H. Layard has lent us a valuable clue by his discovery, at Koujunjik, of some bas-reliefs which represent the transport of colossal bulls, by means of rollers moving along a narrow embankment evidently reared for that purpose. Thus, the germ-thought of so modern a discovery as our railway communication may have existed in the minds of those acute men of yore!

The Plain of Buka'a, though now under cultivation, is totally devoid of trees, as are also its surrounding mountains. It was therefore with pleasure that I espied groups of poplar, mulberry, ilex, etc., growing in the immediate neighbourhood of the good-sized modern village which has sprung up close around the ancient ruins. Water-springs, too, are plentiful, and Baalbek can boast of a comfortable little hotel, the "Victoria," where my quarters were a pleasing contrast to those of the previous night.

I had suffered much that day from thirst, which I tried to quench during dinner by swallowing an unconscionable amount of weak tea, a hint learnt from an American gentleman; it is certainly a safer drink than plain water if you are not quite sure about its quality. An Englishman and his wife, both artists, were my sole companions in the hotel. They looked poorly, and spoke of the miasma which is prevalent in this district, inducing fever—a frequent drawback in the vicinity of old sites. Noticing, as we dined together, that their glasses were, and continued to be, empty, I began to wonder what their beverage was. Dinner over, and all the resources of my teapot exhausted, I ventured at length to question them on the subject, when I found with surprise that they had actually arrived at the prudent and convenient course of drinking *nothing at all!*—and in such a thirsty land!

Karnak and Baalbek are, in some sort, rivals as regards the grandeur of their ruins and the large area they cover. The first surpasses in antiquity and in the massive grandeur of its colossal constructions; but Baalbek must bear the palm for perfectness of proportion and for elegance of decoration. The Baalbek ruins form a most striking *tout-ensemble*, though one somewhat bewildering to the traveller on his first visit; as are also those of Karnak, owing to their magnitude and ruinous extent.

The sun was scorchingly hot on the morning of May 17th, which I spent among the ruins—more so, indeed, than at any other place which I can remember. I was apprehensive of a sunstroke, and therefore had to hurry my investigations more than I liked. The vast pile stands for the most part on a solid Phœnician foundation; on this have been reared later Roman superstructures, to which the

Arabs have made their own additions. You can only reach the interior now by groping through a subterranean Roman passage; but the original ancient entrance must have been a splendid one on the east side, leading towards the great central Temple of Jupiter, whose six remaining columns, each composed of three single stones, are still full of perfect and most pathetic beauty. Ten of these originally reared their heads in faultless symmetry to a total elevation of a hundred and twenty-five feet. This noble façade, raised on a wall forty feet high, was approached by a steep flight of steps. Time and weather have impressed on the whole a mellow orange tint which enhances its indescribable charm.

Evidences are discernible of the antiquity of the Baalbek foundations, especially at the north-west corner of the ruins, where, into the great outer wall, are built colossal stones of workmanship belonging to the age of Solomon, if not to an anterior period; the three largest measure sixty-four and sixty-three feet respectively in length.

Another of Baalbek's famous architectural and sculptural gems is the "Temple of the Sun," which is not older than the Roman period and contains some of the most richly decorated known specimens of Corinthian architecture. The splendid colonnade, in the same style, which surmounted it, is still in parts well preserved; but one loses the full sense of its lofty proportions owing to the fact that the ground has risen considerably around it. Earthquake has been cruel in Baalbek, and so also has man, in helping to mar the splendid work of past generations. The Arabs have plundered every iron clamp they could get hold of, so that column, entablature, frieze, and cornice have each in turn been hurried to their fall. Many stones also have been removed to aid in the construction of the two large modern churches —one Roman, the other Greek—which have been erected in Baalbek.

Under the familiar name of Baal, *i.e.* "Lord," the sun was early worshipped here, as also in Egypt under other titles. The district became a favourite Roman province, and, under the later emperors, a Christian one and the seat of a bishopric. During the persecution which raged under Diocletian, this Church contributed her Gelasinus to the "noble army of martyrs." But the same sad and too common story must be repeated here, as in so many other parts of Syria; Christian life all died out after the Saracen supremacy in A.D. 633. We may, then, rejoice that, in these latter days, a manifold new life has been springing up round the old ruins, and that, out of the present population of over five thousand, a considerable number are Christians.

On May 18th began the long ride of two days back to Beirût, which I was to break by sleeping at the little inn of Schtora on the Damascus road. This inn furnished my last rural night-quarters on

Asiatic soil. It was quite by haphazard that I could be received into it, as the inn boasts of only two small bedrooms which open inconveniently one into the other. So, on arriving, I was much relieved to find that my usual good fortune had not deserted me, and that I should be the sole inmate that night; though there was just a slight possibility that a commercial man *might* arrive about 11 p.m. I put away the unpleasant suggestion, and, after some deliberation, chose the outer of the two rooms as being the more commodious and airy. Having retired, I was just about to court earnestly

". . . a sleep
Full of sweet dreams, and health and quiet breathing,"

when, lo! an ominous tap at my door; on opening, I was told that *this* time I had "une *mauvaise* chance"—for a man had just arrived who would require one of the two rooms! I was certainly in a dilemma; it seemed that the rash hopes cherished an hour ago were to find now their correction in the restraint of a *pro tem.* solitary confinement! After a brief parley with the amiable *garçon*, I, with his aid, shifted myself and belongings, in a great scrimmage, into the inner den, where I had no alternative but to remain a close prisoner till the unwelcome fellow-traveller chose to vacate. I had enjoyed for many weeks the pleasures of unrestrained liberty, so succeeded in taking this little reverse philosophically, and in sleeping well, spite of sundry small annoyances.

Next day I was able, on horseback, to enjoy in quite a new way the fine scenery between Schtora and Beirût, and my pleasure was enhanced now by the contrasting remembrance of the former diligence experiences on this same road. As I followed the interminable descending zigzags, the blue waters of S. George's Bay, and pretty Beirût with her brilliant red sands, were ever and anon visible in the front distance, greatly increasing the beauty of the return journey. But the ride of eight hours on the hard high-road seemed a very long one, and I was glad to alight once more on Saturday, May 19th, at the Hotel Victoria.

Then had to come partings; the dismissal of the horses and their keeper; and soon after, the good-bye to my trusty Solomon, who conveyed back with him to Mr. Howard at Jerusalem my well-worn and much-appreciated saddle.

Regretfully I took my leave of this interesting Syrian land, and on May 21st embarked in the *Rio Grande* for a thirteen days' steam along the Asiatic coast, towards Greece. I had not much choice in the matter as there were comparatively few passenger-steamers then running, the season being advanced. Bad sailor though I am, the calm, smiling waters of beautiful S. George's Bay allured me into trusting myself upon them in spite of their treacherous character, and they were on the whole very merciful to me during those thirteen days of hot, cloudless sunshine.

Our steamer cast anchor off many places; thus I had the opportunity of landing at Tripoli, Cyprus, Lattaquié, Alexandrette, Mersina, and other ports on the coast of Asia Minor.

It was between 4 and 5 a.m. that, on peering out of my port-hole one bright morning, I beheld, close by, the rocky scene of the Apocalyptic vision; there stood little, yet lofty Patmos, looking like a beautiful dream in that soft early light. Over one of its bare and—but just now—sun-tipped peaks, hovered a single silvery fleece, trailing from heaven its ". cloud of glory."

As we lay off Smyrna for two days, I was able fully to explore it, and also to make thence the excursion to the ruins of Ephesus, now called Ayasalook, forty-eight miles from Smyrna; they are reached in two and a half hours by a railway of English construction, which passes through a fertile, cultivated plain containing many acres of fine fig trees. But, alas! the locust was already flitting busily among the green leaves of the herbaceous plants as I travelled along; they were pointed out to me by an English resident who happened to be in the train, and from whom I gained many scraps of local information.

It seemed strange that not one passenger from our large steamer except myself was disposed to do more than potter about the streets of Smyrna. Thus, in this my last, but by no means least interesting Asiatic land excursion, I still maintained my solitary travelling traditions, having only the escort of a Jewish guide, and, after leaving the train, the aid of a horse to bear me through the tangle of rankest vegetation—home of poisonous snakes—wherein lies, scattered and half buried from view, the *débris* of great Ephesus,—beautiful for situation even yet in her desolation, and once a glorious city, strong in commercial resources and influence, in advanced civilization and art, and in zealous adhesion first to heathen rites, and afterwards to the pure truth of Apostolic Christianity. But all her glories have now alike vanished! With painful interest I rode, for more than an hour, under a scorching sun, through the vast area of ruined sites, many of which can still be plainly identified. All man's work is more or less wrecked and prostrate here amid Nature's stern solitude, wherein no human being any longer exists;—malaria, jackals, and venomous snakes reign supreme to-day in what *was* Ephesus.

I caught sight of Mount Olympus shortly before we cast anchor off Salonika; on June 1st I landed at that port and visited some of its grand early Christian basilicas, now converted into mosques; I fear they have since been partially marred by the destructive fire which occurred soon after my visit.

As we glided on through the Ægean waters, the gleaming white promontory of distant Mount Athos indicated that we were approaching the classic land of Greece,—and, alas! leaving further and further behind the bright and fascinating East:—for regret *would* mingle with the thankfulness with which I was looking forward to revisiting my native shores.

When, at length, the familiar cliffs of Dover came into view, I could realize well that my lonely journeyings in far-off countries were a thing of the past;— however, I was returning with a happy sense of plans accomplished and wishes fulfilled, and with a store of vivid and tender memories gathered from a first personal acquaintance with most ancient and sacred lands.

FINIS.

APPENDIX A.

Prayer for the Land of Egypt.

O Almighty God, Who didst enable S. Mark the Evangelist to establish Thy Holy Church in Egypt, and dost still preserve the light of the Gospel there in the midst of all the darkness, have mercy upon the people of that land; enlighten the ignorant; rouse the careless; recover the fallen; strengthen and confirm the faithful, O mighty Lord God, we beseech Thee; and let the cry of the martyrs come up before Thee, even all those who have witnessed a good confession; and as they were faithful unto death, so now strengthen them that remain, specially Thy servants the Bishops in that land; guide them and us into all truth, for the sake of Him Who is the Way, the Truth, and the Life, Who with Thee and the Holy Ghost liveth and reigneth, one God, world without end. Amen.

APPENDIX B.

Extract from "The Worker," July, 1890.

"One place may be mentioned as having great and peculiar claims upon the Bishop of Jerusalem—that is, the port and ancient city of Suez, which stands at the entrance of the Suez Canal from the Red Sea. At this place there is an interesting congregation, which, when Sunday is slack on the canal, amounts to about sixty persons. Some of these are agents of the P. and O. and other steam companies trading through the canal; others are connected with the railway, and not a few young men are clerks in the telegraph service. This congregation has, for the last seventeen years, maintained a regular Sunday service among themselves. A layman reads the service, except on the rare occasions when a clergyman visits Suez. They have hired, and keep for this purpose only, a large room in the hotel, on which they have spent a good deal of money in fitting it very nicely as a chapel. The Bishop receives constant applications for what they would so much value—a chaplain; and he has met, whilst travelling in Egypt more than once young men who have stopped him and said, " Can you not give us a chaplain for Suez? We have been accustomed to the ordinances of the Church, and sadly feel the want of them." The congregation would raise about £60 a year, were the Bishop able to meet it; but the chaplaincy would cost £250 if for the whole year round, though the Bishop would be thankful to be able to send a chaplain even for the season. This will seem an urgent case indeed, and would that the Bishop could find some one who would undertake the charge of collecting for it."

PRINTED BY WILLIAM CLOWES AND SONS, LIMITED,
LONDON AND BECCLES.

www.ingramcontent.com/pod-product-compliance
Lightning Source LLC
Chambersburg PA
CBHW020240240426
43672CB00006B/590